UNDERSTANDING
REVIVAL

And Addressing The Issues It Provokes

So that we can Intelligently Cooperate with the
Holy Spirit During Times of Revivals and Awakenings
and not Reject His Workings due to Religious
Affections, Physical Phenomena or Manifestations
and that we may not be Caught Unaware
of the Tactics of the Enemy

MATHEW BACKHOLER

Understanding Revival & Addressing the Issues it Provokes - So that we can Intelligently Cooperate with the Holy Spirit During Times of Revivals and Awakenings and not Reject His Workings due to Religious Affections, Physical Phenomena or Manifestations and that we may not be Caught Unaware of the Tactics of the Enemy.

ISBN 978-1-907066-00-9 (paperback)
ISBN 978-1-907066-22-1 (eBook ePub)
ISBN 978-1-907066-99-3 (hardback)

British Library Cataloguing In Publication Data
A Record of this Publication is available from the British Library
First Published in March 2009 by ByFaith Media
Updated in 2014, 2015, 2016, 2017 and 2021.

- Jesus Christ is Lord -

Contents

Page   Chapter

5.   Preface
9.   Understanding Revival – What is it?. 1
17.   Revivals from the Holy Bible. 2
21.   Revival Related Scriptures. 3
25.   What Does Revival Do?. 4
29.   Who Needs Revival?. 5
33.   Views of Revival. 6
41.   The Beginnings and Characteristics of Revival. 7
53.   Reoccurring Experiences in Revival. 8
59.   The Church and Revival. 9
63.   Common Characteristics of Physical Phenomena. . 10
71.   Conviction and Confession of Sin. 11
75.   Revival and the Community. 12
81.   Education, Evangelism and Missions. 13
89.   Supernatural Characteristics of Revival. 14
99.   The Dangers of Revival. 15
111. Persecution and Opposition. 16
121. Enemies of God. 17
127. Misperceptions of God's Workings. 18
133. Human Emotions – Part I 19
141. Human Emotions – Part II 20
151. A Diversity of Views. 21
159. Disunity Within the Body. 22
167. False and Spurious Converts. 23
179. Counterfeit Conversion. .24
185. Preach the Pure Gospel. 25
189. Warnings and Wisdom. 26
195. Hindrances to Revival. 27
205. Why Revivals Cease. 28
209. Revival Merchandise and Memorabilia. 29
219. Why Revivals are Chronicled. 30
227. Evaluating the Past and Looking Forward. 31
233. Appendices A-D
239. Sources and Notes
247. ByFaith Media Books
251. ByFaith Media DVDs

'The works of the Lord are great, studied by all those who have pleasure in them' (Psalm 111:2).

'This will be written for the generation to come, that a people yet to be created may praise the Lord' (Psalm 102:18).

'One generation shall praise Your works to another and shall declare Your mighty acts' (Psalm 145:4).

'Restore us, O Lord God of hosts; cause Your face to shine and we shall be saved' (Psalm 80:19).

Preface

The Lord said, "…And it shall come to pass afterward that I will pour out My Spirit on all flesh. Your sons and your daughters shall prophesy, your old men shall dream dreams, your young men shall see visions; and also on My menservants and on My maidservants, I will pour out My Spirit in those days" (Joel 2:28-29).

It was a nearly two decades ago that the author first tried to find the word 'revival' in a Bible concordance and did not find it. The author had read a few books on the subject and knew that revival was no fallacy or erroneous teaching as it was clearly proven through Scripture and documented throughout Church history. The author quickly realised that the majority of Bible translations did not use the words 'revival' or 'awakening,' but the Scriptural concept of reviving or quickening individuals, communities and nations is found in the Old Testament, and abounded in the New Testament.

In regards to revival, outside of the book of Acts the author knew that there were lots of physical phenomena, human reactions to the Divine Presence, but struggled to find the relevant passages when asked to do so. He knew that Abraham, Moses, Jeremiah, Isaiah, Ezekiel, Daniel and many others had incredible encounters with God and they acted and reacted in unusual ways when God met with them, or when an angel appeared, or in the various acts of obedience to an intercession.

The Word of God reveals many unusual things (see ch. 18, Misperceptions of God's Workings) – the Holy Bible speaks of revelations, physical phenomena (joy, falling, shaking, trembling and weeping etc.), visions, dreams, trances, people crying out, demons manifesting, healings, judgments, people repenting, shouting, singing, rejoicing, dancing, jumping, leaping and whirling, and in any move of the Holy Spirit you can expect to find some of these phenomena, if not most during times of revival to a lesser or greater degree.

The author has read nearly three hundred books on the subject of revival; 'The works of the Lord are great, studied by all those who have pleasure in them' (Psalm 111:2) and felt that he was now prepared to write *Understanding Revival and Addressing the Issues it Provokes*. Whilst the work is not exhaustive, it is fairly comprehensive and for ease of reading and research, the characteristics of revival cover many chapters and are sublisted into numerous relevant categories. Some incidences to the pessimist, may sound so far fetched that the author thought that it was only fitting that an example or two from revival Church history should be included. In all revivals there are multiple common characteristics and reoccurring themes which straddle continents, centuries and cultures – the common threads that weave through the tapestry of revival Church history and it is these, amongst other things that have been brought out in this book. Let us not be alarmed by what we read or see; there is nothing new under the sun and God is in control of all things and all things are under His control.

It was Dr. John White who correctly noted the 'Church's panicky flight at the approach of revival, and the failure to recognise it when God sends it. Revival has dangers. But our fear may lead us to reject what God sends. We must not neglect power because it has dangers.'[1]

We all need to be aware of how the Holy Spirit works during times of revival, the heaven-sent blessing, so that we can intelligently cooperate with Him and thus further the work of any spiritual awakening, rather than impede it by rejecting, resisting or quenching the Holy Spirit. Also, let us not be deceived by the devil's tactics or seduced by those who are of a 'different spirit' and are under Satan's control.

- Dr Martyn Lloyd-Jones said, "Read the history of the past to discover its lessons...there is nothing quite so foolish as ignoring the past."
- Historian, E. H. Carr said, "You cannot look forward intelligently into the future unless you are also prepared to look back attentively into the past."
- Frank Bartleman, the chronicler of the Azusa Street Revival (1906-1909) in America, said, "In order to understand what God is going to do, we must understand what He once did."

Evangelist Seth Joshua saw a localised revival in New Quay, west Wales, UK, in the spring of 1904 which was a great blessing to Evan Roberts when he visited the meetings in May. Joshua was used extensively across Wales in bringing souls to Christ, but especially during the Welsh Revival (1904-1905) which broke out on the last day of October 1904 under the ministry of Evan Roberts. In a lecture, Seth Joshua said, "The world owes everything to the Church and the Church owes everything to revival."[2]

Balanced biblical reflection is always needed during and after revival and unusual things happen which may catch us unaware, whilst some Christians sadly reject all things supernatural because they have suppressed God into a box. Intellectually and emotionally many believers limit God's power to their own finite understanding of the god they have made in their own image. God in a box – is that how we view Him? For the author it was how he once viewed God before he visited his first revival fifteen years ago. It is frequently our preconceived ideas and doctrines that are in the box. God and the Bible should shape our thinking and not any pre-programmed mindset, ideas or opinions.

Would it not be a tragedy if those who had prayed, pleaded and interceded for revival, reject it when it comes? Because it did not come how they had expected or they got caught up in a false 'revival' which was not from God. Through revival Church history, too many Christians, even ministers and missionaries upon hearing of the works of God have stated, "If that is revival, I don't want it in *my* church." Whilst others have initially rejected a move of God (like Andrew Murray, see page 116) because of the physical phenomena, bodily manifestations it has produced; and some, sadly, to the detriment of their church have totally rejected it and thus missed the greatest blessing of God – revived Christians, saved sinners and sometimes transformed communities. History sadly records that during the Welsh Revival (1904-1905), some villages were entirely unaffected as God passed them by, whilst a church of a different denomination in the parish of Barvas where the Lewis Revival (1949-1952) in the Outer Hebrides, Scotland, broke out, rejected the revival entirely and the minister warned his congregation to keep away! They were not the first to do so and will not be the last. But let us not allow God to pass us by.

Charles H. Spurgeon said, "He [God] *can* bless us as He wills and He will bless us as He wills. Let us not dictate to God. Many a blessing has been lost by Christians not believing it to be a blessing, because it did not come in the particular shape which they had conceived to be proper and right."

'There is nothing new under the sun' as Scripture declares in Ecclesiastes chapter one, and the author hopes that by reading this book, the reader may be more aware of the happenings during times of revival without denouncing a genuine move of God as false, unholy fire, counterfeit or a demonic delusion. That the reader might understand how the Holy Spirit moves so that we can intelligently cooperate with Him rather than impede, resist, quench or grieve Him. That we may handle any negative situations in a spirit of love and grace during times of heaven-sent visitations (and outside of it), and not be unaware of the devil's infiltrations and imitations as there is a huge difference between God's dynamics and the demonic, between light and darkness; good and evil.

In many chapters, the author has quoted from revivalists, evangelists, missionaries and ministers; most of whom partook of the fires of revival and tasted the heavenly glories. The opinions of revivalists, the testimonies, observations and experiences of those who participated in revival hold far greater weight than those of us who have not been used in revival. When they speak, we should listen and heed the advice of those who walked closer to the Lord than we do; because if we walked as close to the Lord as they did, then we too would probably see revival. These Christian workers were men and women of faith, and though the vast majority have passed into glory; being dead they still speak; but would it not be foolhardy to ignore their advice and neglect their life lessons and observations, as well as the host of admonitions and warnings in Scripture?

'God is greatly to be feared in the assembly of the saints and to be held in reverence by all those around Him' (Ps. 89:7).

Chapter One

Understanding Revival – What is it?

What is Revival?

Revival is essential for the life and well-being of the Church. Revival glorifies God, vindicates His name, exalts Jesus Christ, gives the Holy Spirit His rightful place in the Church, raises the high and holy standard of the body of Christ and saves sinners who become part of the Church.

Dr. Martyn Lloyd-Jones speaking on revival said, "Suddenly they are aware of this presence, they're aware of the majesty and the awe of God. The Holy Spirit literally seems to be preceding over the meeting and taking charge of it, and manifesting His power and guiding and leading them, and directing them. This is the essence of revival."[1]

The word 'revival' comes from the Latin word 'revivere' meaning to live, to return to consciousness, to reawaken or a renewal of fervour, 'but strictly speaking, it means to bring to life again, to reanimate...' so wrote G. J. Morgan. The Greek word for revival is anazōrpureō, which means to stir up or rekindle a fire which is slowly dying, to keep in full flame. It is used metaphorically when the apostle Paul wrote to Timothy, '...Stir up the gift of God which is in you...' (2 Timothy 1:6). Welsh revivalist, Christmas Evans from the eighteenth century wrote: 'Revival is God bending down to the dying embers of a fire just about to go out and breathing into it until it bursts once again into flame.'

The word 'revival' first came into the English language in 1702; the standard definition being: an awakening in or of evangelical religion.[2] Sometimes the concept of revival is referred to as: a quickening, a spiritual awakening, a visitation, the Holy Spirit descending or a Pentecost etc.

The word 'revival' is not in the majority of Bible translations. Because of this, there are some who would say revival does not exist; or cannot happen, but that is like someone claiming that cars do not exist because the word 'car' or 'motor vehicle' is not found in Holy Writ. The words: trinity, rapture, missions and soteriology, (the doctrine of salvation) are also not found in the Holy Bible – but would we deny the validity and essential truths of their doctrines?

In 1384, John Wycliffe, an Oxford professor, completed the first translation of the Holy Bible in the English language. It had been translated from the Latin Vulgate and was written by hand. With this translation, new words came into the English vocabulary, with about one thousand Latin words being added; whilst other biblical words were thought up to express theological terminology including: sanctified, justified and atonement. I don't think anybody would be so foolish to claim that there was no 'atonement' because it was not in the English language prior to the 1380s – Jesus was the Lamb of God who was slain before the foundation of the world; so conversely, we cannot say that the word 'revival' has no credence for today because it is not found in the majority of Bible translations.

So does revival exist? Both in the Old and the New Testament, by direct word of inspiration, 'revival' is recorded by inspired inference and the concept is clearly seen in the lives or events of individuals and groups (see chapter two). Secondly, we have revival Scriptures; verses from the Word of God, which have been prayed through and pleaded by multitudes of people through the centuries who have acted on the promises (and conditions) of God and seen revival in their church, town or nation (see chapter three). Thirdly, there are thousands of books on the subject of revival in the English language alone; many of which document accounts of revival or are biographies of revivalists. Finally, the author during his time of research has come across more than one thousand revivals and awakenings throughout the world and has merely scratched the surface.

Evangelism Versus Revival

Revival cannot be put together, manufactured or produced. If it can be planned, orchestrated and be turned on or off then it cannot be revival. Revival cannot be worked up, but it needs to come down. Revival is not an organised event, though out of an organised event, such as an evangelistic campaign or during effective evangelism, revival can break forth. The object of evangelism is to seek lost souls, whereas revival revives dry and weary souls, transforms saints, saves sinners and can change entire communities.

Evangelist Dr. Fred Barlow described revival as: 'Heaven-sent, Spirit-given, sin-convicting, soul-saving, politic-purging, society-redeeming and nation sparing....'[3]

In evangelism, the focus is on the evangelist or preacher, and many who profess Christ soon fall by the wayside. But in revival, the focus is on God, and the vast majority of those who profess Christ stay true to Him as abiding fruit.

In effective evangelism, God may bless the work and people will respond to the call of repentance and make a profession of faith. However, in revival there is an overpowering presence of God and regardless of any leaders present, or an appeal to get right with God, the people will be compelled by the Spirit of God to get right with Him. They will repent of their sins, pour out their hearts to the Almighty and call upon the name of the Lord who is mighty to save. He shall see the travail of His soul and be satisfied.

J. Edwin Orr, twentieth century evangelist, revivalist and world renowned revival historian said, "In times of evangelism, the evangelist seeks the sinner, in times of revival the sinners comes chasing after the Lord."

Selwyn Hughes, founder of Crusade for World Revival wrote: 'Evangelism is the expression of the Church; revival is an experience of the Church. Evangelism is the work we do for God; revival is the work God does for us.'

Scottish born evangelist, James A. Stewart saw numerous revivals in Eastern Europe beginning in the 1930s prior to the outbreak of World War II. He also saw revival in Norway in 1947 and a move of God in Milldale Bible Conference (1966) in America. After more than three decades of ministry he wrote: '...Revival results in a great wave of evangelism and ingathering of souls. Revival includes evangelism, but evangelism may not include revival. Evangelism always follows revival, but revival does not necessarily follow an evangelistic campaign. Evangelism seeks the resurrection of sinners who are dead in trespasses and sin. Revival is a spiritual quickening of the life of the redeemed.'[4]

On occasions, revival does break forth during evangelistic campaigns. The giants of evangelism such as Dwight L.

Moody, Reuben Alexander Torrey, Wilbur Chapman, A. C. Dixon, James A. Stewart, Billy Graham, Carlos Annacondia and Luis Palau, all saw revival break forth on more than one occasion during their evangelistic campaigns.

When Christians become revived, they will inevitably be more effective in personal evangelism, being burdened for the lost. The vast majority of Christians unnecessarily live and die without ever seeing a revival – this is a travesty and an indictment on the Church – because God has promised to pour water on the thirsty and floods on the dry ground and He is not a man that He should lie!

What is Revival For?

Revival is the Church being saturated with God – it is primarily intended for the Church so that they can be revived into a true, proper and correct relationship with God. From this, revival begins to affect those who are outside of the Church to a lesser or greater degree. Theologically and historically the river of revival begins amongst the Church (the body of Christ), but will naturally flow outwards and bring to life those who are dead in their trespasses and sins (non-Christians) because God has no pleasure in the death of the wicked. During times of revival, Christians always get revived before sinners get converted because that is a spiritual law of revival.

On very rare occasions, the exception and not the norm, revival can be for those who are completely dead in their trespasses and sins. This is what happened in the case of the city of Nineveh, who repented under Jonah's preaching, (the reluctant revivalist) who declared, "Yet forty days, and Nineveh shall be overthrown!" It was also seen in the Samaria Revival under Philip the evangelist (Acts 8:5-8) and amongst the Angas Tribe in Nigeria in the 1930s.[5]

What Does Revival Do?

Revival is a visitation of the Holy Spirit, a quickening, a bringing to life. It is God rending the heavens and coming down, the hills melting like wax before His presence. It is water being poured out on the thirsty and floods on the dry ground. It is a turning from darkness to light, from the power of Satan to God, a casting off of the works of darkness; thus the light of the world (Christians – Matthew 5:14-16) burns brighter and thus aids the Church to be without spot or wrinkle until the glorious day of His appearing.

The apostle Paul declared '…always pursue what is good both for yourselves and for all' (1 Thessalonians 5:15) and 'the manifestation of the Spirit is given to each one for the profit of all' (1 Corinthians 12:7). Revival, God's Spirit being poured out, is for the reviving of Christians and the benefit of the Church. The Holy Spirit will in turn move hardened sinners to fall before the living God and to call upon His name, because whoever calls upon the name of the Lord will be saved and there is no other name (Jesus Christ) under heaven given to men by which they must be saved.

Revival is generally either 'localised' amongst a Church or community, where many individuals share a common experience of the Holy Spirit descending in their midst, or 'national,' amongst a town, people group, or nation where multitudes share the common experience of the presence of God. A localised revival is a quickening from the Holy Spirit, a visitation from Him, when Christians get revived, but a national revival is where not only the Church or community gets revived, but the town, people group or nation gets transformed and becomes a habitable praise of God.

The quickening, the reviving of Christians is 'floods being poured on the dry ground' (Isaiah 45:3) so that Christians get on fire for God and have renewed consecration and zeal – the Holy Spirit comes to refine, purify and to wash clean, 'a refiners fire and like fullers soap…He will purify…and purge them as gold and silver that they may offer to the Lord an offering in righteousness' (Malachi 3:2-3). Only after Christians have been quickened then a visitation of the Holy Spirit on the community or beyond is possible and very probable as long as the Church keeps praying, seeking and pleading for God to 'rend the heavens' (Isaiah 64:1) and come down – as the Holy Spirit descends to 'convict the world of sin, and of righteousness and of judgment' (John 16:8). God is 'mighty to save' (Isaiah 63:1) and 'He shall see the travail of His soul and be satisfied' (Isaiah 53:11), because 'God has no pleasure in the death of the wicked' (Ezekiel 18:23) but 'desires all men to be saved and to come to the knowledge of the truth' (1 Timothy 2:4), because 'whoever calls upon the name of the Lord will be saved' (Romans 10:13 and Joel 2:32). God has promised: "I will pour out My Spirit on all flesh..." (Joel 2:28) and 'no good thing will He withhold from them that walk uprightly' because He is 'a sun and a shield; the Lord will give grace and glory' (Psalm 84:11), and says, "I will yet for this be enquired of by the house of Israel to do it for them" (Ezekiel 36:37) and the dry bones shall live (Ezekiel ch. 37), because God declares, "Before all the people I must be glorified" (Leviticus 10:3).

One author wrote: 'This is revival from heaven! – When men in the streets are afraid to speak godless words for fear that God's judgment will fall! When sinners, aware of the fire of God's presence, tremble in the streets and cry for mercy! When, without human advertising, the Holy Spirit sweeps across cities and towns in supernatural power and holds people in the grip of terrifying conviction. When every store becomes a pulpit, every heart an altar, every home a sanctuary and every people walk carefully before God – This is revival!'[6]

The Theology of Revival

In times of revival, the fundamental truths of Jesus' eternal Son-ship, the virgin birth, His sinless life, His death, resurrection, ascension, second coming and the judgment (and heaven and hell); alongside, repentance, the new birth, faith in Christ and total consecration are always preached.

Vinet, in his book, *Outlines of Theology* wrote: 'If you learn in a general way that there has been a revival in a place, that Christianity is reanimated, that faith has become living, and that zeal abounds – do not ask in what soil, in what system, these precious plants grow. You may be sure beforehand that it is the rough and rugged soil of orthodoxy [the foundation of agreed belief], under the shade of those mysteries which confound human reasoning.... The revival has preached the total depravity of man and his powerlessness to save himself. The revival has preached salvation by grace and not by works, the necessity of the new birth in order to enter the Kingdom of Heaven and the absolute dependence of man in regards to God. The revival has preached the plenary and essential deity of Jesus Christ as well as His perfect and entire humanity; it has declared that God was in Jesus Christ, reconciling the world unto Himself; and that it is in Jesus Christ alone that we have remission of sins and access to the Father; and that whosever abideth not in Him abideth in death.'[7]

James A. Stewart wrote: 'Revival is an assembly word. Any movement that fails to deliver the local church from its subnormal existence and raise it to a higher elevated position in its ascended Lord has no true marks of a New Testament Revival…. Revival, as presented to us in the New Testament, is not so much an individual experience as a collective experience of a church of born again believers.'[8]
'Renewal is not revival. Local renewal meetings, as important and essential as they are, more often than not, only revive the Christians present and leave the local church untouched.' James A. Stewart wrote: 'God's way of revival is through renewals from within, so that our local churches become the centre of blessing.'[9]

If we understand the previous two quotes by Vinet and Stewart it does make it easier to understand the difference between a revival and an outpouring, such as the Toronto Blessing (1994+) in Canada, the Sunderland Outpouring (1994) in England, and the *Lakeland Outpouring (2008) in America, where the focus is largely on the Church who need to be renewed and refreshed (*or healed), who already understand the essential tenets of truth and thus live by them; but we should all be regularly reminded of these wonderful and blessed essential truths of Jesus and His atoning sacrifice for fallen mankind, because Jesus is Lord! *See page 228.

Revival – A Two-Edged Sword (see pages 160-161)
Revival is a two-edged sword – a blessing for many and judgment for a minority. It is 'a sign that is spoken against' for 'the fall and rising of many' because God's presence will reveal the true state of people's hearts (Luke 2:35). The blessing of revival is to cut free and deliver, for the cleansing, purging, sifting, shaking and restoration of the Church, '…do not despise the chastening of the Almighty. For He bruises,

but He binds up; He wounds, but His hands make whole' (Job 5:17-18). Be warned, the judgment of revival is for a minority of the body of Christ who are unrepentant and wilfully living in habitual sin, those who continually dishonour the name of the Lord, because judgment always begins at the house of the Lord (1 Peter 4:17) and it is the 'Lord [who] kills and makes alive; He brings down to the grave and brings up...He brings low and lifts up' (1 Samuel 2:6-7). The Scriptures declare: 'Utterly slay...begin at My sanctuary' (Ezekiel 9:6). 'Blow the trumpet in Zion...tremble; for the day of the Lord is coming' (Joel 2:1). God said, "I will come to you quickly and remove your lampstand from its place – unless you repent" (Revelation 2:5). God's grace does wear thin and He does take out individuals and shuts churches!

John D. Drysdale was principal of Emmanuel Bible School, Birkenhead, England, in the 1930s. He wrote: 'A revival is a renewed interest in religion, after indifference or decline. A revival is a re-animation from a state of languor and decline. A revival is a period of religious awakening. A revival is restoration to consciousness of life. A revival is voluntary, and determined return to first things, and a whole-hearted honouring of God as Creator, Jesus Christ as our Lord and Saviour, and the Holy Ghost as our Sanctifier.

'A revival, in the first instance, has to do with God's people. Then when the unsaved see God's people taking Divine things seriously, they become alarmed about their sin, and their rebellion against God and many of them are won to God. A revival is...a manifestation of the mighty power of God in turning men and women of every walk of life from their sins, to a life of God-glorifying, and whole-hearted sacrifice and service towards our fellows.'[10]

Rev. William Haslam saw at least seven revivals and is most noted for the Baldhu Church Revival (1851-1854) in Cornwall, England, which began when the Anglican preacher got converted under his own preaching! He said, "Revivals – that is the refreshing of believers and the awakening of sinners – ought to take place wherever the gospel is preached in faith and power."[11]

Chapter Two

Revivals from the Holy Bible

Old Testament Revivals

1. From the godly line of Seth men began to call on the name of the Lord (Genesis 4:26) – they saw their need which is an awakening of a group of people.

2. King Asa became King of Judah and did what was right in the eyes of the Lord. He banished the male and female prostitutes from the land and removed all the idols. He commanded his people to seek the Lord God of their fathers and to observe the Law and the commandments (1 Kg. 15:9-15 & 2 Chron. 14:1-15).

3. The prophet Elijah had a spiritual battle on Mount Carmel, before King Ahab and the four hundred and fifty prophets of Baal and four hundred prophets of Asherah. Once the true altar was prepared; a complete offering was given and Elijah called upon his God and the fire fell! The people fell on their faces crying out, "The Lord He is God! The Lord He is God!" And revival broke out (1 Kings 18:20-40).

4. Jehoiada the priest made a covenant between the Lord, the king and the people that they should be the Lord's people. They also tore down the temple of Baal (2 Kings 11:17-18 and 2 Chronicles 23:16-21).

5. King Hezekiah of Judah reopened and repaired the house of God which had been shut up and neglected for many years, and made a covenant before God. The house of God was then cleansed and sanctified. A big Passover festival was held and all the idols, wooden images, high places and false altars were smashed, cut down and destroyed. The temple worship was reinstated and the Levites got their old jobs back (2 Kings 18:1-8 and 2 Chronicles 29-31).

6. Evil King Manasseh of Judah as a captive in Babylon, humbled himself before God who permitted him to

return to Jerusalem. He removed the idols and foreign gods and repaired the altar of the Lord and commanded the people of Judah to serve the Lord God of Israel (2 Chronicles 33:12-16).

7. King Josiah (whose father and grandfather were evil) saw revival in Judah, when the Book of the Law was found and he acted upon it – by repenting and humbling himself before God. King Josiah, the elders and the people of Judah made a covenant before the Lord to obey His commandments. The temple of the Lord was cleansed and all the false altars and temples of idols were destroyed, and they celebrated with a huge Passover festival (2 Kings chapters 22-23 and 2 Chronicles chapters 34-35).

8. Jonah was called to preach in Nineveh, to the notorious cruel Assyrians, but fled from the call of God. Eventually the prophet Jonah preached in this large pagan city, declaring, "Yet, forty days, and Nineveh shall be overthrown!" The people of Nineveh believed the Word of the Lord. The king commanded his people to humble themselves and cry mightily to God and turn from their evil ways. God saw their humility and contrition and judgment was avoided which upset Jonah! (The book of Jonah).[1]

New Testament Revivals

1. John the Baptist called the people to a baptism of repentance for the remission of sins and told them to bear fruits worthy of repentance. They came to him for baptism and confessed their sins. He told them of the One who was to come (Mark 1:4-5 & Lk. 3:1-18).

2. Jesus was the promised Messiah, the Saviour of the world and was the Anointed One (Luke 4:18-19). At His baptism He was filled with the Spirit and returned from His forty days in the wilderness in the power of the Spirit (Luke 4:1, 14). He preached the Kingdom of God with signs and wonders following, confirming the message and thus proving He was the Promised One (Matthew 11:2-5 and Luke 8:25). The people flocked to hear His teaching (and to be healed) and Jesus had periods of perpetual revival in various cities.

3. The Holy Spirit fell on the Day of Pentecost and people began to speak in tongues. Peter preached and about three thousand people were cut to the heart, being under conviction of sin. They believed on the Lord Jesus Christ, repented of their sins and were baptised in the name of Jesus (Acts chapter 2).

4. Peter and John preached and around two thousand people were added to the Church (Acts 4:1-4), 5,000 less 3,000 from the Day of Pentecost.

5. Through the hands of the apostles many signs and wonders were performed and multitudes became believers in Christ Jesus (Acts 5:12-14).

6. The number of disciples of Jesus multiplied greatly in Jerusalem including many of the priests (Acts 6:1-8).

7. Philip went down to Samaria, preaching with miracles following and multitudes with one accord heeded what he said and became followers of Jesus. There was great joy in that city (Acts 8:5-8).

8. Peter visited Joppa and raised Dorcas from the dead; as this fact became known throughout Joppa, many believed on the Lord Jesus (Acts 9:36-43).

9. Peter and some brethren went to Caesarea and preached at Cornelius the centurion's home. The Holy Spirit fell upon those gathered, they spoke in tongues and were then baptised (Acts 10:23-48).

10. Some of the disciples of Jesus (not the twelve) preached at Antioch to the Hellenists and a great number believed and turned to the Lord (Acts 11:19-21). When news of this revival reached the church at Jerusalem they sent Barnabas to assist in the work & more people were added to the faith (Acts 11:22-24).

11. The apostle Paul and friends preached to the Jews in the synagogue in Antioch at Pisidia. Many of the Jews and devout proselytes followed the teaching of Jesus Christ. The Gentiles then begged that they also may hear this preaching on the following Sabbath and almost the whole town came to hear; this upset the elders of the city, but the Word of the Lord spread throughout that region (Acts 13:14-50).

12. The disciples preached in the synagogues at Iconium and both Jews and Greeks believed. Signs and

wonders were performed and the city was divided against the Jews and the apostles (Acts 14:1-4).

13. Paul and the apostles travelled; the churches were strengthened in the faith and the Church increased in numbers daily (Acts 16:1-5).

14. Paul and Silas went into the synagogue in Thessalonica and preached. A great multitude of devout Greeks and many of the leading women followed them, which led to a riot, as people said, "These who have turned the world upside down have come here too" (Acts 17:1-9).

15. Paul and Silas were sent to Berea and they preached in the synagogue. Many believed, both Greeks and prominent women of the city, but Jews from Thessalonica stirred up the crowd and another riot began! (Acts 17:10-15).

16. Paul preached on Mars Hill, in the midst of the Areopagus in Athens to the pagans, some mocked, but others joined them and believed (Acts 17:22-34).

17. Paul, Silas and Timothy travelled to Corinth and spoke at a house meeting of Justus who lived next door to the synagogue. Crispus the synagogue ruler and his entire household believed along with many of the Corinthians. They stayed there for six months, teaching the new converts (Acts 18:7-11).

18. Paul taught in the school at Tyrannus for two years and all who dwelt in Asia (Minor) heard the Word of the Lord, both Jews and Greeks, but some were hardened and spoke evil of the Way (Acts 19:8-9).

19. In Ephesus, after hearing and seeing the power of God working through the apostle Paul, fear fell on the Jews and Greeks. Jesus was magnified; many who had believed on Jesus Christ publicly confessed their sins and those who had practised magical arts publicly burned their occult books (Acts 19:11-20).

20. Paul was shipwrecked on the Island of Malta. Many people were healed under his ministry including the leading citizen of the island (Acts 28:1-9). There is no recorded mention of conversions, but undoubtedly there were as they thought he was a god (v6) and Paul always preached the good news.

Chapter Three

Revival Related Scriptures

God's Spirit and the Glory of the Lord

- Thus says the Lord, "And it shall come to pass afterward that I will pour out My Spirit on all flesh; your sons and your daughters shall prophesy, your old men shall dream dreams, your young men shall see visions; and also on My menservants and My maidservants I will pour out My Spirit in those days" (Joel 2:28-29).
- The Lord said, "But truly, as I live, all the earth shall be filled with the glory of the Lord" (Numbers 14:21).
- 'Surely His salvation is near those who fear Him, that glory may dwell in the land' (Psalm 85:10).
- '...The Lord will arise over you and His glory will be seen upon you' (Isaiah 60:2).
- 'For the earth will be filled with the knowledge of the glory of the Lord, as the waters cover the sea' (Habakkuk 2:14).

God's Glory and Vindication

- God said, "By those who come near Me, I must be regarded as holy; and before all the people I must be glorified" (Leviticus 10:3).
- The twelve memorial stones were set up, 'That all the people of the earth may know the hand of the Lord, that it is mighty, that you [the Israelites] may fear the Lord your God forever' (Joshua 4:24).
- God said, "For My own sake, for My own sake, I will do it; for how should My name be profaned? And I will not give My glory to another" (Isaiah 48:11).
- 'O Lord, though our iniquities testify against us, do it for Your name's sake; for our backslidings are many, we have sinned against You' (Jeremiah 14:7).

- 'Not unto us, O Lord, not unto us, but to Your name give glory, because of Your mercy, and because of Your truth. Why should the Gentiles say, "Where now is their God?" ' (Psalm 115:1-2).
- '[The] Gentiles...glorify God in the day of visitation' (1 Peter 2:12). See also Ezekiel 36:22-23.

The Holy Spirit and God Descending

- Thus says the Lord, "For I will pour water on him who is thirsty, and floods on the dry ground; I will pour out My Spirit on your descendants and My blessing on your offspring" (Isaiah 44:3).
- Thus says the Lord, "Rain down, you heavens, from above, and let the skies pour down righteousness; let the earth open, let them bring forth salvation, and let righteousness spring up together. I the Lord have created it" (Isaiah 45:8).
- 'Oh, that You would rend the heavens and come down! That the mountains might shake at Your presence...to make Your name known' (Isaiah 64:1).
- 'For behold the Lord is coming out of His place; He will come down.... The mountains will melt under Him, and the valleys will split like wax before the fire, like waters poured down a steep place' (Micah 1:3-4).[1]
- 'He shall come down like rain upon the mown grass, like showers that water the earth' (Psalm 72:6).[2]
- 'Bow down Your heavens, O Lord, and come down; touch the mountains and they shall smoke' (Psalm 144:5).
- 'This is the Word of the Lord to Zerubbabel, "Not by might nor by power, but by My Spirit," says the Lord of hosts' (Zechariah 4:6).

Holiness Scriptures

- 'Who may ascend into the hill of the Lord? Or who may stand in His holy place? He who has clean hands and a pure heart, who has not lifted up his soul to an idol, nor sworn deceitfully. He shall receive blessing from the Lord and righteousness from the

God of his salvation. This is Jacob, the generation of those who seek Him...' (Psalm 24:3-6).

- 'Sow for yourselves righteousness; reap in mercy; break up your fallow ground, for it is time to seek the Lord, till He comes and rains righteousness on you' (Hosea 10:12).
- 'I acknowledged my sin to You and my iniquity I have not hidden. I said, "I will confess my transgression to the Lord" and You forgave the iniquity of my sin. Selah. For this cause everyone who is godly will pray to You' (Psalm 32:5-6a). See also Proverbs 28:13.
- 'Search me, O God, and know my heart; try me, and know my anxieties; and see if there is any wicked way in me, and lead me in the way everlasting' (Psalm 139:23-24).
- 'Let the words of my mouth and the meditation of my heart be acceptable in Your sight, O Lord, my strength and my Redeemer' (Psalm 19:14).
- 'One who turns away his ear from hearing the law, even his prayer shall be an abomination' (Prov. 28:9).

God's Merciful Nature and Reviving

- The Lord said, "If My people who are called by My name will humble themselves, and pray and seek My face, and turn from their wicked ways, then I will hear from heaven, and will forgive their sin and heal their land" (2 Chronicles 7:14).
- '...But You are God, ready to pardon, gracious and merciful, slow to anger, abundant in kindness and did not forsake them' (Nehemiah 9:17).
- 'The eyes of the Lord are on the righteous and His ears are open to their cry' (Psalm 34:15).
- 'Will You not revive us again...?' (Psalm 85:6).
- '...Revive me in Your way' (Psalm 119:37b).
- 'Revive me, O Lord, for Your name's sake! For Your righteousness' sake...' (Psalm 143:11).

Our Responsibility

- Obey the precepts as revealed in the Holy Bible! Jesus must be at the centre of our lives, we need to be living a God-glorifying lifestyle, walking in holiness (1 Peter 1:16), abiding in God's presence (John 15:1-11), being fully submitted to the Father's will, having offered our bodies as a living sacrifice, which is our reasonable service (Romans 12:1-2). Walking in the Spirit (Galatians 5:25) and obeying Him (Acts 5:32).

- Jesus said, "Blessed are those who hunger and thirst for righteousness for they shall be filled" (Matthew 5:6). Are we hungering and thirsting for more of God? Will He not fill those who ask? (Luke 11:5-13).

- Confessions of our sins, the sins of our forefathers and our nation's sins are paramount (Exodus 20:5-6, Judges 2:6-19 and 1 John 1:9). We need to make sure that we are right before God. Unless we deal with the sins of the past it is impossible to move forward into all that God wants for us (Prov. 28:13).

- Does our heart condemn us? Is our conscience pricked with unconfessed sin because we have not kept God's commandments and therefore we are not pleasing in His sight? (1 John 3:21-22).

Covenant-Keeping God – Conditional Promises

- "If My people..." (2 Chronicles 7:14). See page 23.
- "If you will keep My commandments and execute My judgments, then will I do it!" (1 Kings 6:12) AV.
- "Ask of Me, and I will give You the nations for Your inheritance" (Psalm 2:8). This is the Father speaking to His Son, but we can also pray it because the Great Commission is the Church's responsibility and God has no pleasure in the death of the wicked.
- "Thus saith the Lord, the Holy One of Israel, and his Maker, ask Me of things to come concerning My sons, and concerning the work of My hands command ye Me" (Isaiah 45:11) AV.
- "I will yet for this be enquired of by the house of Israel to do it for them" (Ezekiel 36:37) AV.

'The Lord is not slack concerning His promise...but is longsuffering towards us, not willing that any should perish but that all should come to repentance' (2 Peter 3:9).

Chapter Four

What Does Revival Do?

Revival does a thousand and one things and this chapter brings to the fore the essence of revival and includes statistics from revivals of what God has done in the past in different centuries, in many nations on different continents.

Revival and the Trinity
- Glorifies God.
- Exalts Jesus in praise, love and adoration.
- Gives the Holy Spirit His rightful and due place within the Church.

Revival and People
- Revives Christians and brings that which was stale or dying back to life and vigour.
- Brings the brethren into a correct relationship with God and one another; restores relationships.
- Converts sinners, produces saints and draws the backsliders back into the family of God.
- The way of revival is costly and humiliating. It includes dear and costly repentance, often with its exacting demands of open confession (Mark 1:4-5) and restitution (Luke 19:5-10). Leaders above all must not shrink back from paying the price.
- It re-emphasises the liberating release from the guilt and power of sin by cleansing in the blood of Christ.

Revival and the Church
- Transforms, strengthens, unifies, revives, renews and makes strong the Church, the body of Christ, but it may also divide and even split congregations.
- Brings to light that which was in darkness and exposes sin and all motives of the heart.

- Produces an increase of godly sincere repentance, reconciliation and *restitutions *Luke 19:5-10.
- Brings a greater emphasis on the cross of Calvary and the efficacy of the blood of the Lamb that was slain to take away the *sin of the world. *John 1:29.

Revival and Christian Ministry
- Raises up more lay-workers and thrusts forth more labourers into the harvest field.
- Calls more individuals from standard employment into full time Christian ministry. The intakes at Bible Colleges and mission agencies increase as more Christians heed the call of God.
- Brings into being new ministries and occasionally new mission agencies and / or humanitarian works.
- Christian ministries become more fruitful and effective for the Kingdom of God.

Revival and Educational Institutions
- Strengthens Bible Colleges and Training Centres etc., and sometimes leads to founding new ones.
- Revolutionises institutions of learning; often founding them and they owe a great debt to revival. This was best seen in America during the eighteenth and nineteenth century when many, now prestigious institutions were founded by Christians for godly education. See, chapter thirteen, Education, Evangelism and Missions.

Revival and the Community
- Can transform families, places of employment, churches, communities, people groups and islands.
- National revivals or awakenings can transform a nation and uplift society at large. In the past this had brought about social welfare and changes which have been enshrined in law. This was most clearly seen in the Evangelical Awakening (1739-1791) and the fruit of reform that flowed into nineteenth century Britain. Revival elevates society and can change the moral character of a nation.

In 1739, George Whitefield preached in Philadelphia, New England, America. The American philosopher, Benjamin Franklin, in his autobiography wrote: 'It was wonderful to see the change made by his preaching in the manner of the inhabitants of Philadelphia. From being thoughtless or indifferent about religion, it seemed as if the whole world were growing religious.'

In October 1742, Rev. William Halley of Muthil, (shire of Perth) Scotland, UK, who was witnessing a revival which was birthed out of the Cambuslang Revival (1742), in a letter wrote: 'The arrows of the Almighty King are still flying thick amongst us, and wounding the hearts of His enemies, and laying them down groaning at the feet of the Conqueror, crying under a sense of guilt and the frightful apprehension of wrath, and thirsting after a Saviour.'[1]

William C. Conant, in reference to the First American Great Awakening (1735-1760) wrote: 'It cannot be doubted that at least 50,000 souls were added to the churches of New England out of a population of about 250,000, as it is estimated; which makes the remarkable proportion of twenty percent of all inhabitants – a fact sufficient to revolutionise, as indeed it did, the religion and moral character, and to determine the destinies of the country. But this was not all. Perhaps as many converts were made within the churches as without them; and this, as every experienced Christian knows, is a change of double moment to the Church, at once adding strength and removing the most depressing of all burdens. Not less than 150 new congregational churches were established in twenty years.'[2]

An eyewitness from Bicester during the 1860 Revival in England said, "It is not asserting too much to say that a greater number of sinners have been converted to God in Bicester, and within eight miles of it, during the last ten months than have made an open profession of religion during the last two hundred years!"[3]

During the Pingtu Revival (1931-1933) which became part of the Shantung Revival (1930-1932) in north China, a missionary in a letter, dated 15 July 1932 wrote: 'In the densely populated county of Pingtu, Shantung [Province], where the revival began and the churches have become greatly revived, there are now villages in which every family has one or more saved persons, and in some villages nearly everyone has accepted the Lord. Is this not glorious news to all who love the Saviour!?'[4]

In 1952, during a revival in Brazil, in an interior city, the churches gained more additions in a month than in the previous decade.[5]

During the Congo Revival (1953-1957) a missionary wrote to the Worldwide Evangelization Crusade and stated that the Holy Spirit had descended on the 'hard and dry district' amongst the Meje tribe. From the Egbita centre she wrote: 'God has done in a few days things we had never seen in twenty years of labour, but one realises too that nothing has been lost of all the efforts of sowing and reaping. It is as though the Lord has reaped in a day.'[6]

Oswald J. Smith wrote: 'The greatest need of the world and the church today is a mighty manifestation of the Spirit of God. Before the days of Finney revivals [prior to 1821] there were only 200,000 church members in the United States. When Finney ended his ministry [he died in 1877], over three million had joined the churches. The greatest days of the Church have been the days of revival. Nothing can take its place. The best that man can do does not meet the need. Only as God comes upon the scene in revival power are the problems solved.'[7]

In the spring of 1938, a teenage Arthur Wallis was at Moriah Chapel, Loughor; the birthplace of the Welsh Revival (1904-1905). He thought to himself: 'If God can achieve such mighty things in times of revival, and if the spiritual labourers of fifty years can be surpassed in so many days when the Spirit is poured out, why...is the Church today so satisfied with the results of normal evangelism? Why are we not more concerned that there should be another great revival? Why do we not pray for it day and night?'[8]

Chapter Five

Who Needs Revival?

Abnormal and Normal Church

The majority of churches do not reflect the true representation of Christianity as revealed in the New Testament, the Church should be different than a social club and God must be glorified. This is why we need revival.

James A. Stewart wrote: 'Coldness, deadness and backsliding are abnormal and the Church will never become normal until she sees revival. The glorious splendour of the Church which shines out as a result of revival is the true standard our Lord has set up in the New Testament, and this is what He expects to see among His redeemed ones at all times.... A subnormal and backslidden Church is an insult and a disgrace to a holy and powerful God.'[1]

A Bible College student who had heard of several localised revivals in a number of Bible Colleges / Institutes wrote in his diary: 'I dedicated myself to pray persistently that the whole body of Christ might be made spiritual. At present it is far below normal. I find no basis in the Word for expecting those who are Christians to be subnormal! It is my duty to *claim* with thanksgiving the Church's possession of her privilege in Romans 8! May God make us spiritual, deliver us from conscious sin, and make us ever more conscious of sin!'[2]

Bishop Handley Moule, in his description of the normal Church said, "It is nothing less than the supreme aim of the Christian gospel that we should be holy; that the God of peace should sanctify us through and through our being; that we should walk worthy of the Lord unto all pleasing ['fully pleasing Him' Colossians 1:10]. It is the insatiable desire of the soul which has truly seen the Lord, to be made fully like Him by His grace.

"...To displace...self from the inner throne and enthrone Him; to make not the slightest compromise with the smallest sin. We aim at being entirely willing, nay, definitely to will, to know with ever keener sensibility what is sin in us, that it might be dealt with at once by the Holy Spirit. We aim at nothing less than to walk with God all day long; to abide every hour in Christ, and He and His words in us; to love God with all our heart, and our neighbour as ourselves, to live that in no conventional sense, 'no longer to ourselves, but to Him who died for us, and rose again' [Romans 12:1]....'[3]

Jonathan Edwards, a revivalist and theologian from the eighteenth century wrote: 'God hath had it much on His heart, from all eternity, to glorify His dear and only begotten Son; and there are some special seasons that He appoints to that end, wherein He comes forth with omnipotent power to fulfil His promise and oath to Him; and these times are times of remarkable pouring out of His Spirit, to advance His Kingdom; such a day is a day of His power.'

The Antidote is Revival

On 28 September 1935, J. Edwin Orr began a world tour to circumnavigate the globe. He travelled to America, Canada, Australia, New Zealand and South Africa. For the two preceding years he had travelled extensively around Britain, Eastern and Western Europe, into Soviet Russia and as far away as the Holy Land (modern-day Israel) and saw localised revivals in many countries. After World War II, J. Edwin Orr, a preacher and revivalist, became known as a world renowned revival historian. He wrote: 'No one will suggest that the spiritual poverty and smug self-satisfaction...is the ideal of the Lord for the body of Christ. The antidote is revival, and revival must always be the will of God. To refuse to pray for revival (as hopeless) is like impudently telling the Lord that His power is limited.'[4]

'Away with pessimism. It is the sin of unbelief. The pessimist says that revival is impossible. Such are seldom men of faith. They say that revival is impossible before Christ comes. While the Spirit of the Lord is among us, who dare tell Him what is possible and what is impossible. God forgive our unbelief. They will try to justify their statements from Scripture. Tell them all that I challenge them to produce one single verse which proves the impossibility of revival among

God's people. [Orr had just seen localised revival breakout in three Bible Colleges / Institutes in America and three localised revivals in New Zealand – all in a space of three months!]. They will quote, "When the Son of man cometh, shall He find faith in the earth?" Faith is already missing in the earth, but what has that to do with the Church of Christ? Revival is a Church affair. They will quote that we are in the Laodicean Church. The Laodicean Church is the apostate, professing Church – and you and I have nothing more to do with it. The call in the days of Laodicea is, "If any man hear My voice, and open the door" – have not we responded to that? Then we are free from the curse of Laodicea. It is a snare of the evil one to make us despair. Revival is always possible to the obedient child of God....'[5]

'One finds that the pessimist fulfils their own ideas in themselves. ['As a man thinks in his heart, so he is' Proverbs 23:7]. As soon as a man starts talking about the impossibility of revival, his own work is beginning to shrivel up. ['According to your faith be it done unto you' Matthew 9:29]. The man who believes in revival is the man who sees results.'[6]

Max Warren in *Revival An Enquiry* wrote: 'The Church which is true to the Bible knows that sin is a deadly reality in its own life and therefore it must seek the Holy Spirit. When the Holy Spirit comes in sin convicting power, revival takes place and revival is inevitably disconcerting for all that is complacent and sinful in the life of the Church, as well as disturbing for much that is good but falls short of the best.'[7]

Dr. Robert C. McQuilken wrote: 'Let us not limit God in His workings, and let us not fail to be ready for new and great outpourings of the Holy Spirit in the closing days of this age. For the days are upon us when nothing will avail to break through the overwhelming power of the enemy, except supernatural power beyond what most Christians have not known anything about. If the Church was supernaturally blessed of God at its birth, who will say that, in the closing days of its witness here on earth before its translation, it will not be blessed in even a mightier way?'[8]

Leonard Ravenhill wrote: 'Without question, the greatest need of this hour is that the Church shall meet her ascended Lord again, and get an enduement that would usher in the revival of revivals just before the night of nights settles over this age of incomparable corruption.'[9]

In March 1962, Rev. Geoffrey R. King, gave the presidential address at the Annual Assembly of the London Baptist Association. In his closing statements he said, "It is revival that we need – the one thing that can save the situation in our land today, in the world today – the one thing that will really begin to meet the whole situation. For this we must seek, for this we must cry, for this we must wait upon the living God, earnestly, humbly, unitedly, desperately. Our eyes must ever be up to Him for this. Our hearts must ever be lifted up [towards Him] for this is the one and only thing which will really meet our tragic need. But, meanwhile, let us give ourselves assiduously to digging the ditches for the floodtide of quickening which the Lord in His gracious purpose will be pleased to send us. And, while we are intent upon the quickening and the blessing of God upon our labours, who knows if, in His sovereign mercy, He may suddenly rend the heavens and break through upon us with the great thing, the Divine intervention, the outpouring of the Holy Spirit's power, the visitation of God in our time?"[10]

Willis Hoover who founded the Methodist Pentecostal Church in Chile, during the 1909 Chile Revival said, "I believe that the true secret of this whole thing is that we really and truly believe in the Holy Spirit – we really trust Him – we really honour Him – we really obey Him – we really give Him free rein – we really believe that the promises in Acts 1:4-5 [baptised with the Holy Spirit] and Joel 2:28-29 [I will pour out My Spirit on all flesh] is for us."[11]

A friend once asked Evan Roberts of the Welsh Revival (1904-1905) for a message to the churches that were praying for revival. Closing his eyes for moments, he prayed for guidance and then said, "They have the Word and they know the promise. Let them keep God to His promise, Ask and ye shall receive."[12]

Chapter Six

Views of Revival

How does God Work in Revival?

There are differing views amongst Christians as to how we can see revival. It relates to God's sovereignty and man's instrumentality and to what degree are they interconnected? But the common denominator from all sides is that it is the Holy Spirit that does the work as God comes down.

If we are only familiar with the more prominent national revivals such as the Great Awakenings of the eighteenth century in Britain and New England, America; the Fulton Street Revival (1857-1859) or the Welsh Revival (1904-1905) then our perception of revival, how it comes about, the effect it can produce and other factors will be narrowed.

G. J. Morgan in *Cataracts Of Revival* wrote: 'In the hidden ledger of God there is a specific law where every revival works accordingly, and every law runs back to the source of all things, even the wise Lawgiver who planned, the Mind that thought, the Heart that felt – the God that purposed everything in the end to reach the goal of perfection.'

Sovereignty, Instrumentality and Responsibility

- Is it purely God's sovereignty? – If so, do we sit back and do nothing and merely enjoy the ride?
- Is it a combination of God's sovereignty, human instrumentality and our responsibility?
- Does man have any degree of responsibility; some Scriptural duties that have to be undertaken?
- Do we pray revival down or can it be worked up?
- Are there key Scriptures to pray and plead?

Views of Revivals from Revivalists

1. It is totally a sovereign work of God.
2. It is God's sovereignty coupled with man's responsibility. Man applies God's promises.

3. Anybody can have revival at any time as long as the conditions and promises have been appropriated.
4. Preach the pure gospel with unction; exalt Jesus, the efficacy of the blood, the cross, man's sinfulness and the wrath and grace of God and you will see revival.
5. For some Pentecostals, revival can mean a gathering of Christians who receive the baptism of the Holy Spirit (often receiving the gift of tongues, Acts 2:1-11, 10:46 and 1 Cor. 12), or when a number of Christians in a service or conference receive a touch from the Holy Spirit when prayed for by a leader / minister.

The first three views are all part of the same swing of God's revival pendulum. The Holy Spirit descends in the day of visitation; reviving Christians and converting sinners. With point four, there are preachers who have such an anointing on their lives that regardless of their location, they see revival; it is as if they 'carry' the presence of God with them – 'glory carriers' – revival by extension. Often they will have had intercessors prepare the way before them.

The fifth point reveals why many Pentecostal personalities are referred to as revivalists, not because people come under conviction of sin and get right with God, but because Christian receive a touch from the Holy Spirit when prayed for, often with the laying on of hands. However, this can be abused leading to a "bless me," self-seeking attitude. Whilst some leaders minister with a 'different spirit' (2 Corinthians 11:3-4), (often unknowingly), for financial gain or popularity, and a mixture of Divine and demonic can be present.

A sixth point is that some preachers primarily aim at seeing Christians revived so as to build up and elevate the Church; they promote a revival of religion. They preach the Word of the Lord; denounce sin and challenge the brethren to get right before God. The brethren acknowledge their guilt and respond in Spirit-led repentance and confession which leads to contrition and brokenness before the Lord. Christians are revived and this inevitably flows into a community and sinners get converted. This was J. Edwin Orr's method of ministry in the second stage of his world tour (from Sept. 1935) where 90% of results were amongst believers, but he also saw 10,000 professions of faith in a single year!

God's Sovereignty and Human Responsibility

After the resurrection, Jesus sent His disciples to proclaim the good news as part of the Great Commission – "Go into all the world and preach the gospel to every creature" (Mark 16:15) and "Go therefore and make disciples of all the nations..." (Matthew 28:19). To see sinners converted and lives transformed is a Divine-human partnership – we are called to make disciples and to help, train and build up the body of Christ to the praise and glory of God. It is God's sovereignty coupled with man's responsibility and this is how we can see revival in the fullness of time.

In 1970, J. Phillip Hogan gave the presidential address to the Evangelical Foreign Mission Association (EFMA) and stated, "In Acts 5:32 we read, 'And we are witnesses of these things and so is also the Holy Ghost, whom God hath given to them that obey Him.' This indicates that the task of worldwide witnessing is a joint task. It is a cooperative endeavour between the Lord of the harvest and His Church made up of human vessels."[1]

The Divine-human Partnership Quotes

- Rev. William Haslam of the nineteenth century saw at least seven revivals. In *From Death Into Life* he wrote: 'Revivals – that is the refreshing of believers and the awakening of sinners, ought to take place wherever the gospel is preached in faith and power.'

- John George Govan, founder of The Faith Mission (Scotland) partook of several revivals at the end of the nineteenth century. He said, "Without God we cannot, without man He will not."

- Victor Ellenberger wrote *A Century of Mission work in Basutoland 1833-1933*. In reference to the Qalo Awakening (c.1912) in modern-day Lesotho, he wrote: '...The awakening of a whole district under the guidance of a missionary who had joined the mission rather late in life, is a veritable miracle of the power of God in conjunction with the faithful service of man.'

- James A. Stewart saw many revivals in Eastern Europe in the 1930s and 40s, and later in America, he saw one revival. In his book, *Opened Windows, The Church and Revival* he wrote: 'God's sovereignty and man's responsibility never clash in the Word of God. In His inscrutable wisdom and providence God has chosen to do His work in the world through His saints, and has so bound up His purposes with man that He limits His workings to man's obedience.'

- Duncan Campbell of the Lewis Revival (1949-1952), Scotland, in his book, *God's Answers, Revival Sermons* wrote: 'Let me say what I frequently say – that the God I believe in is a covenant-keeping God who is true to His engagements. 'If you will keep My commandments and execute My judgments, then will I do it!'' (1 Kings 6:12).

- Norman Grubb, in the foreword to *Floods on Dry Ground* which documented the Imbai Revivals of 1935 and 1936 in the N. E. Belgian Congo, wrote: 'It clearly demonstrates that revival is not an act of Divine sovereignty apart from human cooperation, but the legitimate outcome of man's compliance with Divine conditions for revival.'

- John Ferguson in his book, *When God Came Down an account of the North Uist Revival 1957-58* wrote: 'God Himself is the source of revival, but it is equally true that His people are the channels through which revival comes...Matthew Henry wrote: 'When God intends great blessing for His people, He first of all sets them a-praying.' And these words bring human responsibility and Divine sovereignty together, where they belong.'

- Miss Eva Stuart Watt's in her book, *Thirsting for God* wrote: 'Let us realise that revival is not a miracle, but like other events, is brought about by fulfilling God's requirements for revival and paying His price.'

- Arthur Wallis, in his book, *In the Day of Thy Power* wrote: 'The Word of God presents to us side by side the two foundation stones of every revival [Acts 1:4, 11, the brethren were united and in prayer] – the sovereignty of God and the preparedness of man. Because we cannot understand how they harmonise is no reason for emphasising one at the expense of the other.'

- Michael Howard has seen at least six revivals in various African countries during the 1980s and 90s. In *Tales of an African Intercessor* he wrote: 'No move of God or mighty revival is His sovereign act. God works and moves by the distinct cry of His people or is prevented by the distinct lack of their cry.'

Rev. C Perren in *Revival Sermons In Outline* wrote: 'Who can question the importance of human instrumentality in the salvation of men, when the Word of God so plainly declares, 'he that wins souls is wise'? 'They that turn many to righteousness shall shine as the stars forever and ever.' 'Let him know that he which converts the sinner from his error of his way shall save a soul from death and shall hide a multitude of sins.'

'While human agency is thus very plainly declared, we should ever remember that all man's work, however zealous and untiring; all his words, however eloquent; all combined forces of the professed people of God, apart from Divine sanction and aid, shall be powerless in bringing one soul to Christ or reinvigorating the Church. Such results are 'not by might, nor by power, but by My Spirit, says the Lord of hosts.' To attain success we must be 'labourers together with God,' labourers not idlers, labourers together with God, not equal with, but under and belonging to Him, in subordination to God as instruments in His hand.

'Great was the success of [Charles] Finney in revivals, and of his preaching it was said, "He preached God's word clear through and without flinching, never muffling the sword of the Spirit, he made it cut to the very marrow." These words may with equal force be applied to Jacob Knapp and Elder Swan, whose labours were blessed to thousands. Thus, in God giving the Word, and in man preaching it, there is a union of Divine and human agency, and without the knowledge of God's Word there can be no revival.

'Divine and human agency in revivals is markedly seen in the efficacy of personal and united prayer. The history of revivals amply proves prayer to be the right arm of every great awakening. To quote Scripture in proof of the necessity and potency of such work would be to transcribe a great portion of the sacred Word.'[2]

Covenant-Keeping God and the Fullness of Time

God is a covenant-keeping God because Scripture declares, 'know that the Lord your God, He is God, the faithful God *who keeps covenant* and mercy for a thousand generations with those who love Him and keep His commandments' (Deuteronomy 7:9). 'God of heaven, O great and awesome God, You *who keep your covenant* and mercy with those who love You and observe Your commandments' (Nehemiah 1:5).

Revival can be seen through God's sovereignty and man's fulfilled responsibility, (the Divine-human partnership), which is revealed in the fullness of time. All things are decreed in heaven (Psalm 119:89), but they have to be outworked on earth. It was Lewis A. Drummond who wrote: 'Prayer opens the door to the fullness of time.' The fullness of time is a series of synchronised events coming together as one, which unlocks and releases all that God has for that particular situation. It was the accumulation of Divine orchestrated events that fulfilled the prophecies of the Messiah: the conception of the forerunner, John the Baptist, the census which resulted in Joseph returning to his home town of Bethlehem, the Virgin Birth, the flight to Egypt and the death of Herod which enabled Mary, Joseph and a young Jesus to live in Nazareth, because 'when the fullness of time had come, God sent forth His Son...' (Galatians 4:4).

The fullness of time, waiting upon God (Jeremiah 14:22b) is revealed when we have prevailed in prayer like the persistent widow because prayer is the prevailing key to answer. But we also have to be living a consecrated life, in obedience to the Master with a pliable and contrite heart.

Our Cooperation is Needed

There are times when revivals seem to be spontaneous manifestations of Divine power and there is no human agency at work; but behind spontaneous moves of God are intercessors; or at least one person who prayed the heavenly fire down as did Elijah on Mount Carmel. '...As soon as Zion travailed she gave birth to her children' (Isaiah 66:8b).

In every revival there is an interblending between the Divine and human agencies. The prayer of the burdened heart is the key that unlocks the heavenlies imploring God to come down and revive His people. In seeing revival, God needs our cooperation and assistance as He chooses to work through human vessels. God had mercy on the inhabitants of Nineveh, but He did not send revival until Jonah went through the city calling the people to "repent" – and they did!

Rev. Duncan Campbell wrote: 'God is sovereign and will act according to His sovereign purposes – but ever keeping in mind that, while God is sovereign in the affairs of men, His sovereignty does not relieve men of responsibility.'

Rev. John Smith, from the early nineteenth century wrote: 'The *mode* of the Divine working is dictated by sovereign wisdom; but the *degree* depends on the faith of the Church. God Himself determines whether He will descend as the dew upon Israel or as the burning flame; but it is for His people to decide whether He shall come upon the single fleece while the rest of the floor is dry, or whether the whole of the camp shall be surrounded and gladdened by the scatterings of angel food....'[3]

George Mitchell chronicled the life of evangelist and revivalist, Jock Troup, who was used in the East Anglia Revival (1921-1922) in England, which flowed into the Fishermen's Revival (1922) in Scotland. Mitchell wrote: 'It is helpful and healthy to learn from revival times that God's emphasis has been on holy people He has mastered, rather than clever methods we can master.'

Our Responsibilities

God is not obligated to send revival if we have negated our responsibilities to 'be holy' (1 Peter 1:16), to 'walk uprightly' (Psalm 15:2) and we *must* have 'clean hands and a pure heart' (Psalm 24:3-6), because without holiness 'no one will see the Lord' (Hebrews 12:14). See also Isaiah chapter 58, Hosea 10:12 and Matthew 5:1-12 for our individual and corporate responsibility towards mankind.

As long as we do not fail to fulfill our part, living up to God's high and holy standard, then God will not fail to fulfill His. This is not trying to twist the arm of God or being presumptuously arrogant, but our covenant-keeping God has declared, "If My people who are called by My name will humble themselves and pray and seek My face and turn from their wicked ways, then I will hear from heaven, and will forgive their sin and heal their land" (2 Chronicles 7:14). 'God is not a man that He should lie...has He said, and will He not do it? Or has He spoken, and will He not make it good?' (Numbers 23:19).

Arthur Wallis in regards to Nehemiah's intercession for Jerusalem wrote: 'Nehemiah was able to prevail in prayer because he held God to be faithful and pleaded His promises. He reminded Him of what He had covenanted to do [Nehemiah 1:4-11] and pressed Him to fulfill it. This is a spiritual lever that never fails to move the Hand that moves the world.'

Praying for revival is taking God's promises as revealed in the written Word, the Holy Bible and presenting His own words to Him and seeking the fulfillment of those Scriptures, because He has promised – but it is foolhardy to pray these Scriptures whilst neglecting those which need to be lived out daily, e.g. "Be holy because I am holy."

If we have not done our part, then we cannot expect God to do His. But if we have done our part, then we can expect God to do His; though the timing and the method may be different than what we expected, as God says, "My thoughts are not your thoughts, nor are your ways My ways..." (Isaiah 55:8), but those of us who wait upon God 'will not be ashamed' or disappointed (Isaiah 49:23). Glory!

Just like the parable of the widow and the judge, 'men always ought to pray and not lose heart...' and 'cry out day and night' to Him (Luke 18:1, 7). And let us not forget the parable of the persistent friend who asked, sought, knocked and received, because God likes to give good gifts to His children (Luke 11:5-13). Therefore, 'be patient, brethren, until the coming of the Lord. See how the farmer waits for the precious fruit of the earth, waiting patiently for it until he receives the early and the latter rain' (James 5:7).

Miss Eva Stuart Watt, Home Secretary of the Sudan United Mission wrote: 'When He [God] finds Holy Ghost men willing to use Holy Ghost methods, things happen beyond the range of human effort or understanding. The Spirit of truth is come to guide us into all truth and, if we are willing, [He] will teach us the truth about this mighty challenge.'[4]

Chapter Seven

The Beginnings and Characteristics of Revival

Prayer in Preparation for Revival

- Revival always begins with a burden. It could be one person or more. They become a watchman who stands in the gap (intercession) on behalf of the land. To some they may appear to be going mad, like Jonathan Goforth of China or Evan Roberts of Wales, as they are so consumed and burdened with revival.

- Those with a burden would have long realised that personal revival always precedes a general revival. They would have got their own lives sorted out before they could expect God to move others en masse.

- Genuine disciples of Jesus Christ will be grieved and burdened over the state of the weak impotent Church, their sin-ridden community, city or country. They will be grieved that God is blasphemed and derided and is not being glorified as He should be.

- They desire Jesus' name to be lifted high and flown as a banner across their land. They wish all Christians could enter into a living relationship with the Holy Spirit, to know Him and His convicting and guiding power as He leads them closer to Jesus.

- God frequently steps in at the last minute, at the darkest hour – if God did not step in with His mercy, then He would have to step in with His judgment.

- Before a revival comes, faithful disciples of Jesus Christ will be praying and interceding for God to move His mighty hand and to pour out His Spirit from on high. They will plead the promises of God as contained within the Holy Bible. It has been said by many a preacher that preceding revival, the word 'O' or 'Oh' is always used in passionate prayer, pleading and interceding as it comes from deep within. Others will cry (Psalm 125:5) and sigh (Ezekiel 9:3-4 & 21:6).

- These disciples will be earnestly trying to live righteous, holy and God-glorifying lives. They will talk, read and *study revivals, awakenings and revivalists and encourage others to seek God for revival blessings. Because what He has done in the past He can do again. *See Psalm 111:2.

An Assurance of Revival

- Someone will go through a period of agony in prayer (travail in intercession) until they get an assurance that God will move in power and send the Holy Spirit (Isaiah 66:8b). It is often a case of: 'Let us not grow weary while doing good, for in due season *we shall reap* if we do not lose heart' (Galatians 6:9). But David Brainerd who saw revival amongst the North American Indians (1745-1746) had practically given up hope as he had his dreams dashed on too many occasions and then within days, revival came.
- This process of assurance is always after a period of intense intercession (Holy Spirit led prayer, Romans 8:26-27, Eph. 3:10, Eph. 6:10-18, 1 Tim. 2:1 & Jude 20). This includes identification, agonising (which can incorporate: weeping, travail, pleading and groaning in the spirit), which results in the assurance (spiritual authority), so that they know without a shadow of doubt that the victory has been won in the heavenlies and will soon be manifested physically through people's lives in their church or town. Because, 'Those who sow in tears shall reap in joy' (Psalm 126:5) – 'Our God shall come...' (Psalm 50:3).
- Missionaries and Church leaders on occasions have also had an assurance by the Spirit of God that revival will come. But, the Kuruman Revival (1829) in Namaqualand (in present day South Africa) amongst the Batlaping tribe of the Bechwanas, caught Robert Moffat and his fellow missionaries by surprise. It was a case of, 'The wind blows where it wishes and you hear the sound of it, but cannot tell where it comes from and where it goes' (John 3:8). For the missionaries it was, 'This is the Lord's doing. It is marvellous in our eyes!' (Psalm 118:23).

- Some people know precisely when revival will come and have dates from the Lord, but this does appear to be the exception and not the norm. For Rees Howells in Rusitu, Gazaland (present day Zimbabwe), he only knew that revival was coming a day before on 9 October 1915. Pentecost broke out on the tenth and lasted for five years! During the Congo Revival (1953-1957), an evangelist, Tomu, visiting the Wamba Mission Station knew that revival would come in three days time. See page 44.

William C. Burns, referring to the Kilsyth Revival (1839) in Scotland, UK, on 23 July 1839 wrote: 'Some of the people of God who had been longing and wrestling for a time of refreshing from the Lord's presence, and who had during much of the previous night, been travailing in birth for souls, came to the meeting, not only with the hope, but with well-nigh anticipation of God's glorious appearing.'

Charles Finney, from the nineteenth century wrote: 'There was a woman in New Jersey, who was very positive there was going to be another revival.' She spoke to the minister and elders to hold conference meetings but they ignored her request. So convinced was she that God was going to move that she employed a carpenter to make extra seats (benches) so that she could hold meetings in her home. 'She had scarcely opened her doors for meetings, before the Spirit of God came down with great power. And these sleepy church members found themselves surrounded all at once with convicted sinners....'

A few months prior to the Lewis Revival (1949-1952), two sisters in their eighties who had been persistently praying for revival into the early hours for months, knew that their prayers had been answered. One of them received a vision of a packed church in their community of Barvas. The parish minister was informed and for at least three months, prayer meetings for revival were held twice a week in a thatched cottage with church deacons and elders in attendance, whilst the sisters prayed at home. Rev. Duncan Campbell arrived in late 1949, after his first meeting, as the people were dispersing the deacon told him not to be discouraged, "God is hovering over; He is going to break through...He is coming. I hear already the rumbling of heaven's chariots wheels." About thirty people went into a cottage to pray and at 3am God came down and swept in which set the community ablaze for three years!

Rev. David Davies and his wife Anne were used in the Congo Revival of the 1950s. In July 1953 they brought a native evangelist, Tomu from *Lubutu, North East Belgian Congo (*the place where revival first broke out in February 1953) to their large mission station at Wamba. On Thursday the sixteenth; the evangelist spoke from Exodus 19:11 'Let them be ready for the *third day*. For on the *third day* the Lord will come...' and on Sunday the nineteenth, God came and revival continued for four years!

Steve Hill, a visiting evangelist to Brownsville AOG Church, Pensacola, America, told the congregation on Father's Day, 1995 that God was going to do something special and within two hours He did – revival lasted for five years!

Steve Hill said, "Religion will damn you to hell because it cannot save you. Don't tell me how much you *know* about the Lord. Tell me if you *know* the Lord. Do you wake up in the morning with Jesus on your heart? Do you go to sleep at night with Jesus on your heart? Do you sing His praises through the day? Is He your love? Is He everything to you? Do you worship Him? Do you know Him?"[1]

J. Edwin Orr wrote: 'If you want to serve God, "Present your body a living sacrifice, holy, acceptable to God" – it is your reasonable service (Romans 12:1). Jesus Himself said, "Why call Me, 'Lord, Lord,' and do not the things I say?" (Luke 6:46). He does not want the lip service of sentimental humbug; He wants the heart service of reasonable honesty. What is more, He needs it. "My son, give me thy heart..." (Proverbs 23:26). If the law required us to love the Lord with all our heart, we should not withhold it under grace. Full surrender is our reasonable service and "the love of Christ constraineth us" (2 Corinthians 5:14).'[2]

Common Characteristics of Revivals

Generally, Christians when referring to manifestations think of the demonic and the activity of the devil, the work of the antichrist. In this book, unless stated otherwise (or from the context in which it is written), the word manifestation(s) refer to physical phenomena, which come from the Spirit of God. Physical phenomena, bodily manifestations are not exclusive to times of revival, though they are greatly heightened during one. Some of the common characteristics of revivals are:

- When revival comes there will be a heightened awareness of God's presence as the Spirit descends on a church, chapel, hall, school, Bible College, university, village, town, island, community or nation.
- Christians will be renewed, revitalised and revived, once they have examined themselves through the eyes of a holy God and put away their sin. The Church (individual members) will be cleansed, refined and purified under the spotlight of the Holy Spirit.
- Many non-Christians will be drawn to a church where a revival is in progress, as if by an unseen hand. Some of whom will have not been inside a church building for decades or if ever. Some will try to leave and will be unable too, as if a glass barrier or restraining hand is stopping them.
- People will be converted inside and outside of the church building or wherever people meet, work or sleep. Some people will not even have had contact with a Christian, but the Holy Spirit will get a hold of them; at work, in the fields or on the road etc.
- There is a deeper reality of the cross of Calvary, the blood of Jesus, and what He has done for mankind, but especially for the individual (see Isaiah 53).
- God is no respecter of persons. People of all ages, from different social and political backgrounds of varying educational and economic levels get saved. Young children to the very elderly. A child of four or six can come under conviction of sin, just like an adult of eighty-four; though God will reveal sin (and Himself) in a way that each can understand.
- Converted teenagers become radical for Christ. They may not dress like us, look or talk like us, but they will press in for the deeper things of God and will not be ashamed of Jesus! The majority of these converts will

stay true to God and be trophies of grace, lasting fruit, the next generation of leaders, evangelists and missionaries etc. Many will have a zeal which has not been tempered by maturity, but that's ok. We learn from our mistakes and we have all been young once.

- Many child converts of revival will have an unusual zeal for God, a capacity to pray and an anointing on their life which can be quite mind boggling. With child-like faith and obedience to the Holy Spirit they can move in the gifts of the Holy Spirit without having any theology behind it. Child preachers can come to the fore, though generally not many, and this also includes young teenage girl preachers.

- It is not uncommon to see 10%, 50% or virtually the entire village or town becoming Christians during a time of localised revival. This was seen during the Northampton Revival (1734-1735) under Jonathan Edwards where amongst 220 families, nearly 700 persons (virtually every adult) became converted. The greatest statistic for a country, of which I am aware, was 25% (of five million population) during the British Great Awakening (1739-1791), though during times of repeated revivals this percentage can rise, as in Nagaland in north east India, where it is reported that 99% of the population (under two million) are now Christian (though this does include Catholics), after revival broke out in 1949, 1952, 1956, 1966, 1967, 1972 and 1976, and the fires of revival were still being felt in 2006.

- There will be a greater degree of Bible reading, an increase in: the quantity of Bibles and Christian literature sold, prayer and Sabbath observances (one day of rest which may or may not be on Sunday) will be more strictly observed; not out of compulsion or coercion, but out of a desire to please the Master and to get to know Him and His ways more.

- Those who are illiterate, even those who are elderly, will begin to learn to read so that they can read the Word of God for themselves, therefore the literacy rate in revival areas will be raised. This was perhaps best witnessed during the Second British Great

Awakening (1859-1860), the Indonesian Revival (1964-1974) and in many developing countries.

- Many secular pursuits, hobbies, interests or even things that people enjoy, though not sinful in themselves are generally disregarded for the greater price of the heavenly things above. Meeting with God is better than the neutral and that which is good.

- In national revivals there will be a great upsurge of lay workers who will assist in the work. These workers as well as ministers will preach a lot more frequently. William Grimshaw of Haworth, England, was the first beneficed clergyman in northern England to exercise an unrestrained evangelical ministry. It began in 1742 and he would preach up to thirty times a week.

- The press and frequently the secular papers alongside news websites and bloggers will write articles about the move of God. Often they are open and honest, but some news reporters will always denounce it as fanaticism, hypnotism, emotional experience or some psychological trick, to pull in the masses. Good as well as bad reports will bring the unconverted closer to what is happening, as curiosity always gets the better of people and as the old saying goes, 'There is no such thing as bad publicity!'

- There will also be those who have genuine concerns and are cautious, perhaps suspicious about what they see around them and are not immediately able to embrace the move of God. Some never will. Whilst others will openly denounce it vehemently.

- Sinners (and saints) will cause opposition and be critical of any move of God, especially in areas where Hindus, Muslims or Roman Catholics live. Often it is the demonic that stirs up the hatred and bitterness. We could say that they are victims, as many have been taken captive by the devil to do his will.

- Where God moves, the enemy always tries to infiltrate and imitate to cause the good that is happening to be spoken of as evil. We must learn to discern between God's dynamic and the demonic.

The Holy Spirit in Revival

- The Holy Spirit, as the third Person of the Trinity will be honoured. He will not be seen as a "thing" or "influence" or an "it," but as a Person, who brings conviction of sin, shows true righteousness, guides into all truth, gives direction and instruction and glorifies Jesus. The Holy Spirit can be 'resisted,' 'grieved' or 'quenched' all of which is forbidden in Scripture and we are commanded to be 'filled with the Spirit,' and He is 'given to those who obey Him.'

- Christians will be filled with the Holy Spirit (if not already) which is a separate and distinct experience from conversion. It can happen immediately or subsequent to conversion as the Holy Spirit cleanses them from all sin and *can* deliver them instantly from past bondages and addictions.

- In many revivals there is often talk of the fullness of the Spirit (sometimes referred to as entire consecration which can lead to entire sanctification). Whatever your preferred terminology, it is not that *you* have the Holy Spirit, but that the Holy Spirit has *you!* There is a world of difference which outworks itself practically into hourly and daily godliness.

William Booth was an evangelist who saw revival in Cornwall in 1861. Four years later he founded the East London Christian Mission, which in 1878 was renamed the Salvation Army. General Booth said, "Only God can take out of your heart the bad temper, pride, malice, revenge, love of the world, and all other evil things that have taken possession of it; and fill it with holy love and peace. To God you must look, to God you must go. This is the work of the Holy Spirit: He is the Purifying Fire; He is the Cleansing Flame."

Evangelist and revivalist, Rev. Lionel B. Fletcher stated that after his conversion, the greatest experience he ever had was when he realised that 'the mighty gift of the Holy Ghost was not only for men of the New Testament days, but was available for men today...the Christians birthright is the power of the Holy Ghost.' Whilst attending a conference in Sydney, Australia, (in which he fully gave himself to God at the after-meeting), Archdeacon Tress said, "God can only fill us to the extent that we yield ourselves to Him. If you yield yourself without reserve to God, you have the right to know that God gives Himself without reserve to you, and by faith you may claim the filling of the Holy Ghost."[3]

The Holy Spirit in Revival (Continued)

- The Holy Spirit on occasions, can come in waves of revival power (touching some groups immediately whilst leaving other groups for other occasions), especially on mission stations which in times past were considerably large, with hundreds of people and are often a community within a community. At the Ibambi Mission Station during the Congo Revival (1953-1957) the Holy Spirit came in three distinct waves. He first came upon the station people, then the schools and then a few weeks later, He came upon the Central Bible School.

- The Holy Spirit will speak to individuals or bring them under conviction for certain acts or ways, which generally they would not respond to, if the issue was mentioned from the pulpit. The Holy Spirit by His loving conviction will make it known that God does not approve of certain things and that they must give them up. The stumbling block in their lives might not be 'open sin,' but the motives of the heart and the reason why the believers do certain things. Perhaps it's pride to impress others, or overeating or overspending etc. as a way of self-comfort.

- Often in revival the Holy Spirit will set a person free instantly from alcoholism, smoking and other addictions, whom may have been bound by demonic forces – whilst at other times He will not *instantly* deliver them. See Alcohol, Smoking & Habits, pg. 76.

- Converts and revived Christians can receive fullness of joy in the Holy Spirit. Not just a few hours of joy whilst only at church, but a daily, weekly attitude of the fullness of joy, at work or at rest in His presence.

- The gifts of the Holy Spirit are always poured out in revival (to a lesser or greater degree), though from revival Church history it does appear that they have been more prominent since the *Azusa Street Revival (1906-1909), leading to the rise of Pentecostalism and very prevalent after the Charismatic Renewal of the 1960s and 1970s.

- In times of revival there are more documented cases of people speaking in an 'unknown tongue' which *is known* to someone within the congregation. It could be as common as a European language of which the person speaking in tongues is completely unaware of, or a little known tribal dialect. This was frequently the case in the Dutch Presbyterian Church in Soe, on the island of Timor during the Indonesian Revival (1964-1974) and recorded at the *Azusa Mission.

- There can be spontaneity; inside and outside of meetings, anywhere and everywhere within the vicinity of the Holy Spirit. Spontaneity in prayer, worship, praise, testimony and sometimes preaching.

- On rare occasions, and for a period of the revival, the Holy Spirit may not call anyone to preach, there could be no preaching at all, although this is the exception and not the norm. There may be lots of praise and worship like what was seen at many of the meetings during the Welsh Revival (1904-1905) and the Azusa Street Revival (1906-1909). For the first two weeks during the Hwanghsien Revival (1932) in north China, there was nothing but confession of sin! A missionary wrote: 'Meetings lasted five or six hours at a time with nothing but confession of sin, one after another bringing out the hidden as well as the known sins of his life. So deep was the work that hours for eating and sleeping passed by unnoticed. And so 'Judgment began at the house of God.' When sin was faithfully dealt with, and forgiveness received, many were baptised with the Holy Spirit. It is like the story in the book of Acts.'

Idols and Temples in Revival

- Where former heathen or animists worshiped idols of stone or wood, upon conversion they would smash their stone idols (or throw them into a deep lake) and burn their wooden ones. During the Shantung Revival (1930-1932) in north China, those who converted to Christ took down their household gods which had been worshipped for generations.

- Upon conversion, all fetishes (a charm embodied with demonic power), charms, amulets, spell books and various occultist paraphernalia will be destroyed, which is an act of renouncing one's old ways and is often done publicly. During the Eggon Revival (1930s) in Northern Nigeria, former spirit worshipers, including spirit priests came and burned their fetishes and followed Christ. On 13 February 1960, during the Dani and Uhundi Revival (1957-1962) in New Guinea, 5,000 Dani & Uhundi, recent converts burnt their charms and 3,000 followed suit the next day!
- In the West, the idols of money, time consuming hobbies or anything that takes priority over Christ have been disregarded as the flesh is crucified under the direction of the Holy Spirit.
- During the Florentine Revival (c.1493-1497) in Italy, at the bidding of Savonarola, the Florentine citizens threw onto the shelves of a giant wooden pyramid their books of magic, carnival masks and costumes, playing cards, dice boxes, the indecent books and pictures and many other things. This great pile was set on fire whilst the people sang hymns and was known as a 'bonfire of vanities.'
- If the majority of former heathen or animists villagers get converted, or most notably the chief of the village, they would often tear down the village temple or chop down the sacred groves. During the first five years of the Indonesian Revival (1964-1974) at least thirty temples were torn down. Temples destroying is also evident in African and Indian revivals and during the Nagaland Awakenings of the 1950s, 60s and 70s.

The Doctrine of Revival

A Christ-less, cross-less, blood-less message will result in spine-less, defence-less and power-less church goers with the nickname Christian, because a fast food gospel message will result in biodegradable believers. The doctrine of any revival *will always* emphasise Christ crucified, the cross, the efficacy of Jesus' shed blood and the judgment. The message will exalt Jesus Christ, the Saviour of the world.

The first Bishop of Liverpool, J. C. Ryle said, "Without Christ crucified in her pulpits, a church is a little better than a dead corpse, a well without water, a sleeping watchman, a silent trumpet, a speechless witness, an ambassador without credentials, a lighthouse with no power, a messenger with no good tidings. Such a church is a stumbling block to weak believers, a comfort to infidels, a hot-bed for formalism, a joy to the devil, and an offence to God!"

A. C. Stanley Smith wrote: 'From the very beginning of the revival [in Ruanda from 1937-1950s] the heart centre of the message was the cross and the power of the blood of Jesus Christ. An ever deepening understanding of these truths has saved the movement from many of the extravagancies of doctrine and practice which so often mar revival movements.'

'We preach Christ crucified...this is the great message of the revival, cleansing and victory through His blood. For ourselves it means death to self, self-pleasing which means lust, and self-seeking which means pride.... The theme of Christ crucified must ever be the basis on which our teaching of both justification [conversion] and sanctification [cleansing by the power of the Holy Spirit] is founded.'[4]

A. C. Stanley Smith also wrote: 'Underlying it all and the inspiration of it all was the profound understanding of and constant emphasis on the cross. This proved to be without a doubt a deep rooted and real movement of the Spirit.... The overwhelming emphasis in the revival was on the sins of the Church, the need for repentance and the efficacy of the blood of Christ for cleansing and life-giving power.'[5]

Leonard Ravenhill stated that it would be folly and a lie to give an aspirin to a cancer patient, telling them this would cure their illness. Ravenhill wrote: 'Equally criminal (in my judgment) is our attempt to appease soul-hunger of the millions around us by sermons that are not Christ-centred, not being born in the burning heart of a yearning preacher, and not wet with the tears of his own travail and anxiety for fallen man.'[6]

Chapter Eight

Reoccurring Experiences in Revival

Reoccurring Experiences in Revival

- Prayer meetings begin to multiply and the numbers attending rise rapidly. The Kilsyth Revival (1839) had 39 weekly prayer meetings and the congregation of Ballymena, during the 1859 revival in Ireland held on average 16 prayer meetings each night! Also 12,000 of Newtownards inhabitants (33%) attended the union prayer meeting! In September, 20,000 gathered for an open-air prayer meeting in Armagh. In July, 10,000 gathered for prayer at the Maze Racecourse whilst in October, the attendance at the Maze Racecourse decreased from 10,000 to 500!
- Prayer meetings are instigated by children and teenagers, and united prayer meetings are held at different churches of different denominations. In days past, and in various cultures it was common to have same sex prayer meetings so that there would be no appearance of evil and no cause of impropriety.
- The Holy Spirit through the ages has descended on schools, bringing children, teenagers and teachers alike into a saving knowledge of Jesus. Often it is like a ripple effect, moving from one classroom or floor to another. On occasions, this effect had travelled outside of the school gates and into the community. See chapter 13, Education, Evangelism & Missions.
- There are always some believers whose faces shine or radiate with the glory of the Lord (like Moses when he descended Mt. Sinai). This could be a revivalist, coming out of their prayer closet, or a new convert, rejoicing in their newfound salvation. This glowing or radiance can last for hours or a few days.
- The consumption of alcohol always drops. Pubs in small communities or even larger towns can go out of

business, whilst the consumption of alcohol will decrease rapidly. Landlords and brewery owners will be furious. Sometimes Christians do become drunk in the Holy Spirit and are unable to stand or become incoherent in their speech. This is not something to be sought, or to be ashamed of. God's work, done God's way will not lack fruit and He knows what He is doing. This was very evident in the Congo Revival (1953-1957) when people were 'intoxicated with joy' and 'drunk in the Holy Spirit' as several missionaries noted. I also witnessed it at the Brownsville Revival (1995-2000) when I visited in the summer of 1997.

- Those who have been under deep agonising conviction of sin, having been 'stricken' by God (many of whom can appear to be in a coma or even dead, that is lifeless) who had led evil lives can be delivered from their demons / evil spirits, as well as being converted to Christ. It appears that the longer a 'stricken person' stays on the ground, immobile, the deeper the work of grace and the greater the deliverance that they receive.

- Revival Church history reveals that most 'stricken people' should be left to God, to fully allow the Holy Spirit to do His deep work in their lives. Trying to bring comfort, speaking 'peace, peace' when there is no peace can be disastrous as they need to know their doomed state before they can receive His grace and abundant pardon. Their torment can go on for days or weeks, but when they are truly converted, it is a work of grace that is very deep and abiding.

- Prostrations can last for days; Church history records that in many of the revivals from previous centuries, people were left out in the open over night or for several nights until they came through to a saving knowledge of Christ Jesus. This may not be appropriate in the city centres in the twenty-first century, but people are still carried from meetings.

- On a few occasions, as the preacher was speaking on the Judgment Day, lightning has flashed across the sky, as in George Whitefield's day, and as witnessed at Rasharkin Presbyterian Church on the seventh June 1859, when lightning filled the church and 500 people prostrated themselves on the floor and 100 came under deep conviction of sin!

- God's grace always reaches down to the worst of sinners. Even those who openly mock God (mock the revival and defy His laws) have been stricken by the Holy Spirit. Some get stricken with the grace of God (Jude 18-23), whilst others become stricken with His judgment. The latter leads to death and an eternity in hell. Sometimes, these God mockers are struck dead instantly, at other times within hours or weeks, often suffering in a most miserable way and under demonic torment. Some will even take their own life like Judas.

- There are always those who were mockers of the things of God (especially those who spoke badly of the revival and publicly maligned the leaders); upon conversion or under the light of the Holy Spirit will apologise and / or retract previous statements.

- In all revivals there will be elements of flesh involved, but this swings on a pendulum from the over-the-top emotionalism to the traditional stale and stagnant, no emotion. We can be just as much in the flesh jumping up and down with our mind not on the Lord in worship as singing from a hymn or chorus book with disdain and hardness in our hearts. The flesh can be one who tries to 'work up' the blessing, one who imitates certain manifestations or those under the influence of the evil one or who have been completely taken captive by the enemy to do his will. On the other side, it could be one who resists, quenches or grieves the Holy Spirit, often by not allowing Him to work in their lives. Their opposition to change could be their comfort zones have been infringed upon, a dislike of: the freedom of worship, protracted meetings, physical phenomena or because the Holy Spirit is moving in a way that they are not happy with, as it goes against their preconceived theology of what happens, should happen and should not happen in revival.

- Sometimes the leaders of certain denominations will not embrace a revival but those within their churches will. Roman Catholics have frequently disdained revivals often believing them to be "Protestant and not Catholic." Some openly mock the Protestant 'excitement' yet still some get converted. During the Argentine Revival (1982-1997), God gave Omar Cabrera a real heart for nominal Catholics. His purpose was not for them to abandon the Catholic Church, but rather they should enter into the Kingdom of God through their faith in Jesus Christ.

- Denominations that hold communion weekends (generally they are traditionally held from Thursday to Monday in Scotland), have on more than a handful of occasions witnessed revival or if they were already seeing revival it was intensified. I put this down to the fact that prior to partaking of communion; we examine ourselves, (get right with God confess our sins and ask forgiveness) so as not to partake in an unworthy manner as 1 Corinthians eleven states. The Shotts Revival (1630) and the Cambuslang Revival (1742), both in Scotland are good examples of this.

- Many of those who have been in revival or converted in times of revival will be led or called into Christian ministry and some will become missionaries in a foreign field. I would go so far and state that if nobody was called into full-time Christian ministry during a period of revival then I would have to question whether or not a revival really took place.

- Ladies and young women have been used in revivals, as revivalists, evangelists, singers, helpers, or intercessors who accompany a revivalist as part of a team. From my research, only around two percent of revivalists are female, though many more partake in the work of revival alongside their husbands such as Catherine Booth of the Salvation Army.

- In many revivals there have been instances of heavenly music, as if the angels themselves are singing in the heavens above and can be heard on earth. These events have happened inside and outside of the church, even in the open fields.

- Fishermen or sailors who have been aboard their trawlers, boats or ships upon coming near port where there is a revival, have been struck by the Spirit of God, whilst others have been converted on the open seas, having had no contact with the revival! This happened amongst the fishermen during the East Anglia Revival (1921-1922) in England, which led into the Fishermen's Revival (1922) when it reached Scotland, and amongst the US Navy at New York during the American Great Awakening (1857-1859).

Revival and Time

- In the presence of the Lord time does not exist, five hours in the presence of the Lord can seem like ten minutes. During the Indonesian Revival (1964-1974) a five hour sermon was common, but could be as long as fifteen hours! This is why revival meetings are so protracted and frequently go through the night, until sunrise. If a revival persists for some time, the leader will usually try to end a meeting in the early hours, or earlier so as to allow those present to get some rest, ready for the next day's work. Worship as well as preaching (if there is any) can go on for hours and hours, without people getting restless.

- During the first two or three days of a major revival, when the Holy Spirit descends in awesome power, some people will not be able to sleep for two or three days or for a week, or will be satisfied with a minimal amount of sleep, say 2-4 hours a night. Some are driven by what I term 'spiritual adrenaline' or 'spiritual hyperactivity.' See pages 109 and 205+. This was noted during the Congo Revival (1953-1957) at several mission stations. When the Holy Spirit descended at the Bible College of Wales, South Wales, UK at Easter 1937, the early hours of the morning seemed as midday to staff and students alike as the presence of God was so real!

- There are times when a revival begins and continues day and night without cessation in one continuous meeting, with people coming and going. This was evident in Mount Hawke Revival (1852) in Cornwall, England, under Rev. William Haslam when a meeting lasted for 8 days and during the Asbury Revival

(1970) in Wilmore, Kentucky, America, which continued for 185 hours, a little over seven and a half days. I know of no continuing meeting lasting longer than eight days, but after the Moravian Revival (1727) in Herrnhut, Moravia, a twenty-four hour prayer meeting was begun which continued unbroken for one hundred years!

Revival and Work

- In past revivals down the centuries there have been many cases where businesses (shops and *factories) have had to close for a period of time. The workers being dismissed for a few days because of God's Spirit falling on the workforce. Firstly, the saving of the worker's souls is more important than profit, see Luke 9:25. Secondly, *it can be unsafe to work amongst heavy machinery, some under such deep conviction of sin can barely think straight, let alone stand up! Thirdly, the workers minds are occupied with something of a far greater importance (eternal issues) than manual work. Self employed persons have also had to take time out.

- Whilst work productivity increases amongst the saved it decreases amongst those under conviction of sin. Though on occasions, within rural districts, production of all sorts will just cease, even harvests of grain have been left uncut as seen at Lurgan, county Armagh, Ireland, during the 1859 revival.

- Workers (who are not under conviction of sin), who are soundly saved will have a greater capacity for productivity. A happy labourer is a productive worker and a converted worker will want to put in an honest days work. This was very evident during the Congo Revival (1953-1957) when natives in several mission stations who had procrastinated in construction work for months, completed buildings in a matter of days! During the Kilsyth Revival (1742) in Scotland, Rev. James Robe stated that the hay harvest was brought in 'a third part of time sooner over the ordinary.'

Chapter Nine

The Church and Revival

Common Characteristics within the Church

- Praise and worship to exalt and honour God will become more real, regardless of our preferred style of worship. In every national revival, (Reformation or renewal) new songs or hymns have been written, composed and sung to the praise and glory of God.
- Some revivalists aim their sermons at stale, dying and dead Christians, before they begin to preach the gospel to sinners (though in most audiences both are present). There is no point in trying to win the lost if they will only be suffocated by dead religion.
- Denominational and sectarian barriers are often broken down as God's people hunger and thirst after righteousness, and aim for unity. For example, Pentecostals and Baptist, Methodists and Presbyterian and Anglican and Congregationalists come together as one in Christ.
- Those with opposing views, Calvinistic and Arminian theology will also rejoice and work together in the harvest to promote the work of God. Sometimes the clergy of certain denominations will not embrace the move of God, but those within their churches will. Brethren will not be focusing on the minor issues of doctrine. They will realise that we are united by our faith in Jesus Christ and not our doctrinal preference. They will focus on the more important task of glorifying Jesus Christ, reaping the harvest and aiding discipleship.
- A greater compassion for the lost, hurting and needy will be manifest in practical social concern and action. It will be love in action and / or social reform.
- Members of the body of Christ will feel that it is their duty, even their obligation to question how another's

walk with the Lord is. 'Let the righteous strike me, it shall be a kindness and let him reprove me, it shall be as excellent oil; let not my head refuse it' (Psalm 141:5), c.f. Proverbs 27:6a, 17. This *should* be done in humility, with a concerned and humble attitude and heart. Giving and receiving a challenge is part of assisting in building up the body of Christ; being concerned for each others spiritual well-being.

- Many revivals have been so life changing in a community, town or city that many of the body of Christ have genuinely believed that they were living in the millennial reign of Christ! Also, some of the leaders or Christians of these large revivals have believed that the revival they were experiencing would be the last revival before the return of Christ, such as the Brownsville Revival (1995-2000), Shillong Revival (2006-2007) and numerous other large revivals from previous centuries. See page 154.

Church Services

- Poor weather will not affect people attending meetings when a revival is in progress. This feature was more noticeable in times past when there was no public transport or when people had to walk over hills and through valleys in driving rain or sleet, through thick snow or over some distance on foot.
- The attendance at prayer meetings greatly increases, resulting in a much higher percentage of committed members per congregation.
- If churches or chapels are kept unlocked people will gather to meet without a service being announced, and when there is a meeting announced people will be there hours before its commencement. If the church doors are locked they will be queuing outside, where impromptu services may begin in worship.
- Church services will increase. For the first fifteen months of the Rusitu Revival (1915-1920) under Rees Howells in Africa, they had two services every day! The Brownsville Revival (1995-2000) had five services per week (four evening services {Wed.-Sat.}

and one Sunday morning service, with a Tuesday evening prayer meeting and afternoon teaching session for church leaders and Christian workers.

- During revival, a leader who is taking a meeting will find it difficult to dismiss the people. Often he (or she) will try several times to bid the people to depart. In the first few days of a revival it is common for an evening meeting to go through until sunrise!

- Most of the older style church buildings during times of revival in the last century were unable to accommodate the masses that attended the services. William Romaine (1714-1795) was dismissed from his parish at St. George, Hanover Square, England, because the parishioners were annoyed at continually finding their pews occupied with strangers! Prior to Health and Safety regulations it was common for churches to be so filled, that people would be standing in the aisles, sitting on the window ledges and even on the pulpit steps! Many church buildings become so thronged with those unable to get in (100s or 1000s of people) that meetings were often held in the churchyard amongst the graves.

- During revivals there may appear irreverent acts, such as the preacher preaching from a tombstone, as did John Wesley from his father's grave in Epworth, England when he was not permitted to preach inside the church. If the preacher is preaching inside a graveyard then the people assembled will be standing on the graves! Some who are spiritually dead in trespasses and sins will be prostrated on the graves of physically dead, crying out for mercy while others are praising the Lord. As an example this was seen in Dunrod during the 1859 revival in Ireland, and at Limavady, where 2,000 people assembled in the graveyard of Drumachose, Presbyterian Church.

- Clear-cut, uncompromising gospel messages will be preached at funerals and if the person concerned had led an evil life, the preacher will tell the congregation so, without trying to appease the family – the truth sometimes hurts, but godly sorrow leads to repentance. Steve Hill, from the Brownsville Revival

(1995-2000) stated that, when a family asked him to take the funeral of their drug-taking, wild reprobate son, he informed them that he could take the service but would not lie and tell those present that, "Johnny was a good boy." Also, Steve will not take a funeral service unless he is permitted to give an altar call.

Notes for Leaders and Church Workers

- Unless the leader is wise and delegates responsibility to others he will soon become worn out, or encounter burnout and have a breakdown. Some have died prematurely for neglect of the human body (deprivation of food and sleep); this has been recorded by many ministers during the 1859 revival in Ireland. Evan Roberts had several breakdowns during the Welsh Revival (1904-1905).
- The leaders within a localised revival, especially ministers, elders, deacons and other committed members of the congregation will find that their lives will change dramatically as there will be extra responsibilities and duties which will need to be dealt with, especially enquirers (those burdened by sin) and interviews with the press and media etc.
- Leaders will have to lovingly rebuke Christians who act in the flesh (trying to imitate the things of God) and on occasions those who oppose the things of God. But we can also be in the flesh by resisting what the Holy Spirit is doing; rebellion is as the sin of witchcraft (1 Samuel 15:23). Do not quench, resist or grieve the Holy Spirit; openly, or in your heart.
- Revival is a revolt from low spirituality. New converts or revived Christians are prone to question the reality of the conversion and commitment of others, but especially those with positions of authority when they see no life or joy. This can cause offence, but one has to wonder why they are asking such a question in the first place! It is a flippant remark to say that they are full of pride when we may be too proud to accept a rebuke.
- Leaders can hinder revivals in many ways. See chapter twenty-seven, Hindrances to Revival.

Chapter Ten

Common Characteristics of Physical Phenomena

Physical Phenomena

Physical Phenomena, bodily manifestations, are always present during any move of the Holy Spirit because we are emotional beings. During revival they affect people to a lesser or greater degree, but should not be sought. Physical phenomena can be varied from weeping to dancing; unrestrained worship to repentance and like Israel during the completion of the foundations of the rebuilding of the temple, it can be difficult to 'discern the noise of the shout of joy from noise of the weeping' (Ezra 3:13). It is what is known as 'Divine disorder' or 'a solemn commotion.' We are commanded to 'let all things be done decently and in order' (1 Cor. 14:40), but what is *now* considered as 'decently and in order;' propriety, is not the same as what we read in the New Testament! See page 132. In times of revival the Holy Spirit is in charge and He does things His way, which to the traditional and ritually observant will appear disorderly.

Puritan revivalist, Richard Baxter of Kidderminster, England, in *Five Disputations* wrote: 'It is better that men should be disorderly saved than orderly damned; and that the Church be disorderly preserved than orderly destroyed.'

Not everything you see in revival is from God. The enemy will always be looking to take advantage and there are always attention seekers. But there can be a danger in hastily reacting to physical phenomena in another and deciding that it is either fleshly or of demonic origin. If it is of demonic origin then the demons ought to be cast out, if they are not already fleeing! On the other hand, if the person's bodily movements are a reaction to God's presence then the dangers lies if we try to suppress him or her and thus hinder the work of God in the person's life and thereby quench the Spirit. There is a difference between genuine emotion felt as the *result* of an experience and attempting to work up an emotion in an attempt to *produce* the experience. The latter is of the flesh, trying to work it up.

Charles H. Spurgeon who saw revival in London in the 1850-60s said, "He [God] *can* bless us as He wills and He *will* bless us as He wills. Let us not dictate to God. Many a blessing has been lost by Christians not believing it to be a blessing, because it did not come in the particular shape which they had conceived to be proper and right."

At the beginning of March 1860, Rev. T. H. Baxter, a United Presbyterian minister from Banff, UK, was in Buckie and Portordon. In his church the following Sunday he gave his opinion of the revival in Scotland from personal observation. 'He did not deny there were improprieties, but if they waited for a revival of religion without improprieties, they never would have one at all. The means, instruments, manifestations and results connected with the revival, so far as he could discern, were similar to those connected with every genuine revival since the Day of Pentecost.'[1]

During the 1930s, revival was sweeping China. Rev. Richard S. Bjorkdahl of the Swedish Missionary Society describes a series of meetings held at Wuchang, during 7-21 October 1934. He wrote: 'Rev. Wu Djen Ming of the Lutheran church in Honan had promised to help us out.... Rev. Wu could not stay the full fourteen days. He had only promised to be with us ten days, and when these were over, we said farewell to him.... After Rev. Wu, we had four days help from the so called Bethel Band, from the institution planted by Dr. Mary Stone in Shanghai. It was composed of two pastors, Chi and Lin, and a singer by the name of Sun. Their aim was mostly to win outsiders. They were very lively and somewhat noisy. They would make sketches on the blackboard illustrating their sermons, they sang and played and sold their books with a good deal of flourish. Some of our members, who had not fully come through during Rev. Wu's meetings, were awakened and helped. People differ much as to nature and disposition, and God has many means at His disposal. *What seemed distracting to me, sometimes even repelling, proved liberating to others.* A very good result of the meetings of the

Bethel Band was the formation of voluntary preaching bands, which have started to go out witnessing about the salvation in Jesus.'[2]

Dr. Martyn Lloyd-Jones in reference to physical phenomena in revival said, "These phenomena [from Acts 2:14-18] are indicative of the fact that some very powerful stimulus is in operation. Something is happening which is so powerful that the very physical frame is involved...the phenomena are not of importance in and of themselves. The phenomena therefore should not be sought, they should not be encouraged, they should not be boasted of. The phenomena if I may use a modern term are epiphenomena [a by-product of another phenomenon], incidental, occasional, concomitance and not of vital essential part.... The body is weak, some bodies are weaker than other bodies, and so when this mighty spiritual power comes there are certain bodies that break down and they should be helped and dealt with in a semi-medical manner. They should be prayed for, they should be pacified, and that is how these great leaders of revival have always dealt with them.... Anybody who tries to work up phenomena is a tool of the devil..."[3]

Dave Roberts, editor of *Alpha* magazine, in his book, *The 'Toronto' Blessing* wrote: 'To suggest that all our physical reactions to a Divine encounter must correspond exactly to a proof-text criteria is to turn the Bible from the story of salvation and grace into the rule book of salvation.'[4]
Roberts also wrote: 'Allowances must be made for congregation members learning to respond appropriately to the Spirit, and for leaders learning to discern between the Spirit, the flesh and the devil. Judgments about a church's conduct on the basis of one meeting do a disservice to those involved.'[5]

Common Characteristics of Physical Phenomena
- Inside and outside of the church building, people, sometimes only a few, whilst at other times it can be hundreds or thousands will be shouting out praises to the Lord, such as "Glory," "Hallelujah," or "Praise the Lord" etc. Often it is as if the person will explode and

so is compelled to shout aloud to the glory of God! Billy Bray from Cornwall of the Twelveheads Revival (c.1824), Cross Lanes Revival (c.1830), the Crantock Revival (c.1867) and at least five other revivals; all in Cornwall, England, was always full of the joy of the Lord. He abounded in shouts and praise and leaped and danced not only at church, but in the street, at the market, even when he was hundreds of feet down the mineshaft at work!

- Holy laughter (and holy joy) is an interesting phenomenon which practically outworks itself through an individual's vocal cords and is expressed on the face of the recipient. It is often uncontrollable and unrestrained and comes from deep down inside a person. Evan Roberts from the Welsh Revival (1904-1905) would often be in the pulpit, laughing and smiling and some thought that this was irreverent. A missionary during the Hwanghsien Revival (1932) in China told the Lord that she did not want any manifestations but only Him. In a few minutes she was on her feet and giving her testimony. She wrote: 'I began, "Who can lay anything to the charge of God's elect?" [Romans 8:33] and burst out so in praise to God that I knew that the Power in me was from above and my heart was filled with holy laughter and praise (Psalm 126:2). Many others have received this blessing, some not in full, some more fully....'
Also, Mr Kiang Fang Nan surrendered his all to the Lord and received the fullness of the Holy Spirit. Great joy and floods of laughter came over him and he praised the Lord for two hours!
- There are always sceptics because of physical phenomena, bodily reactions during revivals. Physical phenomena can be emotional reactions which are transmitted via the body due to the convicting and illuminating power of the Holy Spirit, while some can be of human origin (imitation) or of demonic origin (infiltration & demonic manifestation).
- Physical phenomena can be screaming, shrieking, falling down (prostrations, strikings, swooning, fainting etc.), turning pale, looking fearful or petrified

(visions of hell, Calvary or the coming judgment etc.), perspiring, heaving of the chest, sighing heavily, being unable to walk, incapacitated, immobilised, jerking, trembling, shaking, shivering, rolling on the ground, flaying arms, crying, laughing, praising, shouting, weeping, sobbing, moaning, or groaning etc. When revival came to the Gahini Mission Station in north-east Rwanda in late June 1936, people in many different circumstances would begin to shiver, which led the missionaries, at first to believe that they had some sort of African fever. They soon realised that they were under conviction of sin and in fear of a holy God. I have only read about shivering on two occasions, whereas shaking or trembling is common.

- On rare occasions, those under conviction (see chapter 11) can lose their speech (being unable to communicate in any way, shape or form) sometimes being in a trance-type state and can be physically, as stiff and rigid as a board. This happened to the ringleader of a four man group who intended to disrupt a meeting during the Golant Revival (1854) in Cornwall, England, and was converted the following day. In the Hwanghsien Revival (1932) in northern China, a Communist schoolboy was so convicted of his sins that his body became rigid. He fell against one of his teachers and cried aloud for mercy, being terribly afraid. He was told to pray to God and felt that his very life was being crushed out of him. Teachers and friends prayed for him and urged him to pray. After one hour he did and then for a further hour he confessed his sins and asked forgiveness towards his fellow pupils and found the peace of salvation.

- In a similar incident, during the Shantung Revival (1930-1932) in northern China, a healthy young man, a so-called 'Christian' worker deceived himself and others by insisting he was saved. One night in the courtyard he was suddenly struck down and had to be carried inside, stiff, blue and cold! Missionaries called into his ears, "Confess your sins quickly!" As soon as he could open his mouth he poured out his black sins and stood on his feet again, a forgiven sinner. Several others had God's hand on them in similar ways. Note: Some intercessors have out of body experiences (2 Cor. 12:2) and they can appear dead, being physically cold like Mary MacLean who had been used in the 1939 Lewis Revival, Scotland.[6]

Physical Phenomena, Conviction and Inner Healing

- Jerking, shaking or trembling can be a process that the Holy Spirit uses to literally shake things out of people, bringing inner healing to old wounds and scars. It has been known for people to shake so vigorously that their cowboy boots have come off! The outward is merely a bodily reaction to an inward working and should not be alarming. Whilst some who are overcome by the Holy Spirit are motionless.
- The Holy Spirit during times of revival (and outside of revival) can come in so much power that frail human bodies are unable to cope – it is like electricity flowing through one's body, tingling all the nerve ends, though without any pain. One missionary from the Congo Revival (1953-1957) described it in similar terms when the Holy Spirit came upon her. Sometimes in intercession the body will shake, tremble or jerk as the person is burdened for souls (or other situations) under the anointing and leading of the Holy Spirit – this was testified and recorded by a number of people in both the Brownsville and Congo Revival. One night, Alison Ward testified for around fifteen minutes at Brownsville Church and immediately at the end, an altar call was given, (with no preaching that night) and hundreds came to the front. This unnatural repetitive movement can cause the body to ache (though not painful), as muscles are moved in ways that is not normal for everyday life.
- It is common during revival to see people crying. Crying for joy, crying under conviction of sin or because they are repentant. In times past, when a revival was in the vicinity of a mining community, it was common for miners to come straight out of the pit and attend a service. At other times the preacher ministered in the open-air near the pit, and tears

would be streaming down the miners blackened faces making white gutter lines down their cheeks. This was noted under Billy Bray and other revivalists in the 1820-50s in Cornwall, England, and in the mining valleys during the Welsh Revival (1904-1905).

- People can be under conviction of sin for days, weeks or months as they are in the 'Valley of Decision.' Revival Church history records that people have been under conviction of sin for years prior to a revival, which is greatly intensified during revival. Metaphorically speaking they will either be broken or ground to powder. See Matthew 21:44. Broken by submission or crushed by their rebellion.
- Not all who are awakened (under conviction) come through to salvation. There is false repentance, when a convicted person simulates repentance, or even appears remorseful, sometimes shedding *tears but they are just going through a simulated process with no regeneration. *It could be crocodile tears. Malachi 2:13 reveals that the people were weeping because they gave their offerings with a reluctant heart and were upset because of their loss! Sometimes people are repentant or remorseful because they were caught or found out. Outwardly they appear changed, but they have not come to God and asked His forgiveness. They are either good actors, self-deceived or double-minded. See chapter twenty-three, False and Spurious Converts and chapter twenty-four, Counterfeit Conversion.

Common Characteristics of Physical Phenomena II

- Some people will fall out of the pew or off their seat or fall over if they were standing up as the arrows of the Lord fly forth, bringing conviction which can lead to prostrations. Some Christians will be prostrated but are not necessarily under conviction of sin.
- Some under conviction will wring their hands, heave their chests with emotion, sigh, perspire, shake, tremble, roll on the floor, cry out loud, or jerk, while others who have been struck by the arrows of the Lord appear to be in a coma or even dead –

motionless. Some will be in a weakened condition and will be laid up in bed for days or weeks.

- Some Christians will manifest similar if not identical physical phenomena, as mentioned on the previous page, yet are not necessarily under conviction of sin. The Holy Spirit may be doing a work inside of them, often an inner healing of the emotions from the scars of the past or Divine deliverance from demons. Generally, the wringing of the hands, or perspiring in revival is associated with conviction; unless it's hot!
- If a godly Christian begins to weep, cry and moan (Romans 8:26), it is often a form of identification, how God feels, or compassion for the lost – being burdened. Though they could just be weeping for joy.

In 1956, David Du Plessis, the former General Secretary of the Apostolic Faith Mission, was invited to attend the World Council of Churches as a member of staff. On one occasion, in a rebuttal concerning the criticism of emotionalism in meetings he said, "I would rather see people, any time, weep for sheer joy in the Holy Ghost, than to see them weeping in a theatre because of some 'make-believe' show. I fear we are so afraid of emotionalism that we have caused people to give expression to their feelings in amusements centres."[7]

J. Edwin Orr was in a meeting in Norway, when the Holy Spirit swept in. People wept, confessed sin, others praised the Lord, whilst some knelt or stood and a few trembled. In a rebuttal to claims of emotionalism he wrote: 'Sorrow is an emotion, and if Christians are overwhelmingly sorry for their disobedience, may they not weep? Joy is an emotion, and if someone suddenly realises that his awful sins are forgiven, may he not shout, "Hallelujah?" I have never yet heard of a revival which was *not* accompanied by emotional phenomena. Emotion is not revival, for revival is a deep and abiding work of grace in the innermost core of our beings. But we are only human. I have seen brothers reconciled, and falling into each others arms, weeping. The change of heart was the work of God's Spirit, but I and all others rejoiced to see the outward manifestation of the work of grace.'[8]

Chapter Eleven

Conviction and Confession of Sin

Conviction of Sin (see also pages 68+)

- In revival there will be conviction of sin to a lesser or greater degree. Some will be in great anxiety and deep distress and a small portion of these will be unable to sleep or eat. In China during the revivals of the 1930s they called it sin-sickness!
- Many non-Christians will writhe in agony of soul and be in deep torment until they bow the knee to Jesus Christ, or if they are already a Christian, until they get specific sins out of their life. When George Whitefield preached his first sermon in the last week of June 1735, complaints were laid at the bishop that he had driven fifteen people mad! During the early Salvation Army meetings, the small hymn books would be torn to shreds by those under conviction! Leonard Ravenhill stated that in 1926, at a W. P. Nicholson's meeting he also saw song books torn to shreds by those under conviction!
- In extreme cases those under conviction of sin will beat the floor (or whatever inanimate object is around them); depending on if they are on the floor or sat down etc. Their thumps will be so hard and prolonged that those present will fear that the person will do themselves an injury! Though I have never read of an instance where injury has occurred.
- Those who are under conviction of sin will be encouraged and urged by believers to repent of their sin (sometimes to confess) and to turn to Jesus.
- Some who cry out under conviction will often drown out the preacher's voice; sometimes they need to be removed outside or to another room, and at other times, the cry of the repentant brings conviction to those who are hardened and they too become

convicted of their sins. Some scream so loud and so terrifyingly, it is as if they have been shot, stabbed or attacked by an assailant!

- Not all who are under conviction of sin (those who have been awakened) will come through to conversion and there are numerous reasons for this. See chapter 23, False and Spurious Converts.

Christians under Conviction of Sin

- During revival, Christians will have a sharper conscience and will feel quick conviction for seemingly minor offences, (though in God's eyes, sin is sin). I remember reading about one person who wrote a letter during a revival and decided not to dot the i's and cross the t's. This person came under conviction and remedied the letter. For some, this will appear extreme, but God is always looking at the heart and motives and diligence is very important.
- Christians will be more spiritually sensitive, not wanting to grieve the Holy Spirit and will mourn over their sin, realising that they have injured Jesus.
- Christians will be broken and humbled before God, as they see Him afresh in all His holiness, majesty and splendour. In such a spiritual state, they will also be broken that their sin nailed Jesus to the cross of Calvary – their sin, our sin, put Him there.
- Christians will come under conviction for sins of commission – what they know is wrong and still do.
- They will also come under conviction for their sins of omission – what they know is right or should be done and did not do. Neglect of prayer, Bible reading, careless in word or action or neglecting widows and orphans etc. During the Shantung Revival (1930-1932) in China the sin of robbing God in tithes and offerings (Malachi 3:8-10) appeared to be quite common and was even paid in arrears!

Confession of Sin

- There will always be confession of sin, frequently in public meetings. These confessions are prompted by the Holy Spirit and aid the joyous release of forgiveness. But, some confess whilst in the flesh.

- There is a danger in public meetings in getting caught up in the atmosphere and openly confessing sexual sins without the prompting of the Holy Spirit. People can be unknowingly used by the enemy to cause harm or shock sensitive people or introduce ideas not already there. Wisdom is needed; but especially when members of the opposite sex are present.
- The public confession of sin is a humbling process and also a way of accountability. In oriental countries, such as Korea, China and Japan; it would appear that confession of sin is harder because, culturally speaking, the person will 'lose face' (one's credibility).
- During the Pyongyang Revival (1907-1910) in Korea and the Shantung Revival (1930-1932) in China, incidences occurred where indigenous Christians had to confess their sins of being prejudiced against the foreign missionaries. This type of prejudice does seem more common in oriental countries. Sometimes it is also the Western missionaries who have had to confess their incorrect attitude of superiority, especially in Oriental, Asian and African countries. After confession a greater level of unity is achieved and a true blessing can flow (Psalm 133).

There is a world of difference between saying "sorry," which is often meaningless and without heart and asking someone's forgiveness for a wrong that has been done against them which is humbling. If we do not deal with our sin in private, when revival comes we will have to deal with it in public! Deal with it now, rather than blush in public.

Rev. D. R. Wahlquist of the Swedish Missionary Society, described a series of meetings at Macheng, Hupeh, about fifty miles north of Hankow. The meetings were held from 22 September to 5 October 1934, under the leadership of Pastor Liu Dao Sheng and meetings were afterwards held at the various outstations under the leadership of the missionaries and local workers. Rev. Wahlquist wrote: 'The winds of revival which have been blowing over wide areas of

China have also come to our field, the martyr district, where the blood of the martyrs now bears its richest harvest. No wonder our heart rejoices with an unspeakable joy.

'Sins as black as night have been confessed, such as child murder, fornication, etc. One woman had killed six girls during the course of her wedded life. Another had killed four, etc., etc. The latter was the widow of a church member. As long as the husband lived, she cared nothing for God, but now she was gloriously saved. Some tried in the beginning to confess their sins in a lump. "Forgive me all of my sins." Or they tried to mention only the 'small' sins. But peace did not come in that way. Only when each individual sin was mentioned by name, whether 'small' or 'great,' and when no sin was purposely hidden, could assurance of forgiveness come, and the heart be filled with peace and joy. Many sought us privately for confession and prayer. We sang frequently a little stanza: "The sins of the heart pour out, pour out; *your* sin's account make clear, make clear!"[1]

Dr. William Newton Blair, missionary to Korea, witnessed the beginning of the Pyongyang Great Revival (1907-1910). In his book, *The Korean Pentecost* he wrote: 'Then began a meeting the like of which I had never seen before, nor wish to see again unless in God's sight it is absolutely necessary. Every sin a human being can commit was publicly confessed that night. Pale and trembling with emotion, in agony of mind and body, guilty souls, standing in the white light of that judgment, saw themselves as God saw them. Their sins rose up in all their vileness, till shame and grief and self-loathing took complete possession; pride was driven out, the face of men forgotten. Looking up to heaven, to Jesus whom they had betrayed, they smote themselves and cried out with bitter wailing, "Lord, Lord, cast us not away for ever!" Everything else was forgotten, nothing else mattered. The scorn of men, the penalty of the law, even death itself seemed of small consequence if only God forgave. We may have our theories of the desirability or undesirability of public confession of sin. I have had mine; but I know that when the Spirit of God falls upon guilty souls, there will be confession, and no power on earth can stop it.'[2]

Chapter Twelve

Revival and the Community

Revival and the Community

- During revivals (unless it is only a localised revival in a church) crime will drop; the police and local magistrates will notice the effect, though not all in authority will acknowledge the decrease of crime as a work of God. During the Welsh Revival (1904-1905), many magistrates were given white gloves, a rare British tradition, as there were no cases to try!
- Wrongs will be righted; restitution and reparation where applicable will be commenced.
- It is not uncommon to find whole families turning to God in times of revival, but like a conversion at any time it can also split a family, as some stubbornly refuse to surrender their lives to Christ. See page 142.
- There will be a greater freedom to worship in public. Especially before the popular advent of motor cars, it was common to hear passengers on trains or buses singing hymns, as well as pedestrians, as they were going to and from revival meetings.
- There is always a social impact (ministry of helps), where those converted want to do more to reach and help their fellow man, e.g. temperance societies, missionary organisations, orphanages, change or implementation of laws etc. Sometimes this impact is immediate, at other times these ministries are birthed during or after a revival from those who were converted, transformed or influenced by it. This was very notable during and after the Evangelical Revival (1739-1791) in Britain, where godly men and women (including MPs, Lords and Ladies) and ministries were raised up to elevate society.
- There is a notable increase in the number of Bibles, Christian: literature, merchandise and resources sold,

as Christians are revived and the young converts (as well as older ones), hunger for more biblical truth. They will also apply the teaching in their lives.

- Many young converts will frequently advance from milk to meat in a short space of time, as if being fast-tracked by God in a greenhouse environment of accelerated growth. The biblical principles that have taken us years or decades to learn, they may learn in as little as a few weeks or months.

God's Mercy and Compassion

- God's compassion and mercy is frequently demonstrated to those who appear least *deserving such as murderers, God mockers, drunkards, wife beaters, habitual adulterers and blasphemers, as they come under dreadful conviction and get saved. *None of us deserve God's mercy; it's His grace – all are guilty sinners before a holy and just God.
- God's judgment (and mercy) is sometimes demonstrated towards mockers and blasphemers who are in the midst of their rants. They are struck down whilst under the sound of the preacher. Instant death or conversion is not unknown! Some are so tormented that they take their own life. Some of these deaths are not instantaneous (see Ezekiel 11:1-2, 13), but within hours, days or weeks and some die most horribly and painfully. George Whitefield was in Yorkshire, standing next to a pair of gallows and was about to preach on Hebrews 9:27, 'It is appointed for man to die once and after this the judgment' when a shriek was heard and a person dropped down dead. A few seconds later another person within the crowd made a shriek and dropped down dead – apparently the open-air audience were very attentive after that!

Revival, Alcohol, Smoking and Sinful Habits

- During revival, the consumption of alcohol always drops and thus trade declines. Pubs, drinking houses and bars in small communities or even larger towns may go out of business as the consumption of alcohol decreases. Landlords and brewery owners will be furious. Charles H. Spurgeon in July 1859, speaking in London about the Ulster Revival (1859-1860) said, "In the small town of Ballymena, [Ireland], on market day, the publicans have always taken one hundred pounds for whisky and now they cannot take a sovereign all day long in the public houses." A few years after the North Uist Revival (1957-1958) in the Outer Hebrides, Scotland, the local press reported 'that the drinking trade in North Uist has been ruined!'

- Inevitably those who were former drunkards or social drinkers upon conversion will find themselves on a better financial footing. This was more evident during the revivals in the eighteenth to early twentieth centuries in Britain when people were a lot poorer, they did not get a fair wage and often wives and children were shamefully neglected and ill treated.

- When the owner of a drinking establishment gets converted, they will always stop selling alcohol and close the establishment down. They prefer to lose money and change their profession rather than prop up an institution which leads to unrighteousness and assists in a number of vices. During the Congo Revival (1953-1957), those who grew palm trees from which palm wine was obtained, cut them down at a great financial loss to themselves.

- During the Indonesian Revival (1964-1974), Christians refused to partake of communion, as wine was used. On the Island of Timor there were no grapes grown so the church used tea and sugar. After some time they felt they should use what Jesus used. One church at Soe, saw water turning into non-alcoholic communion wine on sixty occasions since October 1967! One other church saw the same miracle happen on ten occasions.

- Often in revival the Holy Spirit will instantly set a person free from alcoholism, smoking and other addictions if they have been bound by demonic forces, whilst at other times He does not instantly deliver them – for whatever reason. Billy Bray was a drunkard for seven years and was set free from his alcohol addiction immediately. But for some time, he still smoked a pipe which was part of Cornish culture in the 1820-50s. He came under conviction and gave up his pipe but compromised – he began chewing tobacco! Under conviction he struggled with his tobacco craving, but by the grace of God was able to give it up. Conversion and forgiveness of sins do not put away bad habits – that is the choice of the believer who wants to declare that Jesus Christ is *Lord* of their life. Because either He is Lord of all, or He is not Lord at all. The flesh must be crucified daily. Billy Bray saw at least eight revivals from 1824-1867.

In the early 1930s, Nikodemo Gatozi, a government herdsman from Ruanda (now spelt Rwanda) went to Gahini where he accepted the Christian faith, but he did not know the meaning of the cross and death to sin. One night while taking family prayers he read Luke 21:34 'Take heed...lest at any time your hearts be overcharged with surfeiting and drunkenness...and so that day come upon you unawares.' A. C. Stanley Smith wrote: 'God's arrows of conviction pierced his heart;' he could read no further. 'At that moment he saw himself as a sinner and in danger of the judgment. He arose, poured out the beer that was hidden in his house and smashed his pipe to pieces. From that moment he was truly born again and became on fire for God.' Months afterwards, in 1932, he offered to work for God at Kigeme for the Church Missionary Society Ruanda Mission.[1]

In one district in Ruanda, sometime between 1941 and 1946, though probably nearer the latter, 'the move against all intoxicating drink was so effective that the Government in one district assessed its estimate for the beer tax receipts at twenty percent lower than the preceding year.'[2]

Bill Butler, one of the team at the heart of the East Africa Revival (1930s-1950s) wrote about a chief in Ruanda, a nominal Christian who had been baptised and confirmed, yet he was 'notoriously evil' and 'a heavy drinker, with many concubines' who was 'suspected of dabbling in witchcraft.' During a mission, sometime after 1947, the chief got converted. He went home and returned the concubines to their respective homes and made financial provision for each of them; reinstated his 'ring wife' as he described her and also poured away the 'calabashes of drink' and burned his witchcraft charms.[3]

Rev. William Haslam of the Baldhu Church Revival (1851-1854) wrote: 'Conversion and forgiveness of sins do not put away present bad habits. Such a master habit as this [referring to drinking alcohol] requires a direct dealing with. 'Zaccheus was a man who had been led astray by the love of money; when he was saved, he put his idol away from him at a stroke. This is the first thing to be done and if it is done in the power of one's first love, it is a more easy task than afterwards. But it must be done with a firm and whole heart; not, "Lord, *shall I give* the half of my goods to feed the poor?" but, "Lord, behold the half of my goods *I do give*." ... "I do here and now give up drink [smoking, greed, lust etc.] and will totally abstain from it henceforth." This is the first step, and the next...is to carry out the determination in the Lord's power and not in our own. The resolution and determination once made must be given over to the Lord to be kept by Him; not by our own effort and energy, but with perfect distrust of self and in dependence upon Him to enable us to keep it. Without this there is no security whatever for anything more than temporary success, too often succeeded by a sorrowful fall. The flesh is too strong for us, and even if it were not so, the devil is; these two together, beside the lax examples of the world, are sure to overpower the weak one. Young Christians need to put away at *once* the sin, whatever it is, that 'so easily besets' them, or they will be entangled by it. There is no real and thorough deliverance except by renouncing sin and self too, giving up and yielding to the Lord.[4]

Revival, Business and Finances

- There is also a decline in attending theatres, dancing halls, the cinema and other places of amusement. During Charles Finney's campaign in Rochester, New York, America, in 1830, the only theatre in town was converted into a livery stable. 100,000 people were reported to have joined a local church and there were 150,000 professions of faith!
- In smaller villages and even towns, revival Church history records that more visitors than inhabitants can

swamp a location. As one example, during the Cambuslang Revival (1742), there were 900 inhabitants of this town near Glasgow, Scotland, but when George Whitefield along with twelve other preachers came for the communion weekend in August; 30,000 people turned up, a little more than thirty-three times the population and some even came from afar away as Ireland and England! Those who did not bring enough provisions (e.g. food) had to either share others or purchase them.

- When news of a revival becomes known, Christians will travel vast distances to go to where God is moving. With the advent of trains, cars and planes and with disposable income this has made travel much easier than in previous centuries. Some go to get revived or blessed, others to check the reports out for themselves, whilst for many they know that it will probably be the only time that they will ever be in a revival and take the opportunity while they can.

- These visitors will naturally spend their money on hotels, B&Bs, food, petrol / gas, spiritual resources etc., and the community benefits with new jobs being created. During the Brownsville Revival (1995-2000), which the author visited; the local pizza takeaway, just across from the church could not keep up with demand! One outlet of a restaurant chain gave ten percent of its profits to the Brownsville Church after the evangelist, whilst preaching, said that they ought to for all the trade that was going their way!

- During revival, Christians always become more generous and liberal in their giving. The finances will in some shape and form frequently filter into the community and church. In many revivals this has included: employing new staff, social aid, paying off the church mortgage/debt, being able to afford repairs to the church building, purchasing new(er) church vehicles and supporting budding evangelists and new missionaries etc. In 1907, when the Holy Spirit came to All Saints parish hall, Monkwearmouth, in Sunderland, – 'it burned up the debt' as the plaque on the outside of this former Anglican hall declares.

Chapter Thirteen

Education, Evangelism and Missions

Some educational institutions have been founded in revival, others witness localised revival, whilst still others are caught up in revival. Sometimes, revival in an educational institution is like a ripple effect, moving from one classroom or floor to another. On occasions, revival has travelled outside of the gates of the educational establishment and into the community and even further afield.

Localised revivals in an educational institution such as a school, college, Bible College / seminary, missionary training centre or university have been more prevalent in the eighteenth to nineteenth centuries, but during the mid 1930s and early 1950s and 1970s there was an explosion of Bible College / seminary revivals across America.

Revival and Educational Establishments

- When revival comes to a Bible College, seminary or school then classes will be suspended for a period of time, from the morning or afternoon off, up to a week. The school of the Holy Spirit in times of revival is better than the most educated and anointed of professors or lecturers. The Bible Institute for women and girls at Tsingtao, China, saw revival in 1934. Miss M. Clara Sullivan, a faculty member wrote: '…The work of the school continued, but class work, Mr. Scholz definitely reminded all, was not then, nor at any time, of prime importance, the most important of all being a right relationship with God and with one another. And more were led to repentance. We believe all have benefited.'
- When revival comes to any Christian school, Bible College or seminary; cases of discipline will greatly diminish; much to the pleasure of staff. The worst of pupils under the chastening of the Holy Spirit can be

transformed into a true saint within days! However, for some it may take a little longer to transform their mind to that of Christ, and to crucify the flesh.

On the sixth day of the Asbury College Revival (1970) in Wilmore, Kentucky, America, (a continuation of a service that had lasted 120 hours) more than one hundred adults, faculty and locals alike got right with God and each other during the Sunday service. Professor of Bible at Asbury College, Howard A. Hanke, in the book, *One Divine Moment – The Asbury Revival* wrote: 'The spiritual and social healing which occurred on that Sunday morning has solved more problems than any other event in the town for many years.'[1]

In 1904, Principal Philips of Newcastle Emlyn College, Wales, UK (of which Evan Roberts was a student) gave his students a week's leave to attend daily meetings held by the renowned Welsh evangelist, Seth Joshua at Newquay, North Wales, where the Holy Spirit was moving. Philips said to his students, "You'll learn more in one week of revival than a year of theological study."

In a house meeting, some university students were probing a travelling preacher over *their* various views of activities that *they believed he* considered sinful. After an open discussion on various questionable activities, the preacher turned to the students and said, "Did you ever feel constrained of the Spirit to go to —? Just you try and say grace [or God's blessing] before – the same as if you say grace before meat." [C.f. John 8:29b, Jesus said, "…I always do those things that please Him"]. The students trying to justify their position responded, "Is it a sin to go once a week?" "With your own words I condemn you," replied the preacher. "You spend three and a half hours at – each week. Do you spend three and a half hours on you knees per week?" The students admitted their prayerlessness. "Well, if you did pray half an hour each day these questions would never arise. The main point is to remember that the sins of worldliness are surface products of deeper sins, the spiritual sins. Get right with God, and you will get a passion for souls filling you to overflowing and crowding out any desires for questionable things. Tell me, how many souls did you win for the Lord last year? *None.* And yet you dare argue about what is proper for Christian living – why you are not living on the Christian plane yet."[2]

Revival at Schools and Colleges

- It is possible to see the entire atmosphere of a school or college changed during a time of visitation of the Holy Spirit. Briercrest College in Canada would vouch for that when the Holy Spirit came in late 2006 and the students in 2007 began praying for a deeper work, a true revival – the campus was transformed.
- Mission schools were very popular in Africa and China, especially in the nineteenth and twentieth centuries. On a few occasions, some school pupils (notably teenagers) ran away and left the school during revivals at a mission station, because they did not want to confess their sins before God.
- At other times, school children on mission stations have gone back to their villages during holiday time and brought blessing to their pagan villages! Some have also, brought back with them new students for the mission school. At Imabi Mission Station during the first year of the Congo Revival (1953-1957), two hundred and twenty boys left for a month's school holiday and returned with thirty new students!
- When the Holy Spirit turns up at a state school, pupils may be suspended for 'mucking around' or playing the fool. The Holy Spirit would come upon them (or their non-Christian friends) in the classroom or the hallway; some would jerk and shake, others would fall over and it could not be humanly stopped.

On Wednesday, 6 September 2006, dnaindia.com had an article which was entitled: 'Meghalaya school students exhibit 'unusual' behaviour.' Meghalaya is a province in north east India with Shillong as its capital. The report states: 'The Meghalaya government is looking into reports that a number of students from Christian schools in the state were exhibiting "unusual behaviour" like uncontrolled weeping and convulsions. There have been reports during the past few weeks that students of 15 schools in Shillong and other institutions in the Khasi and Jaintia hills region were fainting, weeping, chanting hymns and having convulsions.... Deputy Chief Minister, Donkupar Roy who is in charge of education, said the government was watching the situation but wanted the heads of institutions to handle the matter.'

Before the Brownsville Revival (1995-2000) only three out of the thirty-two junior high schools in the area had Christian Unions, within two years, they all had them, some of which were 250 strong! Students in class would be touched by the Holy Spirit and collapse on the floor and many of the schools had separate rooms where these pupils could be placed. Countless testimonies of people poured in over the years and the healing power of God was very evident.

Richard Crisco, Brownsville's youth pastor had for many years tried to get to meet many of the principals from the local schools but to no avail. Prior to the revival, the Brownsville Church had one hundred youth and within two years they had five hundred attending. After a process of discipleship they found that after two years, ninety percent of the youth converts were still going on with the Lord.

Soon, school principals started to phone up Richard Crisco and invite him out for lunch. After the third time, a principal explained that the administrators and the principals of the different schools had come together and informally decided that they needed to seize the opportunity. Richard Crisco was asked to hold Youth Rallies on a Tuesday night, every month in a different public school. The principals told him that they would announce that the Brownsville youth team would be in on a certain date and the rest was left up to him.

At one Youth Rally, seventy people were converted. The sports coach had a list of the ten worst sinners; promiscuous girls, heavy drug users and prideful sports stars and all ten had been converted! Dr. Michael Brown retelling the story said, "He [the coach] was in a state of shock."

At one school, some students decided to have a prayer and praise time during break and the Holy Spirit came and prostrated one of the fourteen year old boys. His mates carried him to his typing class and the teacher was not amused. She asked two boys (non-Christians) to carry their classmate to the principal's office. As they were doing this the power of God hit them! Dr. Brown went on to say that different principals phoned up Brownsville Church asking them what to do. Whilst some Christians phoned up Brownsville and were "flipping out" because they heard that people were shaking and falling over at school, wanting to know if it was true. But as Dr. Brown stated, when these same kids were going into school carrying guns, dressing like prostitutes, guys with multi-coloured hair, cussing at the teachers, getting kicked out of school, séances in the hallways, pornography in kids lockers, gangs etc.; these concerned Christians were not getting worked up about it, some of whom were their own children. "You know what's nice," said Dr. Brown, "God knows how to make Himself real to a young person."[3]

Evangelism and Mission Work

- During revival, evangelism always takes on a new and important responsibility for every layman and woman and children are no exception! New converts are also the best evangelists, as they give their testimony and talk about their salvation by God's grace and their faith in the atoning work of the Lord Jesus Christ. Their lives are living testimonies to all they meet and to all who know them.

- New converts become the newest (and often best) evangelists and desire their friends, family and work colleagues to come and meet God for themselves. There is also a new boldness for seasoned Christians, realising that life is short and the Lord will come at anytime and if He did, their unsaved friends, associates and neighbours would be weighed in the balance, found wanting and damned for all eternity in the fires of hell.

- There will be places where no preacher or missionary has travelled to, yet there could still be a fledgling Christian community or church. Often it is by people 'gossiping the gospel.' One of the community has got saved and gone home and shared the little of what they know and others follow. This has also been known to happen on the mission field outside of revival. In spring 1829, some lumbermen from

Pennsylvania, visited Philadelphia where Charles Finney was holding evangelistic meetings and they got converted. They returned home to an area known as the lumber region and five thousand in that district were converted along an area of eighty miles, and there was not a single minister of the gospel there!

- At other places, heathen will come under the influence of the Holy Spirit and will decide to follow the One true God. During the Gold Coast Revival (1875-1878), Thomas Freeman's wife wrote to him from Anamabu, (also spelt Anomabo, approximately ten miles from Cape Coast along the Gold Coast in modern-day Ghana) asking him to return as the chapel congregation was overflowing into the streets. She wrote: 'One of our sisters, reports that, as she was passing along the street, she met a group of about twelve heathen people, men and women, from the fishermen's quarter of the town, who were saying, "We will go to chapel to be Christians; we will go and give ourselves to God omnipotent." '

- Greater numbers than normal are obedient to the call to Christian ministry during times of revival and this leads to more labourers being trained and then thrust forth into the harvest field. See Matthew 9:35-38.

Revival by Extension – Evangelism, Fire-Carriers

- During revival, people love to give their testimony and tell others what God has done for them, as a trophy of God's grace. Often visitors from another town who have tasted of the heavenly fire, upon giving their testimony in a place where revival has not yet started, will become a fire-starter in that church or community. If they are asked to pray for believers (the laying on of hands) they will soon realise that they have received a level of anointing which has been transferred to them which can bless others.

- In many of the revivals from Church history, groups of evangelists, lay workers or prayer bands, travel from one 'hot spot' to a spiritually dead location to help ignite the flames of revival, to stir the Christians to pray (or to encourage those who already are) and to hold meetings or campaigns.

- When people hear of what God is doing in another town or country, this acts as an encouraging stimulus to pray for God's Spirit to come to their location.

- Often, teams of people (or individuals) who have been revived will travel to another location as evangelists, singers or to give their testimony and revival often breaks out. This was seen during the Asbury College Revival (1970) which led to Anderson College Revival (1970) which in turn led to about fifty other localised revivals as individuals or teams of students were asked to go and speak in other colleges and churches across America and beyond!

- In many Asian revivals of the twentieth century, revival bands (laypeople evangelistic teams) were designated and grouped together by the leadership of a church to evangelise. The Indonesian Revival (1964-1974) had at least seventy-six evangelistic bands in operation by 1966, which also included some children's teams whom themselves decided to evangelise. The Shantung Revival (1930-1932) in China, also saw children's bands. These bands have been most prominent in China, Japan and Indonesia. The reason why these bands of laypersons were almost exclusively confined to Asian countries was because many of the people lived off the land. They were not tied to any nine till five job which would have prevented them from going away from home for a few days to weeks at a time, and because of their communal culture and tight-knit family bonds, other kinsfolk would take up the slack in the fields or farms. In 1925, Paget Wilkes, founder of the Japan Evangelistic Band was preaching at a conference during the Shanghai Revival (1925) in China, when Andrew Gih heard the call to form the Bethel Worldwide Evangelistic Band, who went across Asia.

Revival and Infant Churches

- On occasions, revival has come to an 'infant' Church when the missionaries have either been expelled from the nation, as in the Nagaland Revivals (1949-1952) which brought about the Nagaland Awakening (1950s), or when the missionaries had handed over the administration control of the Church to the indigenous believers, as in the Pyongyang Great Revival (1907-1910) in Korea. In both these instances the young Churches threw themselves upon the Lord for strengthening and guidance.

- Similar to above, the Imbai Revival (1936) in North East Belgian Congo, came just before the missionaries were told to close the Imbai Mission Station because the Belgian Government would not allow the WEC to have more than twelve European-run stations. The missionaries prayed for revival so the Imbai Church (named after its tribal leader) would not crumble, but stand because their dependence was more on the missionaries and their tribal leader, rather than on Jesus Christ.

- The China Awakening (1927-1937) did wonders for the Church in north China. The Japanese invaded in 1937, and during the revival God raised up Chinese men and women and prepared the indigenous Church to be self supporting; independent of its Western founders. God knew what He was doing as many Western missionaries were interred under the Japanese invasion / occupation and died during World War II. Later, all missionaries were expelled from the country which was under Communist rule.

- During the Ruanda Revival (1937-1950s), the Ruanda Mission Church (founded by the Church Missionary Society), '...transformed the spiritual life of the Church, [and] could not fail to affect its organic life too. Perhaps the first sign of this practical outcome of deep religious experience was seen in the love towards self-support,' so wrote a senior missionary to Ruanda. The Ruanda Mission had begun in 1921 at Kabale on the Uganda / Ruanda border. 'By 1941 the church work at Kabale was fully self-supporting and they began to bear the [financial] burden of the Evangelists' Training School.'

Chapter Fourteen

Supernatural Characteristics of Revival

The Untold Secrets of Revival

There are experiences that happen during times of revival which for many reasons are not talked about or never published. The apostle Paul was caught up to the third heaven and was not permitted to utter certain things (2 Corinthians 12:1-4), whilst John was not permitted to write about the utterance of the seven thunders (Revelation 10:4).

After the Mukti Revival (1905-1906) in India, Helen Dyer in her book *Pandita Ramabai* wrote: 'Some few saw visions and experienced the power of God and things too deep to be described.'

Eva Stuart Watts, in her book *Floods On Dry Ground*, writing about the Imbai Revivals of 1935 and 1936 in the Belgian Congo, wrote: 'When the natives were out in the forest in the morning for communion with the Saviour, things happened about which they could scarcely speak afterwards, experiences of the utterable joy of His blessed presence.' But she was able to write about the experience of Lily Roberts, a missionary who saw revival. In an open vision, the heavens were opened and she saw Jesus.

The revivalist, James A. Stewart, thirty-three years after he saw his first revival in Latvia, in 1931, in his book, *Opened Windows – The Church and Revival*, wrote: 'Because of the sacredness and the glory of the experience of revival it is not easy to speak on this subject to any group of Christian workers unless they have been prepared by the Spirit to receive the message.'

P. S. Bristow in the introduction to *The Lewis Awakening* by Duncan Campbell, (a booklet) wrote: 'I have before me Mr. Campbell's own accounts of the work, received from him from week to week, and I can only say that his much restricted accounts in these pages gives but a glimpse of the great manifestations of Divine power witnessed throughout the island. For personal reasons the vivid details of experience in the lives of individuals is withheld. Could they be suitably narrated, they would be thrilling to read.'

Rev. Gordon I. Thomas, in the foreword to the aforementioned booklet wrote: 'Story after story could be told of incidents that are in the realm of the miraculous and which indeed are positively breath-taking to hear. Practically none of these has been mentioned in this booklet....'

Charles Finney wrote: 'If anything is to be said about revivals [writing about it during the lifetime of the revival], give only the plain and naked facts, just as they are, and let them pass for what they are worth.' He went on to cite an example of how a minister published a self promoting letter in the paper and the revival waned and died. He wrote: 'Some, under pretence of publishing things to the praise and glory of God, have published things that savoured so strongly of a disposition to exalt themselves – making their own agency stand out conspicuously – as were evidently calculated to make an unhappy impression.' Finney concluded with the fact that one church had a revival and around five hundred were converted who filtered into various churches, but they never made it public knowledge through the papers. On several occasions he was asked why. He wrote: 'I could only reply that there was such a tendency to self-examination in the churches that I was afraid to publish anything on the subject.'

We should not seek supernatural experiences, nor glory in physical phenomena, but also, we should never deny them or try to dust them under the carpet. In times of revival, supernatural events orchestrated by the Holy Spirit are largely manifested. We are encouraged to 'desire the best gifts' and 'desire spiritual gifts' (1 Corinthians 12:31 and 1 Corinthians 14:1) though we should not be seeking signs or the miraculous in themselves, but seeking God and giving Him the honour that is due unto His name. All the glory must go to God, for whatever He is doing in a person's life which often reacts with a physical response as soul and body are interlinked.[1]

Let us not be confused over God's dynamics and the demonic. In any meeting where God is moving, a person's face may be contorting, but let us not be hasty in our judgment, are the demons manifesting or fleeing?

In revival or whenever the Holy Spirit moves demons are frightened and may cry out and depart from a person. It is a clash of two worlds, the Kingdom of Light and the kingdom of darkness. Whilst at other times they will publicly manifest and it is the Church's responsibility to bind the strong man and to cast them out in the mighty name of Jesus Christ.

Supernatural Events of Revival

Everything to do with revival is supernatural as it is a move of the Holy Spirit. The following items are just a glimpse of what God has done and can do in revival, though some of these supernatural events should be the norm, as revealed in the book of Acts and so do the Church Fathers and beyond in their respective writings of Church history.

- Certain persons, (Christians and non-Christians) men, women and even children will have dreams and visions. Some people have visions of hell, the lost, of heaven or of the Saviour etc. Generally speaking, during revival, Christians have had visions to give extra impetus to the work of evangelism, whereas non-Christians have had visions to either show them where they were going (hell, the judgment of God) or visions of the Saviour (the mercy of God).

- Unusual visions: During the Shillong Revival (2006-2007), Iba Warjri, an eight year old girl came out of a church building, looked up at the moon, which looked like a close cloud and saw a vision of Jesus in the cloud. Outside of revival, I know a man whom whilst in Wales, UK, was looking out of a window up at the sky. He saw the face of Evan Roberts (the Welsh revivalist) with a big grin on his face in the shape of a cloud. This vision lasted for several minutes until it faded away. The man was so taken back by what he had seen that it never occurred to him that it was a vision, as he initially believed it was a sign in the heavens that could be seen by all.

- There will be prophecies. Often speaking about the nearness of the Second Coming (very prevalent in the last two hundred years) and the call to get right with God, to be ready for Jesus Christ's return as in the Shillong Revival (2006-2007) in India. In connection with this there have been those who have prayed, "Oh, Lord, wait a year or two before coming to give these people time to repent." This was what a lady prayed during the Hwanghsien Revival (1932) which was part of the Shantung Revival (1930-1932) in China. Prior to the Welsh Revival (1904-1905), Evan Roberts after receiving a vision of hell; a fiery bottomless pit surrounded by impenetrable walls with countless numbers of people surging towards it, pleaded that hell's door be closed for one year so that they might have opportunity to repent. George Fox had a vision of an 'ingathering of people' and William Booth had a vision 'of the perishing lost,' both were impetuses for their future revival ministries.

- To a lesser or greater degree, the supernatural hand of God will move. Anything from instant healings, instant deliverance from demonic powers, to angels appearing or hearing angels singing or supernatural lights, such as orbs appearing. On occasions, Jesus Himself has appeared or a special fragrance wafts through the room or building as God's presence can be smelt. During the Shillong Revival (2006-2007) one man filmed angels flashing across the sky on his camera phone and I've seen the clip.

- It is not uncommon for non-Christians to fall, drop or sink to the ground under agonising conviction of sin (though some do appear peaceful), being stricken by God. Some shake, tremble or jerk; others appear to be unconscious, in a coma or even dead, lifeless. They can stay in that state for hours or days, and have to be carried from the meeting or the field, depending on where God struck them.

- Some Christians will agonise in prayer for the lost, being burdened by the Holy Spirit. Their prayers will be of great intensity. Those under such burdens may fall to the ground and groan in the Spirit. Others will perspire (even when it is cool) and be as in great agony of soul. David Brainerd who saw revival amongst the North American Indians (1745-1746), knelt in the snow to pray. He prayed with such intensity and passion that the heat he generated melted the snow as he sunk lower into the ground! It was also said of the apostle James that his knees were like camels knees!

- Some of the physical phenomena during revival can be that non-Christians lose their sight, hearing, ability to speak or the ability to walk for a period of time. Some Christians can become drunk in the Spirit and have to be carried from the meetings; others are incoherent for a time – intoxicated by the Spirit of God. We do not need to be alarmed at these things.

Rare Supernatural Events

- Buildings have been shaken in past revivals as the Holy Spirit comes down as in Acts 4:31. This was witnessed during the Lewis Revival (1949-1952) when a granite house shook like a leaf as Duncan Campbell and others were inside praying. At the village of Phiro, Wokha District, Nagaland, during the 1960s, a building was physically shaken by the power of God. Others have felt the wind of the Spirit as He blows through a meeting, sometimes as a hurricane as in the Congo Revival (1953-1957).
- On rare occasions, when the Holy Spirit has descended, people have seen flames of fire as on the Day of Pentecost. Prior to the Azusa Street Revival (1906-1909), in late February 1906, a house church was started at William Seymour's lodgings in North Bonnie Brae Street. When the Holy Spirit descended, many witnesses believed the house itself was literally on fire and the fire brigade was called out! At the Mukti Mission, India, in June 1905, immediately before the Mukti Revival (1905-1906), one of the senior girls woke her teacher and informed her that one of the girls had received the Holy Spirit. The senior girl said, "I saw fire, ran across the room for a pail of water, and was about to pour it over her when I discovered she was not on fire!" Tongues of fire were also seen on 22 September 1957 in the town of

Wokha, Nagaland, flickering above the roof of a church as the congregation were inside praying.

- On very rare occasions, the 'fire of the Lord' can appear. In 1959 in Nagaland, pastor Kegwahi Kent of the Sendenyu Baptist Church was at his home praying for the nations when the fire of God descended and illuminated his entire house. In the Ulster Revival (1859-1860) at county Antrim, an old Roman Catholic woman was in her garden in the afternoon when 'a perfect flood of light as she imagined bathed her dwelling.' She rushed inside, cried out in mercy and 'fainted away.' She woke up saved! In Nagaland during a worship service, a member prophesied that God would send a pillar of fire as a sign and that all must confess and repent of their sins, but also that it would burn down an unbeliever's home. That night, between 8-9pm a pillar of fire shone above the church with pure light, yet it cast no shadow or reflection. The pillar soon vanished, but the thatched home of an unbeliever called Tesinlo Khing was in flames!
- On very rare occasions, during times of intense worship amidst revival, people or buildings can hover or lift off the ground! In 1954, during the Nagaland Awakening of the 1950s, in a village called Phiro; the church lifted off the ground about two to three feet as the believers were inside praying. Unbelievers saw this and the majority repented of their sins and turned to the Lord whilst some hardened their hearts! In a public meeting, Michael Howard, who has seen at least six revivals in Africa during the 1980s and 1990s, told those present that he was in a church service and some of the members, including himself were literally hovering in the air, levitating about a foot off the ground whilst worshiping the Lord!
- Also, the Holy Spirit has been recorded as lifting people over the heads (or backs if they are kneeling) in a church meeting and placing them at the front of the church – the place generally designated for sinners to come to public repentance and confession of Jesus Christ as their Lord and Saviour. I have only

found this in print twice out of nearly three hundred revival related books. At one service at the Ibambi Mission Station in the North East Belgian Congo in 1953, the entire congregation were prostrated before the Lord, 'screaming out their sins' when 'the head printer seemed to fly through the air over the backs of the people, landing on the floor, where he began crying out his sin.'

In a video interview which can be viewed online, Leonard Ravenhill, who was in his eighty-fourth year was recalling how in 1932, whilst in Wales, UK, as a Christian worker in his mid twenties, he was introduced to Major Russell of the Salvation Army, who was in his eighties. Major Russell had shared an office with General Booth and told Ravenhill that in the early Salvation meetings, altar calls were never given. The old Major hesitantly told the following incident to young Ravenhill who told him that as he was a link to the past, so he would be a link to a future generation. After the preaching, General Booth would look at the workers and in a gruff voice, tell them to pray. Major Russell stated that at one meeting on a Sunday evening in a theatre on the Strand in London, after the General had told them to pray three times, people were literally transported, "bodily over their heads" by the Spirit and landed down at the front at the penitent form!

Carol Arnott speaking on *The 700 Club* to Pat Robinson, retold the incident that in a conference in north Australia, "When the Holy Spirit fell" the wife of a Pentecostal superintendent who was sat down was "taken up, did a double backflip and landed two rows back!"[2]

Revival and the Human Intellect
- On very rare occasions, and only during the duration of the revival, God may give a person the supernatural ability to be able to remember everything they hear or have ever read so as to be able to teach more ably – supernatural intellect. This ability which is instantaneous is removed just as quickly as it has come. I have only read of this experience twice and two years is the longest duration I have come across. David Morgan the

Welsh revivalist, just prior to the outbreak of the Welsh Revival (1859-1860) awoke at 4am and realised that the Holy Spirit had illuminated his faculties so that he could remember everything of a religious nature that he had ever learnt or heard!

- God can give remarkable stimulus to a person's mental powers and spiritual graces, which can last longer than the duration of a revival. Whilst this is not a rare feature, as it is similar to the one above, I have included it here. The Holy Spirit gives them boldness to pray publicly or to evangelise whereas before they were afraid to. In the Ulster Revival (1859-1860) in Ireland, there are several recorded instances of this. In a sense it is like Jesus on the road to Emmaus with the two disciples when He opened their understanding and expounded the Scriptures to them (Luke 24:25). During the Imbai Revival (1936) in the Belgian Congo, after a sermon on Isaiah 58, even old women, who could not read and were not given to such consecutive thoughts, were able to use and pray every clause in order (from Isaiah 58).

- It has been known that during times of revival, the Holy Spirit has changed illiterate people into literates, *without study and sometimes angels have assisted! *This was prominent during China in the revival of the 1950s. There is at least one recorded instance of this in Nagaland Awakening during the same period for a man called Jihlo Bukh.

- At other times, illiterate people will learn to read. During revival in the Sudan, which was part of the East African Revival (1930s-1950s), Bishop Oliver Allison of the Sudan asked one native pastor at a crowded congregation, "How is it that those elderly people seem to be able to read their Bible so well? How did they learn? The pastor stated that they were some of the Praising Ones (the name given for the converts during the revival – because they praised the Lord so much!) and that we (the pastor and the people) thought that they would never be able to learn to read, "But since they were 'revived' they have been so keen to read their Bible that they have learned to read in their special classes. It is the work of the Holy Spirit."

- On occasions, missionaries under the anointing of the Holy Spirit can preach fluently in a foreign tongue, but in normal day-to-day communication their ability is poor. Iba Warjri, an eight year old girl, from Nogrim Sadew, (17 miles from Shillong in India), could not speak the Khasi language well and therefore usually used her own dialect. But during the Shillong Revival (2006-2007) when she had a revelation from God, she could speak it fluently! This has also happened outside times of revival during evangelistic preaching.
- In 1994 at a conference in Hamilton, Canada, a 'little girl' prophesied over John Arnot in perfect rhyme!

Revival Miracles

Having read so many books on revivals there are not many miracles in the Bible which have not been repeated and recorded in revival Church history. Though I am unaware of waters dividing, axe heads (or similar) floating or the dead being raised through a dead man (Elisha's bones, 2 Kings 13:21). Outside of Scripture I have never read about a shadow healing the sick. Raising the dead is more common!

The Indonesian Revival (1964-1974) is perhaps the most supernatural revival the world has ever seen, with many personalities involved, followed by the Nagaland Revival of the 1950s and 1960s amongst tribal people.

In Indonesia, Muslims were affected as were nominal Christians and the animists or heathen. During the Indonesian Revival (1964-1974) under the Indonesian 'umbrella,' multitudes were converted and set free from demonic oppression and curses and sorcery were defeated. The blind saw, the deaf heard, the lame walked, the lepers were healed, the dead were raised, the waters were calmed, the rain was commanded to stop; all in the name of Jesus. Others were protected from the rain as it fell ten feet all around them and they continued to walk for miles in this state, whilst one team crossed a 300 yard wide river in flood which was from 20-30 feet deep, the water did not go above their knees and their feet touched the bottom! People received visions and dreams, words of knowledge, prophecy and extraordinary discernment – knowing the secrets of men's hearts; whilst others received songs from God, a few were taught by angels (being illiterate) and Jesus even appeared to others. Some of the missionary teams ate supernatural food (manna from heaven), another team had flames of fire over the churches where they preached at. When revival first came to Soe, on the island of Timor, an entire village saw flames above the church, others saw supernatural light, which guided their footsteps by night, one mission team was transported by the Spirit (Acts 8:39), others witnessed food multiplying, and food not going-over in the tropical heat. In one place the house shook as they prayed (Acts 4:31). At least two churches saw water turning into non-alcoholic communion wine – this happened at two churches on at least ten and sixty occasions.

In the early 1970s, Dr. Kurt Koch wrote a rebuttal that his book, *The Revival In Indonesia* contained falsified reports. In the small folder he wrote: 'I do not have a mania for miracles...even the extremism of many Pentecostal churches and of the new so-called charismatic movement is an abomination to me [he disliked Christians speaking in tongues *page 73.]...yet there are miracles which I consistently affirm, the miracle that God's Son is Saviour, the miracle of the filling with the Holy Spirit.... The history of revivals shows us that at the beginning of many revivals miracles have appeared. This occurred in Wales in 1905, in Korea in 1906-1960, in Uganda in 1927, in Ethiopia among the Wallamo 1937-1948, in Timor in 1965-1969, as well as in other places. I have travelled throughout the world. I have always asked the Lord for the ability to discern that which is genuine from that which is false.

'The miracles are not the essential things. To be sure, every mania for miracles is dangerous. Yet it has pleased God to bring about many miracles at the outpouring of the Holy Spirit. All revivals are characterised by similar phenomena. Moreover the miracles in Indonesia have decreased in number since the illiterate people have learned to read the Bible. This is a healthy development.' More of Dr. Kurt Koch's rebuttal can be found on pages 123 and 124.

Chapter Fifteen

The Dangers of Revival

Is it From God or the Devil? Judging and Discerning

The enemy tries to undermine all that God is doing and has done. During times of revival there are inevitable elements of the demonic and the flesh as he infiltrates and imitates. Equally unfortunate is that all too often some people give the devil too much credit – something supernatural happens and they attribute it as from the evil one, as if God's supernatural power has ceased! Whilst the devil can counterfeit (e.g. a healing) yet these same people say that God cannot or will not heal! God is the originator of the supernatural whilst the enemy is the infiltrator and imitator. Has the devil more power to deceive us than God has to heal us? Who has the greater power? Let us not be confused over God's dynamics and the demonic.

Many Christians are too hasty to judge and say a work is of the devil (or his demons) whereas it could well be the finger of God. Often all we see is what John Arnott of the Toronto Airport Christian Fellowship calls a 'snapshot,' where a person is being touched and affected bodily, but the snapshot is just a moment of time and the fruit will show forth later. We need to learn to distinguish between the holy and the unholy, the clean and the unclean and separate the precious from the vile before we start denouncing people or a work as counterfeit. We have a preconceived mindset, a bias towards thinking the worst ("Who sinned, this man or his parents?" – "Neither" – John 9:1-3), which is the opposite of 1 Corinthians 13:4-7, 'love...thinks no evil.' Alarm bells start ringing and all too often we jump to the wrong conclusion and miss the best. 'It is the Spirit' that 'searches all things, yes the deep things of God' (1 Corinthians 2:10b). So we have to be spiritually in tune with God to appreciate what He is doing. God is too complex to understand. Most of us cannot even understand the opposite sex, let alone God!

Zecharias was in the temple serving the Lord and came out mute. Was the devil attacking him because of his devotion and service towards the Lord? No, it was because he disbelieved the Word from the angel of the Lord that his wife Elizabeth, who was past the age of child-bearing was to have a son. He was mute for at least nine months until his son, John (the Baptist) was born (Luke 1:5-25, 57-64).

Saul the persecutor of the Church who had endorsed the stoning of Stephen was sometime afterwards struck to the ground and blinded – was it the devil or God's judgment? Neither, it was how God revealed Himself to the persecutor of the Church so that Saul, later renamed Paul, could be converted. He was blind for three days and went on to become the Church's best promoter (Acts 9:1-19).

We should be cautious, but not hasty in our judgments, childlike, but not childish. We are to 'test all things' not reject all things and 'hold fast what is good' (1 Thessalonians 5:21). We should not 'throw out the baby with the bath water' to use a contemporary phrase, but to take the best and leave the rest. We should be 'swift to hear' but 'slow to speak' (passing judgment) and not angry or full of wrath because of what we see (James 1:19). God is more than capable of looking after His work, but 'every move of the Spirit needs to be pastored in a responsible way,' so wrote John Arnott. Just like in the book of Acts, the book of revivals and *riots! *See page 132. Church leaders were present or summoned to supervise, watch over, correct and rebuke where necessary as did Peter during the Samaria Revival, he denounced Simon, the former sorcerer for his sin of simony (Acts 8:18-24).

If God comes and meets with you then it is very probable that what has happened on the inside (an inner healing or sifting and shaking) will express itself on the outside to a larger or lesser degree, be it mildly or wildly! But 'if God is in control can we really be out of control?' so wrote John Arnott. Sometimes God may touch you in such a way that you have little choice in how you respond. See page 230.

In late 1995, during the Toronto Blessing in Canada, Christian sociologist, Margeret Poloma interviewed a cross-section of people who had fallen under the power of the Holy Spirit. About one thousand people were surveyed, each of whom had time to reflect on their experience. It transpired that 92% stated that they were now more in love with Jesus. The second highest statistic revealed that 82% were more motivated and excited to share the good news. John Arnott went on to say how people had attributed so much in the church meetings as demonic, 'but loving Jesus more and wanting to tell others about Him doesn't sound like the devil's doing, does it?'[1]

John Wimber said, "In my experience all who have been overcome by the Holy Spirit – whether they fell over, started shaking, became very quiet and still, or spoke in tongues – thought the experience was wonderful and that it drew them closer to God. They found that prayer, Scripture reading, caring for others and the love of God all increased."[2]

Has God lost His power? Cessation Theology

It is unfortunate that some Christians reject all things spiritual but notably the gifts of the Holy Spirit, believing that either the gifts are not for today (cessation theology), that God's power has diminished or that the gifts ceased at the death of the last apostle. But 1 Corinthians 12:7 informs us that 'the manifestation of the Spirit is given to each one for the profit of all' – that is for the corporate benefit of the body of Christ; has God therefore ceased to be concerned about the Church, His Bride and no longer wants to benefit her?

I am a firm believer that either we believe all of the Bible or nothing. If one part is false or no longer applicable then all of it is no longer applicable, and let us not be confused over the Old and New Covenants. If one portion of the New Testament has been abrogated then who is to say that other parts have not also? The first formal recognition of a fixed list, or canon, of New Testament writings can be dated to about the middle of the second century, though it took longer for both East and West to agree on the 27 books of the New Testament. These books (or letters) were inspired by God and are just as applicable then, as when they were written and therefore are still valid for today.

If we disregard, say prophecy, as "not for today," one of the nine gifts of the Holy Spirit as recorded in 1 Corinthians 12, then it is only fair that we disregard prophets as "not for today." Prophets are part of the five-fold ministry of Ephesians 4, so it is only right, fitting and proper, if we hold to this view to also exclude teachers, evangelists, pastors and apostles! Dare we say that? But if we do, should we not go all the way and disregard all of the Pastoral Epistles as they were also written by the apostle Paul. But 'the Scripture cannot be broken' as Jesus reiterated (John 10:35b) and 'the Word of the Lord endures forever' (1 Peter 1:24-25).

If the gifts ceased at the death of the apostles then why not the responsibility towards the Great Commission and our command to 'love' as revealed in 1 Corinthians chapter 13; how can we disregard portions of one chapter (1 Corinthians 12) and not the subsequent one? Rather inconsistent isn't it? Or what about the preceding chapter (1 Corinthians 11) on propriety of worship and the Lord's Supper? Do we also say it has been abrogated and sweep it under the carpet as not for today? Dare we tell the Holy Spirit what He can and cannot do and how He is to go about it, just to keep us happy? Is Jesus Christ no longer the same yesterday, today, and forever? (Hebrews 13:8). Our 'faith should not be in the wisdom of men, [self imposed doctrines and opinions] but in the power of God' (1 Corinthians 2:5). *Signs of Revival* by Dr. Patrick Dixon (1994) documents the gifts of the Spirit through twenty centuries of Church history, whilst *Holy Spirit Power* by Paul Backholer is about the Holy Spirit.

Jesus speaking to Nicodemus (a Pharisee), about being "born again" told him plainly, "We speak what We know and testify of what We have seen and you *do not receive* Our witness. If I have told you earthly things and you do not believe, how will you believe if I tell you heavenly things?" (John 3:11-12). Nicodemus did eventually believe and assisted Joseph of Arimathea in taking Jesus down off the cross (John 7:50 and John 19:39).

Jesus spoke on the parable of the rich man and Lazarus when each had his own reward in the afterlife, the rich man in hell and Lazarus at Abraham's bosom. The rich man was in terrible torment and asked Abraham to permit Lazarus to dip his finger in water and to cool his tongue, but as there was a gulf fixed between the two it was impossible. The rich man then asked for Lazarus to be sent to his father and five brothers so that they would not end up in hell. Abraham told him that they have Moses and the prophets, let them hear them (the Scriptures − in the Old Testament), but the rich man wanted Lazarus to be raised and *then* they would believe. Abraham said, "If they do not hear Moses and the prophets, *neither will they be persuaded* though one rise from the dead" (Luke 16:19-31).

In John 5, Jesus healed a paralytic at the Pool of Bethesda on the Sabbath day and told him to take up his bed and walk. The Jews persecuted Jesus and 'sought all the more to kill Him because He not only broke the Sabbath, but also said that God was His Father, making Himself equal with God' (verse 18). Jesus plainly told those gathered, "You search the Scriptures, for in them you think you have eternal life and these are they which testify of Me. But you are *unwilling* to come to Me that you may have eternal life" (John 5:39-40).

Sometimes it is impossible to get through to people, to those who only believe what they want to believe, whose hearts have been hardened. We are told not to give what is holy to the dogs; to try to convince some people of biblical truths is like casting pearls before swine (Matthew 7:6) and we should not speak in the hearing of a fool who will only despise the wisdom of our words (Proverbs 23:9).

It is also important to mention that 'the natural man does not receive the things of the Spirit of God, for they are foolish to him; nor can he know them because they are spiritually discerned, but He [God] who is spiritual judges all things...' (1 Corinthians 2:14-15). If we presume to judge another, then with the measure we use, it will be measured back to us (Matthew 7:1-2). It is also advisable to remove the plank of our preconceived ideas before we speak to a brother or sister about his or her speck of sawdust (Matthew 7:3-6).

Beware of Deceivers

Jesus said, "Take heed that no one deceives you..." and even in times of revival we must be on our guard. Those who say that they cannot be deceived, already are! Also, not all signs and miracles are from God. Jesus said, "For false Christs and false prophets will arise and show great signs and wonders, so as to deceive, if possible, even the elect" (Matthew 24:4-5, 24). The apostle Paul wrote: 'I fear, lest somehow, as the serpent deceived Eve by his craftiness, so your minds may be corrupted from the simplicity that is in

Christ,' by those who preach another Jesus, another gospel and who have a different spirit (2 Corinthians 11:3-4).

Satan has many followers infiltrating the church, false apostles and false teachers (2 Corinthians 11:13-15) and in times of revival, there is no exception. There are also those who will deny the power of God even in the day of visitation (2 Timothy 3:1-9). Whilst some so-called 'believers' are known as tares, wolves or accursed children (Matthew 7:15, Matthew 13:24-30 and 2 Peter 2:14-15). Jesus warned of false prophets who will come in sheep's clothing but inwardly they are ravenous wolves. By their fruits we will know them (Matthew 7:15-20). Jesus also said, "If you abide in My Word, you are My disciples indeed. And you shall know the truth, and the truth shall make you free" (John 8:31-32).

In 1743, in the midst of the American Great Awakening (1735-1760), Jonathan Edwards published the *Treatise Concerning the Religious Affections* as he saw froth without fruit – stirred emotions, but not changed lives and it was this minority that were bringing the work of God into disrepute.

Warnings from Scripture

- 'Even if we, or an angel from heaven preach any other gospel to you than what we have preached to you, let him be accursed' (Galatians 1:8).
- '...In latter times some will depart from the faith, giving heed to deceiving spirits and doctrines of demons' (1 Timothy 4:1).
- '...There will be false teachers among you, who secretly bring in destructive heresies...many will follow their destructive ways because of whom the way of truth will be blasphemed. By covetousness they will exploit you with deceptive words...and their destruction will not slumber' (2 Peter 2:1-3).
- 'For certain men have crept in unnoticed, who long ago were marked out for this condemnation, ungodly men, who turn the grace of God into licentiousness and deny the only Lord God and our Lord Jesus Christ' (Jude verse 4).
- The apostle Paul said to the Ephesians, "...After my departure savage wolves will come in among you, not

sparing the flock. Also from among yourselves men will rise up, speaking perverse things, to draw away the disciples after themselves" (Acts 20:29-30).

- 'Do not be carried about with various and strange doctrines…' (Hebrews 13:9).
- Jesus said, "Not everyone who says to Me, 'Lord, Lord,' shall enter the Kingdom of heaven, but he who does the will of My Father in heaven" (Matthew 7:21).

The Deceived Revivalist

Less than a year before the armistice of World War I (1914-1918), Spanish flu swept the world. In Basutoland, (modern-day Lesotho), Africa, entire villages were wiped out. The life of the Basuto was at a standstill and travellers were no longer met on the roads. Schools and churches were closed by public order and gatherings were not permitted.

Victor Ellenberger wrote: 'Many believed that it was the end of the world and were resigned to their fate…. In many places the natives tried to come together in the open, so intense was the need which they felt of drawing near to God. In that respect, that calamity awakened latent spiritual needs among many Basutos and produced a fairly strong revival.

'One of the agents of that revival was – perhaps in spite of himself – a man…named [Walter] Matita…who had been busy for several years already with a campaign of evangelisation throughout the land, was able, chiefly through speaking to the populace about the resurrection, to move their hearts and to resuscitate numerous conversions…. By mingling the supernatural with the practical, he made out, amongst other things, that he had gone through death; that whilst dead he had been taken up to heaven through innumerable worlds. That an angel had then taught him to read and to write and that finally he had been allowed to appear before Moshesh [the father of Basutoland, who died in 1870], who had expressly charged him to return to earth and to call the Basutos in his name to become converted.'

Matita held many other views, especially in regards to the future 'which he hid from the credulity of his audience; but later, when he threw off the mask and wanted to establish a sect of which he would be head, namely the sect of the 'Followers of Moshesh,' or another, that of the 'Possessed of the Spirit,' recruits for which he reckoned to get among those who had been converted through his appeal and whose names he kept, it happened that the great majority of them refused to follow him and they came to swell the ranks of our churches, 'having given themselves up to God, not to man.'

'Indirectly that man who pretended to be one of us and the movement he inaugurated, proved to be a magic stone for the Church at that critical time, for they made it possible for us to remain united and to victoriously resist an attack *perfidiously launched against our work, [*playing one side against each other] even as deeply as the native pastoral body....'[3]

Whilst Walter Matita began in the faith, somehow, probably gradually, he was led astray, yet the majority of those converted under his ministry stayed true to the faith, and that is a testament that those who sat under his preaching were truly born again of the Spirit of God, as they rejected his heresy when it later arose. Their allegiance was to Christ.

A Revivalists Spiritual Bankruptcy

In 1892 there was a revival amongst the Japanese on the Pacific coast of the USA. In 1913, Paget Wilkes, founder of the Japan Evangelistic Band who was no stranger to revivals wrote: 'Some of those who are today the most spiritual leaders in Japan were saved at that time.' Among the new converts 'was a man remarkably converted, whom it was soon evident that God had chosen him as a special instrument.'

This convert from the revival was much used amongst his own people in America, but some years later, he returned home to Japan and was appointed as an English teacher in a large mission school. Paget wrote: 'Almost at once a revival followed; both teacher and students were convicted of sin in no ordinary degree. Many were converted and saved of the Lord.'

After leaving the mission school, this unnamed Japanese revivalist was appointed the pastorate of a country church, where 'he was induced to read books of modern criticism, [also known as higher criticism, where everything in the Bible is questioned] in the hope, we presume, of making himself more intellectually fitted for the task.' He soon lost 'all his old fire and evangelistic zeal...and the result was spiritual bankruptcy.' He shortly afterwards resigned his position and returned to America, having been robbed of the 'solemn fear of God, the quick sensitiveness to sin swiftly disappeared' and he was found to be without 'life and power.'

In 1911, one of Paget's personal friends who himself was a convert of the 1892 Revival, and 'had been very intimately acquainted' with the revivalist 'in the early days of his Christian life' visited America for some special meetings. After making inquires as to the whereabouts of his old friend, 'he learnt to his amazement and sorrow that he was keeping a house of shame in the town of ——.' This backslidden revivalist reluctantly met with his old friend through a mutual acquaintance and after being implored told him the story of his downfall which is how we know about it today.

The backslidden revivalist said, "You may pray for me, if you believe in it, but I have given up all that sort of thing long ago." The old friend dropped to his knees and 'poured out his aching heart for this poor deluded and unhappy soul.'[4]

The lessons we can learn is that it is possible for the elect to be deceived (Matthew 24:24) and we must be careful what we fill our minds with. Whilst we are called to give honour to whom honour is due, we should never idolise revivalists or attach too much value to the use of human instruments as they, like ourselves, are human and prone to make mistakes.

The Devil and Revival

- When God moves, the devil likes to rear his head and cause opposition. Christians, who may be unspotted from the world, can still come under the influence of the evil one. If those who have received God's grace can cause problems, how much more the graceless! The opposition from the conservative Baptists during the Nagaland Awakenings (1950s and 1960s) in India, were most cruel indeed, from those who thought they were doing God a favour, because what they saw did not line up with their theology.

- Opposition towards a revival comes from all quarters, though revival Church history records that during revivals in India in the nineteenth and twentieth centuries the opposition generally came from Hindus.

During China's phenomenal Christian growth over the past one hundred plus years, opposition came from the Boxers and then the Communists. During the Indonesian Revival (1964-1974) the opposition came from the predominant Muslim population. In the Koran (Qu'ran), leaving the faith is punishable by death. Whilst most Hindu families have no qualms with their relatives putting their faith in Jesus Christ, baptism into the Christian faith will! During the 1859 Irish Revival (Ulster Awakening), in many localised towns and communities where Roman Catholicism was strong it was the Catholics who opposed the 'Protestant' move of God. The Established Church: Roman Catholic, Church of England, Egyptian Orthodox and Ethiopian Copts have also persecuted those who have been "born again" within their denominations; the latter two in the past one hundred years.

Demonic Dangers with Revivals
- The devil is a liar, a deceiver and a great antagonist of the Son of God, and despises all things from God and of God. He will try to deceive and beguile us so we must put on the full armour of God, stay close to Jesus Christ and have a deep understanding of the Word of God. There is also the two-pronged danger of either being too proud of the revival, "Look at *us*, what *we* have achieved," or too worldly within the revival! Beware of self-exaltation, self-glory, self-promotion and slipping or sliding into sin – keep to the narrow road and close to Jesus.
- The devil is an imitator and an infiltrator though he cannot produce fruit in a person's life. John Wesley, discussing enthusiasm (physical phenomena) at Rev. John Berridge's church in Everton, England, wrote: 'In some, nature mixed with grace,' and that 'Satan mimicked this work of God.' George Whitefield, talking generally about young people in revival wrote: '...others were guilty of great imprudences.'
- Even within a revival there will be those who prophesy, but not of the Spirit of God, it could be demonic or of the flesh. It is the leader's responsibility to address the situation and the person concerned, to rebuke the devil and to protect the flock.

- Depending on the country and area, during revival there could be witches, warlocks, witchdoctors, Satanists, or shamans turning up at the meetings to do spiritual battle. It may be chanting, incantations, casting spells, cursing or placing accursed objects etc., in and around the church building – even cursed money in the tithe/offering bag. They should be challenged in the name of the Lord. Intercessors remember, 'we do not fight against flesh and blood, but against principalities and powers...' (Ephesians 6:12). Some of these children of the devil will get converted, some will not.

Physical Dangers with Revivals
We have just read about the dangers from others who are not what they appear, or those who have been taken captive by the evil one, but we also need to be careful of ourselves! An author from the nineteenth century writing about the Evangelical Awakening (1739-1791) wrote: 'When men's feelings are roused to a high pitch of excitement, it is not always easy to keep them within the bounds of prudence and reason.' Beware of allowing your emotions to run away with you. There are natural dangers due to the human makeup. We cannot abuse natural laws, which are there for our benefit and expect our bodies to stay strong when we neglect ourselves, physically, spiritually or mentally.

- Extensive and prolonged revivals, those that go on for months or years (and the longer the better) are exhausting. Evening meetings can continue until the sun rises, but it is unwise to rise up early and to go to bed late. There is a big danger in being so excited about the things of God, 'spiritual hyperactivity' that people neglect to rest, sleep and eat at sensible times. See page 205. This can lead to burnout or a physical breakdown which is what happened to Evan Roberts during the end of the Welsh Revival (1904-1905). Duncan Campbell during the Lewis Revival (1949-1952) took eight meetings in twenty-four hours!
- Daily life still goes on, children have to go to school and most adults have a job to hold down. Do not neglect the necessities of life and sleep is essential.

We dishonour God by doing shoddy workmanship when we have the ability to do better. Work *and* rest!

- Sometimes a well-meaning leader may begin to interfere with the revival, having good intentions and pure motives, but interference and not allowing God to do what He wants to do, resisting can quench or grieve the Holy Spirit and thus the revival can cease.

- A leader must have great discernment during revival and be sensitive as to when to address an issue and when to keep quiet and allow the Holy Spirit to point out the error; otherwise a young convert could be crushed, rejected and lost forever. If you want to see fruit, don't damage the blossom. As an example, speaking about women dressing inappropriately (modesty and decency, especially in warmer climates where less is worn and more is revealed), has frequently been addressed from the pulpit in general terms. But at the Brownsville Revival (1995-2000), after stating, "Some of you dress like prostitutes," the leaders would state that they were talking to those who were older in the faith, not new converts, as the older ones should know better. Also a new convert who has been rejected and down-trodden all their life, upon radical conversion will be very emotional and will have uncontrollable joy. They should not be restrained with their joy in the Lord and shouts of "Hallelujah," "Glory" or "Praise God" – it's the only way they know how to express it – Jesus is looking down from heaven smiling on them and shame on us if we frown on them. See Psalm 5:11, 29:9, 47:1, Isaiah 44:23, Romans 15:11 and 1 Peter 1:8.

- A church or small village could be overrun with visitors, seeking to have an encounter with God – this is a good thing, but your church could get swamped with people, having protracted meetings, day in, day out and this will take its toll on the workers, buildings and property. You could also have car parking problems. People will be queuing to get inside church but the neighbours may not appreciate it. In recent revivals, security guards and nursery carers have been employed to assist in people management.

Chapter Sixteen

Persecution and Opposition

Jesus was sinless, perfect and went about doing good, yet He was hated and despised by many. There were at least ten attempts on His life prior to His crucifixion! See Luke 4:24-29, 19:47 and 20:19, John 7:19, 30, 44, 8:37, 59, 10:31, 39 and John 11:53. Jesus said, "If they persecute Me they *will also* persecute you" (John 15:20). Therefore all disciples of Jesus Christ will suffer persecution in some form because of their allegiance to the King of kings and Lord of lords.

Leaders of revival will suffer persecution and some encounter attempted assassination! Many attempts have only been in the hearts and minds of the perpetrators who have turned up at a meeting with a sword, knife or gun etc., but have been struck by the mercy of the Spirit of Grace and Supplication and repented of their vile intentions.

On one occasion, a gun was pointed at Daniel Rowland, the eighteenth century Welsh revivalist; the trigger was pulled but it failed to fire, on another occasion they tried to blow him and his congregation up with gunpowder!

George Whitefield was attacked in his lodgings by a 'seeking' gentleman wielding a sword, the revivalist cried, "Murder, murder!" and people came to his rescue!

The Methodists of the early eighteenth century were a despised sect and were accused of being Deists, Jesuits and Puritans; being in collusion with the Pope and even workers of the devil because they preached salvation by faith and not of works! As the decades passed and especially towards the last two to three decades of John Wesley's life (d.1791), it became easier for those who were known as Methodists. In some towns and villages, John Wesley was escorted into the district as if he were royalty, with people lining the streets. It was a far cry from when he was shouted at, spat at, pelted with mud, stones and even dead pieces of cat! On one occasion, a bull was let loose in the crowd when he was field-preaching! At other times, drunken horsemen would ride through the crowd and it was not unknown for the parson, the Church of England vicar, to employ mobs, ply them with drink, and encourage them to bang drums, to drown out the preacher's voice, tell them to get up to other mischief and encourage them to riot! In Barnsley, Yorkshire, 'bating the Methodist' as one author wrote: 'was a favourite pastime with those of the rougher sort.'

On many occasions, the houses in which John Wesley or other Methodist preachers were lodging at or preaching in were damaged; stoned or firebombs were thrown through the windows. On a few occasions, walls or even the house itself was torn down by the violence of the mobs! John Wesley could hold his own, though he was of short stature (five feet and weighed under 126lb) and would try to find the ringleader and confront him. On most occasions they would be subdued and sometimes converted! One such person was a pugilist (boxer) who became Wesley's bodyguard for a time and as a new Christian, he threatened "to lump" anyone who tried to disturb the peace when Wesley was in town!

John Knox who became the Scottish Reformer, used to carry a two-handled sword to defend his master, George Wishart who was a fiery preacher and prayer warrior. Wishart ordered Knox to leave him in January of 1546 knowing his fate, saying "…One is sufficient for sacrifice."

John Wesley had no qualms in speaking to the local magistrates in seeking for justice and financial compensation for damages caused to his hosts. If the magistrate was in collusion with the rioters he would go higher up the chain of authority and get his justice. If the offenders were repentant over their actions then he would not press charges, but compensation for damaged property was always expected.

Rhodesian born, Michael Howard, has seen at least six revivals across Africa during the 1980s and 90s. He has had stones thrown at him. At one checkpoint in Moçambique, a rebel soldier put a gun through the open window of his vehicle and threatened to kill him. Howard thrust it away and declared to the soldier that he could not kill him! He got out his vehicle and preached the gospel to the soldiers. I believe there were about twenty soldiers present and they all got down on their knees and were converted!

Carlos Annacondia from the Argentine Revival (1982-1997) after a meeting in La Boca, in 1985, was celebrating his birthday with his ministry team when some hoodlums approached and threatened them. One of them pulled a knife and ran towards him. Pablo Bottari shouted, "I bind you in the name of Jesus" and the young man fell to the ground subdued. Someone once said that you cannot have a true [open-air] revival without a riot! The apostle Paul can confirm that statement – read the Acts of the Apostles.

Prior to 1998, on one Saturday night at Brownsville Church, during the Brownsville Revival (1995-2000) a toxic gas bomb was ignited within the church. The back of the church had to be evacuated and the air conditioning shut down. At the same time a bomb of the same type was released in a nearby grocery store and those within the store became very ill, though those at the church suffered no ill affect.

In March 2003, Bill Wilson of Metro Ministries in America, was mugged on the streets not far from the ministries headquarters. A gun was put in his mouth and in the struggle that ensued he was shot and the bullet went out through his cheek. He was back to work as normal within a few days!

Some modern-day high profile men of God do have bodyguards whilst others live in high security monitored homes. During the Brownsville Revival (1995-2000), Steve Hill had a bodyguard who kept close to him when off the platform praying for people during the services. It is better to be safe than sorry. Also, high profile churches and especially mega churches have security guards. This is practical wisdom and I would not be surprised if some ministers wear an executive stab / bullet-proof vest which are very discreet and can be worn under a suit.

Todd Bentley of the controversial Lakeland Outpouring (2008) also known as the Lakeland Revival or Healing Revival which was beamed live to 215 nations of the world via God TV and webcasts, openly stated about the death threats and hate mail he had received. He said, "I can't go out or be in the park with my children without at least ten people coming up to me; *most* of them friendly." His wife (whom he later divorced) also needed security when she went out.[1] See also Appendix C for further examples. We should not put God to the test, but be wise and discerning.

Within some churches and chapels in Britain, they have a space in front of the pulpit called the "Big Seat" where the elders sit and face the congregation. This was birthed from the occasions where people would try to mount the pulpit and assault the preacher!

On more than one occasion I have been told that God would never let any harm come to His people. I responded to one person who held this view and did not quote the Scriptures: 'All who desire to live godly in Christ Jesus will suffer persecution' (2 Timothy 3:12), nor, 'The souls of those who have been slain for the Word of God and for the testimony they held' (Revelation 6:9). I explained that if we get in a car and drive away without putting on our seatbelt and were involved in an accident, could we expect God to protect us when we did not take the relevant safety precautions? Regardless of the fact that it is illegal to drive without wearing a seatbelt in many countries, by not belting up, you not only endanger your own life, but others. Even Jesus for a time did not walk in Judea, but moved to Galilee because He knew the Jews would try to kill Him (John 7:1).

On Sunday, 10 December 2007, Matthew Murray, entered the east entrance of the New Life's Church in Colorado Springs, America, firing his rifle. In the car park (parking lot) he had killed two teenagers, injuring their father and others. Murray was carrying two handguns, an assault rifle and over 1,000 rounds of ammunition. About 7,000 people were on the church campus at the time of the shooting.

Jeanne Assam, a member of the church and a security guard who is licensed to carry a weapon, identified herself and shot the gunman dead. When asked by a reporter if she felt like a hero, Assam said, "I wasn't just going to wait for him to do further damage."

New Life's Senior Pastor, Brady Boyd called Assam a real hero because Murray had enough ammunition on him to cause a lot of damage...she saved the lives of 50 to 100 people. Boyd said Assam was the one who suggested the church beef up its security on Sunday, following the Arvada shooting earlier in the day, where a gunman killed two YWAM workers at their missionary training centre. The pastor credited the security plan and the extra security for preventing further bloodshed. There were fifteen to twenty security people at the church. On the Sunday the guards were doubled to twelve instead of the usual six, all of whom are church members and volunteers. Only those licensed to carry weapons do so.

Revival and Persecution

- Revival sometimes precedes a time of judgment or persecution. This is to prepare the Church for the hardships to come; this was clearly seen twelve years after the revival in the Belgian Congo of 1953 when civil war tore the country apart.
- At other times, amidst persecution revival can break-out; this was most clearly seen in the Indonesian Revival (1964-1974), the Nagaland Awakenings (1950s and 1960s) and the revival in China from the twentieth century onwards, where the Church has seen phenomenal growth during great tribulation.
- Also, revival can cause persecution; this is what happened during the Eggon Revival (1930s) in Northern Nigeria, when former spirit worshipers, including spirit priests came and burned their fetishes and followed Christ. But this persecution purged the Church and the opposition came from the senior tribal leader who was financially hit by the lack of offerings to the spirits, which became his property.
- Sometimes persecution comes from the Church, as the leadership with its traditions, rituals and rote, fail to understand the move of God. When revival broke out in the church in 1960 during the Nagaland Awakening in North East India; some Christians who had an assurance of salvation returned to their village in the northern Sumi territory and were stoned, beaten, tortured and their Bibles were taken from them. One day, in the same location, the villages joined together with three others and stripped fifteen women revivalists to the flesh and paraded them naked before all the people – these shameful acts were carried out by the so-called Church, by people who professed to be Christians! But, by the patient witness and love of these Christians, some of whom

had the gift of healing; within a few years the whole village was touched by the fire of revival!

Opposition from the Old and the New

- There is a danger that some of those who witnessed the last move of God may oppose a new move of God. This is because it looks different than the previous one. Jesus stated that new wine must have new wineskins and that those who have tasted the old *do not immediately* desire the new, because they believe the old is better (Luke 5:38-39). In 1941, the Warden of Bishop Tucker Theological College, Uganda, who had himself been blessed through the aftermath of the Welsh Revival (1904-1905) had little sympathy which he deemed a 'subversive movement,' the Balokole (saved ones) of the East Africa Revival (1930s-1950s). He had embraced one move of God, yet rejected another. See page 118.
- There will always be opposition to revivals and new moves of God. There are always a minority of Christians who resist change.
- It is not uncommon for some of those who have prayed for revival to reject it when it comes, as it did not line up with their preconceived ideas.
- Revival can come so unexpectedly and in a guise which may be different than what is expected or perceived, that it is initially rejected and / or not believed to be from God. In 1860, Andrew Murray was the new minister of a Dutch Reformed church in Worcester, Southern Africa. He had been praying for revival. A prayer meeting of sixty young people led by his assistant was being held in the hall when Divine thunder rolled in and shook the building – revival broke out! Murray was summoned and amidst all the unusual manifestations of loud and also murmured intercession, he told the congregation to be silent – he was ignored. Thrice he tried to calm and stop the congregation, not realising it was the answer, he and many others had been praying for. Bewildered, Murray walked out of the hall and exclaimed, "God is the God of order and here everything is in confusion!"

It took some time before he was convinced that this was the nature of the Divine visitation.

- Others will stand aloof when revival comes, not being sure whether it is from God or the devil. This aloofness, even among leaders or missionaries may only last for a day or two, as what happened at a few of the WEC mission stations during the Congo Revival (1953-1957). But when revival came to the Union Seminary in Shekow, China, in 1933, the students embraced it, heart and soul yet the teachers stood aloof. Rev. Erling Gilje from Denmark, noted: 'There was so much in the revival methods and manifestations that they did not understand.'

- Revival within a denomination, network of churches or a mission organisation can make people impatient of the organisation that seems so powerless, because it is not fully embraced or endorsed and / or certain key leaders stand at a distance with a critical, sometimes even scoffing attitude. During the Ruanda Revival (1937-1950s) which flowed into the East Africa Revival (1930s-1950s), the Balokole (saved ones) and Abaka (those on fire!) caused tension in the early 1940s amongst the Church Mission Society (CMS) Ruanda Mission which was Anglican. It nearly split the CMS Mission in East Africa because the Balokole and the Abaka continually questioned the reality of those who professed Christ when they saw no life. For senior leaders to be told that they were not born again or that they had not the Holy Spirit was deeply resented by many, whilst for others it was a God-sent rebuke and a wake-up call. A missionary noted that 'it sometimes arose out of confusion between the truths of justification [conversion] and sanctification [a deeper work of the Holy Spirit giving victory over sin, (holiness) and fullness of joy].'

In 1945, A. C. Stanley Smith in his book, *Road to Revival – The Story of the Ruanda Mission* wrote about the revival at Mukono Theological College (1936) in Uganda. Thirty-two years later, Bill Butler in *Hill Ablaze* wrote about prayer for revival beginning in 1939, by some twenty-five students at the Bishop Tucker Theological College at Mukono – they are the one and the same college. In 1936, the Diamond Jubilee of the Uganda Church (Anglican) was approaching and the Bishop knew that the greatest need for the Church was revival and planned that missions should be held throughout the diocese.

Bill Butler stated that most of the students of the Mukono Theological College in 1936 had no assurance or clear understanding of salvation, and 'most reflected the attitude widely prevailing in the Church of Uganda at that time; that provided they were baptised and confirmed and not *discovered* in any particular wrong doing, they were Christians. Stealing in the College was rife and to some extent, were drinking and immorality.'

A. C. Stanley Smith wrote: 'The key to the whole situation in Uganda was the Theological College at Mukono, where the Christian leaders of the Church were trained. Here was the place where revival needed to start' and it did!

The sad thing was that the Warden of Bishop Tucker Theological College had himself been blessed through the aftermath of the Welsh Revival (1904-1905), but had little sympathy which he deemed a 'subversive movement.' He had embraced one move of God, yet rejected another.

The Warden implemented three new rules: No student was to leave his dormitory before 6am; they were forbidden to meet together in groups of three or more and no student was permitted to preach inside the College without the Warden's permission. Most of the students were married men, with years of Christian service behind them and not accustomed to flouting authority. They pleaded with the College authorities to rescind the rule. Though after prayer and fasting, in the half term holiday, they knew it was better to obey God than man, and met once again at 4am to pray for revival and worship the Lord.

After their expulsions in late 1941, their licenses to preach in the Church of Uganda were withdrawn. They were branded as 'rebels,' but this event proved to be God's means of scattering them across Uganda, for revival was to breakout in the late 1940s, and these former students, amongst others, would be the revivalists across East Africa. God is sovereign and He is in charge of all things.

A. C. Stanley Smith wrote: 'Every movement of the Spirit sweeping through a lifeless church makes some people impatient of the organisation which seems so powerless. It would be so simple to break away and start afresh. We are convinced that there are far too many denominations as it is.[2] The Church in Ruanda is clear that God's will for us is to live out the new life within the Church of which we are already members. Our Mission is a Church of England Mission. We believe that communion with the Church not only ensures for the African Church a share in the rich heritage of the past, but supplies a basis which can be both broad and flexible enough to allow the indigenous Church free scope for development under the guidance of the Holy Spirit.... We do not transport the whole Church of England system into Africa. The main essentials of its organised life and its doctrine ensure that the African Church shall have the heritage of the past; but we plead for simplicity that there may be room for truly African expression in the worship and form of the Church.'[3]

The Incompatibility of the Old and New School

- Jesus said that new wine, must be poured into new wineskins, thus preserving both, otherwise the skin will burst and the wine will be spoilt (Matthew 9:17 and Mark 2:22). In revival, views of what God can do, cannot do or will do may have to change. Otherwise the Holy Spirit will do a work and could pass us by and that would be a tragedy.

- There is a danger that those who embrace the revival, the new school, reject the traditionalists, the old school. By not seeing eye-to-eye, the new school may unwittingly break the spirit of unity by not having the bond of peace. The Evangelical Revival (1739-1791) had lots of different personalities and views; see Appendix A. As Christians it is wrong to reject brethren who are unable to embrace a move of God. If they are born again, then they are part of the family of God. Some people have all their lives been taught a certain doctrine or been loyal to their denomination, or a member of *their* church for decades and are simply unable to accept certain things, or are bound, or hold dear to their traditions. If we denounce them (or vice versa) then surely we are only hindering the fulfilment of Jesus' prayer in John 17 – "That they may be one" (verse 22). If we do not "love one another" as brethren, then how will the world know that we are Jesus' disciples? (John 13:34-35).

- Even during revival when the Holy Spirit begins to move, there are those who reject His gifts – simply believing that the gifts of the Holy Spirit ceased at the death of the apostles. There is no Scripture to back this up; quite the contrary, and nearly two thousand years of Church history disprove it. See pages 101+.

- Some denominations will embrace the fruits of revival such as: revived or renewed Christians, new converts and transformed lives, yet still vehemently hold to *their* doctrine – though it does differ from member to member. They may still reject the Reviver – the Holy Spirit, or when the revival has ceased will go back to the way things were prior to the revival. This is especially true in regard to women who were raised up in revival with powerful ministries and afterwards were no longer permitted to speak in church.

Leaders who Disapproved of Elements of the Revival

President of the Norwegian Lutheran Mission in south western Honan and north Hupeh, Rev. Olav Espegren, writing from Nanyang in January 1934, noted: 'That the revival is still going forward at all of the stations in that field... In a couple of places there have appeared signs of an ecstatic movement resembling heathen "spirit-possession." In this condition they will claim to speak on God's behalf, dispense forgiveness of sins, etc. Also he mentions signs of the Pentecostal movement which had taken firmer hold to the east. He voices surprise that the Chinese, who are so practically minded in the affairs of the world, can be swept off their feet so easily when it comes to religious things. A very subtle temptation comes in the form of a desire for holiness; and the fullness of the Spirit and holiness seem so easily achieved through this one ecstatic experience. He emphasizes the need for responsible shepherds who... exercise authority.' See point 4, under ch. 16 on page 243.[4]

Chapter Seventeen

Enemies of God

Enemies of God, haters of the cross of Christ are scattered throughout the Bible (Philippians 3:18) and engraved on the pages of Church history, therefore should we expect it to be any different today or any less during times of revival?

An enemy is not necessarily one who is on the outside, but can be on the inside, in the same way that the secret services or members of the MI5, CIA or FBI become part of the group as they gather intelligence or have an informer. See Neh. 6:10, Gal. 2:4-5 and Jude verse 4. See page 168. Tobiah hated the Jews yet wormed his way into the temple of the Lord and even set up his home! (Nehemiah 13:4-9).

Demons (evil spirits) cannot hide before the manifest presence of God and they will frequently rise to the surface and expose themselves, often to the dismay of the person who is manifesting under these demonic influences or those present. Jesus at the beginning of His ministry cast out 'an unclean spirit' from a man who was crying out. The man convulsed and the demons cried out with a loud voice (via the man's voice box) before it was expelled (Mark 1:21-26). These demons should be cast out or off a person by the brethren in the mighty name of Jesus Christ of Nazareth. During times of revival, under the Holy Spirit's dealings or when God's presence descends, some will writhe (or other physical manifestation) on the floor and sometimes the demons will flee by themselves and thus look for a new home. At other times, these open manifestations, shrieks or slithering etc. reveal to the body of Christ that a person has demons and needs to be delivered in Jesus' mighty name.

It is also needful to point out that an enemy can be one who sits in silent opposition with a smile on their face but with anger and bitterness in their heart. The silent opposition, by not jumping into the River of God can reveal their lack of commitment to the things of God. Sitting on the fence like

Humpty Dumpty is not permissible; if you fall off on the wrong side then you will damage yourself and cause a lot of the Lord's soldiers to focus their time on you (because of your opposition) which would be unproductive. Jesus stated that we are 'either for Him or against Him,' there is no place in between, that is the sin of indifference. If we are for Jesus then we are for the things of God, the Father, the Son *and* the Holy Spirit. Let us not reject the Spirit, as Jesus came to destroy the works of the evil one so that we could have abundant life (John 10:10, Hebrews 2:14 and 1 John 3:8). Jesus promised the Holy Spirit to those who believe in Him and that they would do greater works (John 14:12-17 & John 16:7-14), but if we reject Him, we insult the Spirit of Grace and trample the Son of God underfoot (Hebrews 10:28-29).

There will be those who pray earnestly and persistently for revival who will reject it when revival comes, because it did not come how they had anticipated it. Religious rulers had been praying for the Messiah to come for over one thousand years and when He came (Jesus), many rejected Him, because He did not fit in with their preconceived ideas, regardless of the fact He fulfilled the prophecies and signs concerning Himself as stated in the Scriptures, which they proclaimed to follow and ritually observed.

Sadly, there are some people, even brethren, who have an unteachable spirit; they have a know-all attitude and a pre-programmed mindset and will not listen to truth, reason or even Scripture. When Jesus was resurrected, some 'worshipped Him;' whilst 'some doubted' (Matthew 28:17).

Some people are only happy in promoting their denomination, or pet doctrine to the exclusion of everything else and as the Proverbs declare, 'A fool has no delight in understanding, but in expressing his own heart' (Proverbs 18:2). It is like casting pearls before swine (Matthew 7:6), and fools despise the wisdom of words (Proverbs 23:9). If you have been on a Christian forum, you would have undoubtedly come across these type of people. They do not ask questions because they are unsure, they ask so that they can give their own opinion or distorted view regardless of any other point of view, without Scriptural backup, and they are adamant that they are right and everyone else is wrong. Let us also remember that 'any fool can start a quarrel' (Proverbs 20:3) and we are to 'avoid foolish and ignorant disputes, knowing that they generate strife and a servant of the Lord must not quarrel but be gentle' (2 Timothy 2:23-24).

Non-Embracers of Revival

Dr. Kurt Koch in a rebuttal that his book *The Revival In Indonesia* contained falsified reports, in a small folder wrote: 'In all revivals there are people, indeed even pious people, who stand beside the revival and are not caught up by it. God performs mighty deeds and pious pastors and Pharisees stand alongside cursing or criticising. At all of God's special acts there were those who stood alongside. The disciples of Jesus testified that the Lord had arisen. He had appeared among them. The Pharisees said that the disciples had stolen His body and now they were spreading these lies. Whomever has not himself been seized by the spirit of revival and by the Holy Spirit will not understand a revival (1 Corinthians 2:14). What we declare and write often reflect the condition of our own heart. One can possess a good deal of orthodox theology and yet stand alongside.'

Opposition Towards Paul and Barnabus

Whenever you do the work of God you can expect opposition even when the work is going well and bearing fruit. The apostle Paul and Barnabas were on their first missionary journey when they encountered opposition, in most of the places that they went, from Jews and Gentiles, the religious and the non-religious.

Paul preached in the synagogue in Antioch, in Pisidia, with great success, 'many of the Jews and devout proselytes' heeded their message (Acts 13:14-43). On the following Sabbath, 'almost the whole city came together to hear the Word of God' but the Jews seeing the multitudes, 'were filled with envy; and contradicting and blaspheming, they opposed the things spoken by Paul.' Both Paul and Barnabas 'grew bold' and stated that as the Jews rejected the truth they would 'turn to the Gentiles' and more people were won to the Lord. 'But the Jews stirred up the devout and prominent women and the chief men of the city, raised up persecution against Paul and Barnabas and expelled them from their region' (Acts 13:44-52).

In Iconium, Paul and Barnabas entered the synagogue and preached the Word of the Lord and 'a great number of multitudes of Jews and Greeks believed. But the unbelieving Jews stirred up the Gentiles and poisoned their minds against the brethren.' They stayed there a long time preaching with signs and wonders following. But 'the multitude of the city was divided; part sided with the Jews, and part with the apostles.' But when both Jews and Gentiles violently attempted 'to abuse and stone them' they fled to the cities of Lycaonia (Acts 14:1-6).

Paul preached on Mars Hill, in the midst of the Areopagus in Athens, to the pagans, 'some mocked,' but 'some men joined him and believed' (Acts 17:22-34). Paul also taught in the school at Tyrannus for two years and all who dwelt in Asia (Minor) heard the Word of the Lord, both Jews and Greeks, but *some were* hardened' and 'spoke evil of the Way' (Acts 19:8-9). See page 132 – the devil instigates riots.

True or False

The spring 1973 issue of the *Conservative Baptist* periodical published an article entitled 'Indonesian Revival: True or False?' written by Dr. George Peters following his investigation of three recently published accounts of revival on the island of Timor, Indonesia.

One of the books under discussion was *The Revival In Indonesia* by Kurt Koch, translated from the German. In a rebuttal in a four page folder which accompanied the book, Dr. Kurt Koch wrote: 'In the above article the claim is made that Dr. Peters undertook "to investigate the information first-hand." Which first-hand witnesses does Peter cite? He names his authorities, a German and Dutchman, professors of a theological institute in Kupang. Christians in Kupang, Timor who are capable of judging the matter explained that these two men are a great problem for the church in Timor, for they have brought to Timor a modernistic and neo-rationalistic [the new theological doctrine that human reason rather than Divine revelation establishes religious truth] type of theology and have planted this type of theology in the hearts of their students. These two men are not first-hand witnesses, but rather third-rank witnesses. From the beginning to end they have taken a critical position over [and] against the revival.

'In addition to these men Pastor Daniel is also named. Pastor Daniel is the leader of the central ecclesiastical district in Timor, which has its headquarters in Soe. He is, in fact, a good man. I spent two weeks with him in Batu as well as an additional two weeks with his congregation in Soe. I have spoken ten times in his church. Yet, he also is not a first-hand witness, but rather a second-hand witness. I personally heard him testify that for a year he had assumed the attitude of a critical observer towards the revival which was taking place. Only after a year of critical observation was he convinced of the genuineness of this revival and overcome by its spirit.'

Dr. Peters explained that Dr. Kurt Koch's book is "the result of listening to tape-recorded stories," and that he "*did not witness any miracles." Dr. Koch's wrote: 'The truth of the matter is I have never listened to a single such tape...*that again is falsehood. I have experienced a miracle of healing in myself. I have been present when the Lord performed miracles in others. I have also heard many testimonies from reliable witnesses who have experienced miracles.

'Why does Dr. Peters accept negative theologians as witnesses and not the chief witness, Petrus Octavianus, the most powerful spiritual leader in the revival, a man who also possess academic credentials.

'Dr. Peter states that I [Kurt Koch] had come too late to be able to examine the events of the revival. Again this is a falsehood. Between the years 1963-1969 I was in Indonesia five times including the great miracle period at the beginning of the revival. Dr. Peters was there in 1972 or 1973. Not I, but rather Dr. Peters arrived too late. Or does time run backwards for Dr. Peters? Is 1965 later than 1972?

'Dr. Peter writes, "Without them (the ministry of Dr. Middlekoop and Pastor Daniel) the revival...could never have come." That is the height of falsehood. Pastor Daniel himself stated at a conference in Batu that he had originally been opposed to the gospel. Dr. Middlekoop does not have a good reputation among the believers in Kupang and in Soe. He was a great hindrance to the revival.'

Old Testament Enemies

- Various kings of Egypt (Exodus 1:12-14 and 5:14).
- Korah, Dathan, Abiram and On, Israelites, rebelled against Moses' leadership and they died by the hand of God alongside their families (Numbers 16:1-35).
- Tobiah and Sanballat tried to lure Nehemiah into a trap and even sent letters to try to frighten him (Nehemiah 2:19 and Nehemiah 6:1-19).
- Geshem the Arab despised the Jews, laughed them to scorn and tried to do mischief against Nehemiah (Nehemiah 2:19 and Nehemiah 6:2).
- Jannes and Jambres resisted Moses (2 Timothy 3:8).
- Jesus spoke about the Jews' forefathers who shed the blood of the prophets (Matthew 23:29-33).

New Testament Enemies, Deceivers and Stray-ers

- King Herod tried to kill the promised King, the Messiah and ordered the death of all the males in Bethlehem who were aged two or under (Matt. 2:16).
- Judas betrayed Jesus (Matthew 26:14-16, 47-49).
- Simon the sorcerer was converted and baptised during a time of revival! He tried to buy the ability to impart the Holy Spirit. Peter declared, "Your heart is not right in the sight of God...you are poisoned by bitterness and bound by iniquity" (Acts 8:9-23).
- Hymenaeus and Alexander 'suffered shipwreck' after rejecting the faith (1 Timothy 1:19-20).
- Hymenaeus (as above) and Philetus strayed concerning the truth and spread malicious lies, thus overthrowing the faith of some (2 Timothy 2:16-18).
- Demas 'having loved this present world' forsook the apostle Paul (2 Timothy 4:10).
- Alexander the coppersmith did the apostle Paul much harm and resisted his words (2 Timothy 4:14-15).
- Some professing believers are insubordinate, they are deceivers who profess to know God 'but by their works deny Him' (Titus 1:10-11 and 18).
- Diotrephes, a self promoting leader of the church told his congregation lies and expelled those who followed elder John (3 John 9-19).

Chapter Eighteen

Misperceptions of God's Workings

The Unusual Workings of God

Some aspects of God's workings seem easier to understand than others. There is a very present danger of trying to keep God in a box by subconsciously defining what He can do, cannot do, and what He will do and will not do. Intellectually and theologically we know God can do anything, but somehow, in our finite minds we limit an infinite God to our own understanding, without even being aware of it until we are in the presence of God in true revival power.

Some of the things that go on in revival can appear strange and unorthodox, notably the physical phenomena – but then the Bible does have some very unorthodox characters and the Scriptures do reveal strange events: John the Baptist was dressed in camel's hair; he ate locusts and wild honey and to the crowds thundered forth, "Repent" and was the first person in the New Testament to see people confessing their sins (Mark 1:4-6). Hosea was called of God to marry a prostitute and Isaiah went naked and barefoot for three and a half years; both these prophets and their intercessions were a sign against Israel. Jesus overturned the tables of the money changers at the temple, at the beginning and end of His ministry; Peter pronounced to Sapphira that she will drop down dead, just like her husband Ananias, who tested the Spirit of the Lord and lied to God. Jacob, the deceiver (later renamed Israel) wrestled with God, Jeremiah wore a wooden yoke for a period of time and Ezekiel ate food by weight and water by measure and lay on his side, paralysed, against a wall as part of an intercession for more than a year.

Principles which Defy Logic and Divine Paradoxes

Divine principles are different than those of the world. When God is at work; logic, theories and predetermined rules all have to give way to a higher law – the law of the Divine.

A paradox is defined to be a tenet or proposition contrary to received opinion, and seemingly absurd, but true in fact. The Bible is full of paradoxes: for God's thoughts and ways are on a higher plane than ours and therefore may appear impossible or even absurd from our perspective, yet are part of God's wonderful plan.

With God nothing is impossible as God can turn unreality into reality and turn nothing into something. God delights in doing the unexpected, the unpredictable and overturning the laws of probability and science, and this frequently happens during times of revival.

Biblical Paradoxes

- We reign by serving (Mark 10:42-44).
- We rest under a yoke (Matthew 11:28-30).
- We see unseen things (2 Corinthians 4:18).
- We triumph by defeat (2 Corinthians 12:7-9).
- We glory in our infirmities (2 Corinthians 12:5).
- We are exalted by being humble (Matthew 23:12).
- We become great by becoming little (Matthew 18:4).
- When we are weak then we are strong (2 Cor. 12:10).
- We become free by becoming slaves to God (Romans 6:17-22 with Romans 8:2).
- We live by dying to self (John 12:24-25 with 2 Corinthians 4:10-11).
- We possess all things by having nothing (2 Corinthians 6:10).
- If we lose our life for Christ's sake, we will find it (Matthew 16:25).
- We conquer by yielding (Matthew 5:5 with Romans 12:20-21).

God Defying Rules of Nature and Science

- The children of Israel's garments did not wear out in the wilderness (Deuteronomy 8:4).
- Moses and Israel were fed with manna from heaven for forty years (Exodus 16:4-5, 14-17, 31, 35) and they lacked nothing (Deuteronomy 2:7).
- Gideon's three hundred men defeated an army as numerous as locusts (Judges 7:7-22).

- Joshua prayed for the sun and moon to stand still so that Israel could finish their battle. The sun did not move (the earth's rotation ceased) for about a day and they finished the battle (Joshua 10:11-14).
- The prophet Elijah was fed by ravens with bread and meat and drank from the brook (1 Kings 17:4-6).
- The widow's oil and flour was multiplied which fed Elijah, the widow and her son (1 Kings 17:8-16).
- Elijah was anointed by the hand of God and outran King Ahab's chariot (1 Kings 18:46).
- Elisha helped a widow who was in debt; oil was miraculously multiplied into jars (2 Kings 4:1-7).
- A man brought twenty loaves of bread to feed one hundred men, the man of God told them to eat and they still had some left over (2 Kings 4:42-44).
- An iron axe head fell into the water and under Elisha's anointing it floated (2 Kings 6:1-7).
- Because of a band of raiders, a dead man was hastily let down into Elisha's tomb and upon touching his bones was brought to life (2 Kings 13:20-21).
- The shadow on the sundial went backwards by ten degrees (2 Kings 20:9-11 and Isaiah 38:7-8).
- Esther, an orphan was raised by Mordecai and she married the heathen world ruler of the day and saved her race from annihilation (book of Esther).
- The Lord hid Jeremiah and Baruch the scribe from the King of Judah who was unhappy about the prophecies he had given (Jeremiah 36:26).
- Meshach, Shadrach and Abednego were not burnt or singed in the fiery furnace (Daniel 3:8-30).
- The feeding of the five and four thousand, the miraculous multiplication of food (Matthew 14:15-21, Matthew 15:32-38 and Matthew 16:8-10).
- Jesus instructed Peter to go fishing and to take the coin out of the fish's mouth which would be enough to pay both their temple taxes (Matthew 17:24-27).
- Jesus turned water into wine (John 2:1-10).
- After the Ethiopian eunuch's baptism, Philip the evangelist was caught away in the Spirit and was put down in a town called Azotus (Acts 8:39-40).

Divine or Demonic Origin?

At one mission station during the Congo Revival (1953-1957), the missionaries thought a hurricane was coming as the wind of the Spirit blew through the building and came upon many. During the revival, numerous shy native ladies shouted, "Hallelujah!" at the top of their voices. Others shook all over and collapsed on the floor in groans and travail as intercession for souls was birthed in them, whilst others groaned and writhed under conviction of sin. Some people in different mission stations saw holy light or a bright light as part of a vision. People were slain in the meetings and would tremble and jerk uncontrollably or perspire and fall off their seats and roll in the mud in agony of soul. At first some of the missionaries were naturally hesitant about these manifestations – were they from God or not? Dave Roberts, editor of *Alpha* magazine wrote: 'Open-minded doubt is biblical. Closed-minded unbelief is what God abhors.' But as people came through to victory and testified of their sin in front of all, knowing that they had been pardoned by God through the shed blood of Jesus Christ, the wavering and hesitant missionaries knew it to be a genuine heaven-sent revival.

Some in the meetings in the Congo would try to imitate the manifestations of the Spirit as seen upon other people, whether by shaking, jerking or just getting over-excited in the flesh, trying to 'work up' the blessing. One flaky person claimed to be the Holy Spirit and was sharply rebuked, but the people had a teachable spirit and were able to receive correction from those in leadership. The elders, missionaries or those in charge of the meetings rebuked those who were in the flesh and instructed accordingly as there is a difference between hindering the Spirit and working with the Spirit. Those with positions of authority who negate their responsibility which has been entrusted to them, to exhort and to correct in the spirit of meekness and humility, thereby sin and grieve the Holy Spirit when they fail to do their duty. Also, other mentally disturbed people were set free from demons, by the power of God, in the name of Jesus Christ.

A senior missionary wrote: 'Grieve not the Spirit. Criticism, or attributing to the flesh that which is of the Spirit, can hinder revival tremendously; let us not be guilty of either.'[1]

During the 1859 revival in Ireland, there were many people claiming the work to be from the evil one. One country boy who had been affected by the revival stood on a stone and addressed the people in a street in Coleraine, saying, "Some people call it the work of the devil. All I can say to this is, that up to last week I have been serving the devil as well as I could, and I am sure he was well pleased with my service; but if he is employing me now, he is so far changed that I would not know him to be the same man!"[2]

A. C. Stanley Smith wrote: 'The years 1940-45 were times of much conflict arising out of the [Ruanda] Revival [1937-1950s]. The Muyebe Convention [of 1942] opened with a scene of wild tumultuous welcome of the Africans coming from the CMS stations. It took place in full view of the European delegates and many of them were shocked at what seemed to them hysteria or worse.' An African leader said, "What is the matter with you Europeans? Down below [where the majority of the delegates were] there are souls blessed and saved; but up here [on the platform] you are all anxious and worried."
    A. C. Stanley Smith wrote: 'They felt rebuked and yet they were passing through a conflict which if won would mean much to the whole cause of Christ. The African joy was a bit too exuberant; but the Europeans had to learn to leave the African to express his joy in an African way and to sing to his own rhythm.'[3]

A. C. Stanley Smith noted that among the Ruanda missionaries during 1941-1946 'there was a great deal of distressing division' and at one time there were three parties: 'Those who threw themselves right into the Revival Movement confident that the Holy Spirit would deal with the difficulties; a central group, who while rejoicing in the movement as of God, were critical and apprehensive of some of its features and so felt excluded from real fellowship; thirdly, those who were so troubled at what they thought were dangerous and evil tendencies in practice and in doctrine as to feel they must take strong measures of control.'[4]

God can sometimes appear disruptive and God will disturb us out of our religious rituals and comfort zones – but the "disruption" of God in times of revival produces abiding fruit and what is considered 'decently and in order' today, is a far cry from the first century Church! See page 63. Peter preached at Cornelius' house and in the midst of the sermon the Holy Spirit fell upon them and they spoke in tongues, thus disturbing the meeting (Acts 10:23-48). It was similar to what happened on the Day of Pentecost when the people began to cry out and three thousand were saved!

The Devil Instigates Riots

The Bible is full of instances where the enemy is aroused at the things of God and pours out his vengeance through men and women against God's servants. The prophet Micaiah was punched on the cheek for telling the prophets via the Lord that they had a lying spirit and were therefore deceived. Jezebel killed hundreds of the Lord's prophets and followers; Jeremiah was put in the stocks and also placed in a dried up well, whilst his messages from the Lord were ignored for twenty-three years as he spoke the Word of God. Jesus was whipped, beaten and then crucified and Stephen became the first Christian martyr. The apostle Paul was stoned, whipped, beaten and imprisoned on numerous occasions.

Saul (later renamed Paul) believed he was doing the work of God, persecuting the followers of Christ; with a flash of light he fell to the ground and whilst on the floor, Jesus asked him, "Why are you persecuting Me?" 'Trembling and astonished' Saul asked what he should do and when he opened his eyes he was unable to see (Acts 10:1-9).

The apostle Paul and Silas went into the synagogue in Thessalonica and preached. A great multitude of devout Greeks and many of the leading women followed them, which led to a riot. The people said, "These who have turned the world upside down have come here too" (Acts 17:1-9).

Paul and Silas were sent to Berea and they preached in the synagogue. Many believed, both Greeks and prominent women of the city, but Jews from Thessalonica stirred up the crowd and another riot began! (Acts 17:10-15).

Chapter Nineteen

Human Emotions – Part I

The Human Emotions

During times of joy and happiness, people are known to shout, jump, clap, dance or shed tears (or a whole host of other physical responses) in their emotional excitement; whether it is passing your driving test, accepting a proposal of marriage, receiving a letter stating that you've got a promotion, a phone call informing you that you have been accepted into an orchestra, hearing that your wife is pregnant, receiving an answer to a prayer, watching your country win the World Cup or your rugby club beating your rivals etc. Now, if people can get excited about these (and some are more excitable than others) then can we expect anything less, if not more, when God the Holy Spirit turns up and touches lives?

'...Whom having not seen [Jesus] you love. Though now you do not see Him, yet believing, you rejoice with joy inexpressible and full of glory' (1 Peter 1:8).

It has been said that if a person is void of emotions they are either emotionally bound or have hardness of heart. God made the emotions and if He did not want them expressed then He would have not have created us this way. He would also never have permitted the Psalms, with their exhortation and shouts of praise which can only but move the emotions.

During revival, when God turns up and His Spirit is poured out from on high, when He comes down and the hills melt like wax before Him, when He pours water on the dry and barren land, when He begins to fill those that thirst after Him and His righteousness, then you can expect the presence of God to externally affect people's bodies in different ways. If physical phenomena happen in the natural, such as when Samuel went to Bethlehem 'and the elders of the town trembled at his coming' (1 Samuel 15:9) then how much more when the Holy Spirit comes and meets with Christians and non-Christians during times of heavenly visitations? I expect all of us have been nervous at a job interview or perhaps before a vital test, but how much more will we tremble in the presence of a holy God when He comes?

During the triumphal entry into Jerusalem, Jesus refused to silence a 'whole multitude of disciples' who 'began to rejoice and praise with a loud voice' and told the Pharisees that if the people kept quiet 'then the stones would immediately cry out' (Luke 19:37-40).

When the Holy Spirit comes there can be many physical responses as the human body encounters the tangible presence of God. The Israelites were petrified when God descended on the top of Mount Sinai and the mountain shook and blazed with fire. Moses' face radiated God's glory when he met Him. Isaiah saw his uncleanness before a holy God and cried out, "Woe to me." The priests who dedicated the temple under King Solomon were unable to perform their duties as the glory descended. Hannah in her intense prayer for a child was perceived to be drunk by the undiscerning Eli. When Jesus was transfigured before the three disciples, Peter was so dumbstruck that he did not know what to say; John, on the island of Patmos heard a voice as of a trumpet and numerous people throughout the Bible received visions, had dreams or were in a trance as God met with them.

I have heard it said by well-meaning, godly Christians that when they were converted they received it all. Personally speaking, I did not. I was 'born again' at age ten and later baptised in the Holy Spirit, but my shadow does not heal the sick like the apostle Peter (Acts 5:15) and my handkerchief or apron does not carry healing power like the apostle Paul (Acts 19:12-13), therefore I have to conclude that there is much more to see, witness, experience and receive in God, for God and with God in Jesus' mighty name. And to God be the glory for the great things He has done, because He alone is worthy of all glory, honour, praise and adoration.

Sir Isaac Newton towards the end of his life upon being congratulated on his lifetime achievements responded, "I have been like a little child playing with pebbles on the beach while the great ocean of truth lies unexplored before me!"

Godly Extremes

During times of revival there are always godly extremes, some will shout to the Lord, while others will be still in His presence, some will stand whilst others will be prostrated before Him. Some will dance, others will kneel. These natural godly emotions, during the same period of time (say within a meeting) will affect each person differently. These feelings and emotions will come and go, but as long as we continually walk in obedience to the Master, the inner experience will remain. God must continually be glorified and after we have met with God, our character and life will be changed – for the better, it will be abiding fruit.

When God meets with a person He can do a number of things: bring inner healing, show them their son-ship, their adoption into the family of God, the fact that they are justified, sanctified, forgiven and made righteous because of what Jesus has done on the cross of Calvary. For many, these concepts are only intellectual and not heart-birthed in the inner man, but especially during revival these doctrines become living. God may refresh a person, renew them, heal them, mend them, bend them, soften them, commission them or reveal more of Himself and anything else He wants to do. It is God coming and meeting with the inner man, Spirit to spirit as God deals with the soul.

May God 'give to you the spirit of wisdom and revelation in the knowledge of Him, the eyes of your understanding being enlightened; that you may know the hope of His calling, what are the riches of the glory of His inheritance in the saints' (Ephesians 1:17-18). May God 'grant you, according to the riches of His glory, to be strengthened with might through His Spirit in the inner man...being rooted and grounded in love, may be able to comprehend with all the saints what is the width and length and depth and height – to know the love of Christ which passes knowledge; that you may be filled with all the fullness of God' (Ephesians 3:16-19).

In December 1841, David Livingstone was at Kuruman Mission Station in Southern Africa, which had seen revival in 1829 under Robert Moffat. In a letter he wrote: 'I have been quite astonished again and again at their [the natives] calmness. In cutting out a tumour, an inch in diameter, they sit and talk as if they feel nothing. 'A man likes me never cries,' they say, 'they are children that cry.' And it is a fact that men never cry, but when the Spirit of God works on their mind they cry most piteously. Sometimes in church they endeavour to screen themselves from the eyes of the preacher by hiding under the forms [pew seats] or covering their heads with the karosses as a remedy against their convictions. And when they find that won't do, they rush out of the church and run with all their might, crying as if the hand of death was behind them.... It is not to be wondered at that they should exhibit agitations of body when the mind is affected, as they are quite unaccustomed to restrain their feelings. But that this hardened being should be moved mentally at all is wonderful indeed. If you saw them in their savage state, you would feel the force of this more.'[1]

The Baldhu Schoolmaster – Praising Loudly

The Baldhu Revival (1851-1854) in the parish of Kea, near Truro, Cornwall, England, began when its vicar, Rev. William Haslam, a High Churchman, got converted under his own preaching in mid October. After the Christmas holidays, the Baldhu schoolmaster and his wife returned to the parish in January 1852. Rev. William Haslam wrote: 'They came back full of disdain and prejudiced against the work and even put themselves out of the way to go from house to house, in order to set the people against me and my preaching.'

'The master was particularly set against "excitement" and noise. He said, "It was so very much more reverend to be still in prayer, and orderly in praise; it was not necessary to make such an unseemly uproar!" I had however discovered that *the people who most objected to noise had nothing yet to make a noise about*, and that when they had; they generally made as much or more noise than others.

'If a house is seen to be on fire, people cannot help making an outcry; which they do not when they only read about it. Witnessing a danger stirs the heart; and when people's eyes are open to see souls in eternal danger, they cannot help being stirred up and crying out....'

'We read that 'the whole multitude of the disciples began to rejoice, and praise God with a loud voice, for all the mighty works that they had seen' (Luke 19:37) and we are told, over and over again, in the Psalms, to 'praise God with a loud voice,' and to 'shout.' When we lift up our voice, the Lord can stir our hearts; and surely the things of the Lord have more right, and ought to have more power, to stir and arouse the soul of man, than a boat-race, or a horse-race, or a fictitious scene on the stage. I think people would be all the better for letting out their hearts in praise to God. It may be it is trying and exciting to some, but perhaps they are the very ones who need such a stimulus, and this may be the best way to bring it out.'

The schoolmaster still attended the services and took notes. One Sunday, Rev. William Haslam preached on the text, "Cut it down; why cumbereth the ground?" (Luke 13:7) and the schoolmaster was heard to say, "Thank God that I am not cut down yet" and then proceeded for the first time to the after-meetings in the schoolroom. Rev. Haslam found the schoolmaster on his knees, crying out, "Oh, I fear there is no mercy – the sentence is surely gone forth against me, 'Cut him down! Cut him down!' " and 'then the poor man howled aloud in his distress. The people prayed for him with shouts of thanksgiving, while he threw himself about in agony of mind, and made a great noise, which only drew louder acclamations from the people. In the midst of this tremendous din he found peace, and rejoiced with the others in unmistakable accents, and as loud as the loudest.' The next Sunday, during the service, the schoolmaster, quickly left church, leaped over a wall and then over a hedge and ran into a field, shouting all the time – it was discovered afterwards that the *Prayer-book* was now full of meaning!

Rev. William Haslam wrote: 'The schoolmaster became a very earnest Christian, and took much pains and interest in the religious instruction of the children. There were several revivals in the school while he was there, and many of the children were converted.' And soon his wife and her sister were also converted.[2]

Cornish Culture in the 1850s

In 1880, Rev. William Haslam, who had seen at least eight revivals, wrote in reference to the Baldhu Revival (1851-1854): 'In Cornwall [in the 1850s], Cornish folk did not think much of a meeting unless it was an exciting and noisy one.

In the schoolroom, evening by evening, the Lord wrought a great work, and showed forth His power in saving many souls. I have seldom read of any remarkable manifestations in revivals the counterpart of which I did not witness in that room; and I saw some things there which I have never heard of as taking place anywhere else. I was by this time [late October 1851] not afraid of a little, or even much noise, so long as the power of the Lord's presence was evident. The shouts of the people did not hinder me, nor did their loud praying, nor their hearty responses....'

'It may be asked, why did I permit such things?... I lived amongst a people who were accustomed to outward demonstrations.... It was just a question, in many cases, of *no work, or of decided manifestations*. We could not help people being stricken down, neither could they help it themselves; often the most unlikely persons were overcome and became excited, and persons naturally quiet and retiring proved the most noisy and demonstrative. However, it was our joy to see permanent results afterwards, which more than reconciled us to any amount of inconvenience we had felt at the time.

'When the power of God is manifestly present, the person who hears the noise, as well as those who make it, are both under the same influence, and are in sympathy with one another. An outsider, who does not understand it, and is not in sympathy, might complain, and be greatly scandalised. For my own part, I was intensely happy in those meetings and had become accustomed to the loud "Amen's," that I found it very dull to preach when there was no response.'[3]

Billy Bray – Dancing and Shouting

Billy Bray was born in Cornwall, England, in 1794. He began his working life as a tinner, but later became a miner. For seven years he was a drunkard and his oaths and blasphemes were so foul and smelt of sulphur that his companions thought they came from the very pit of hell! He was a natural liar and used to tell stories to amuse his companions and was full of wit and sarcasm. Billy was converted in 1823 and was soon put on the Bible Christian preaching plan (circuit). He built three chapels by hand and saw at least eight revivals from 1824-1867.

Shortly after his conversion Billy Bray said, "I was very happy in my *work*, and could leap and dance for joy under ground as well as on the surface. My comrades used to tell me that dancing, shouting and making so much 'to do' was not religion. But I was born in the *fire* and could not live in the *smoke*. They said there was no need to leap and dance, and make so much noise, for the Lord was not deaf and He knows our hearts." And Billy would reply, "But you must know that the devil is not deaf either and yet his servants make a great noise. The devil would rather see us doubting than shouting."

Billy Bray's biographer, F. W. Bourne wrote: 'To any person who objected to the meetings on account of their noise and uproar, and many have objected to them on that account, he thought it quite enough to say that when the foundations of the second temple was laid, 'all the people shouted with a great shout' and 'that the people could not discern the noise of the weeping of the people, for the people shouted with a loud shout and the noise was heard afar off.' '

One day Billy Bray came into a friends house in Devonport, praising the Lord aloud, saying, "I've just seen a poor man down here with crutches and useless legs, and I haven't been able to help praising the Lord ever since for my sound ones!" See Acts 3:1-8, the lame man healed at the temple.

In 1866, a district meeting was held at Hick's Mill. Mr Oliver in describing the triumphant death of a woman said she died shouting, "Victory." Billy Bray responded, "Glory! If a *dying* woman praised the Lord, I should think a *living* man might."[4]

Shouting and Dancing for Joy

In 1864, Billy Bray wrote his 49,000 word, one sentence *journal*. In 2004, having been deciphered and punctuated it was collated alongside other notes and stories and published as *Billy Bray in his own words*. Billy Bray wrote: 'Now we must have a full joy ourselves to know what a full joy means. Some professors [of religion] get poor tempered when the Lord makes His children happy, and instead of praising the Lord with them they speak against them. It is no new thing to hear preachers, as they call themselves, speak against the power of God: such as shouting and dancing, and praising with a loud voice. The reason is because they do not feel it in themselves, and then they condemn it in others. Some time ago I was in a Primitive Methodist chapel, and there was two men in that chapel so happy that they was shouting and dancing for joy. The dear Lord had made them very happy, and that was not the first time. If we do not shout and dance for heaven, what shall we shout and dance for? I was very glad to see them so happy, and I was happy with them.'[5]

Preacher Rebuked by God

Billy Bray in his *journal* wrote about a circuit preacher who lived in the same area as himself in an area of Cornwall, England. The unnamed preacher was encouraged by an old woman to rebuke a happy convert called WS. WS was at the back of the church, praising the Lord. Billy wrote: 'He was shouting and praising God with a loud voice, and there was an angry old woman by me [the preacher]. She said to go back and stop WS from making such a noise. "When I [the preacher] was going back to stop him, the Lord said, 'Cry out and shout all ye inhabitants of Zion, for great is the Lord in the midst of thee' (Isaiah 12:6). When the Lord said so to me, I did not go where WS was, but went back where the old woman was."

'Then WS was shouting and clapping his hands and praising of God. The old woman said, 'Go back and stop WS from making such a noise.' "I was going back to stop him, and the Lord said to me, 'Clap your hands, all ye people. Shout unto God with the voice of triumph.' That is the forty-seventh Psalm. When the Lord said so to me, I could not go back to WS, so I went back to the old woman again."

'Then WS was stamping with his feet and he was making a great noise. The old woman said to me, 'Go back and stop WS from making that noise, for he will frighten all the people.' There is no Scripture for stamping. As I was going back the third time to stop WS, the Lord spoke to me and said, 'Stamp ye the *residue of My people' [*c.f. Zephaniah 2:9 and Zechariah 8:11, AV.]. When the Lord said that I could not go back to WS.'

Billy Bray concluded: 'WS was a very good man and was not ashamed to own his dear Lord, and his dear Lord was not ashamed to own he.'[6]

Chapter Twenty

Human Emotions – Part II

Humans are emotional beings – it's the way we have been designed and in times of revival, or any move of the Holy Spirit, these emotions will be heightened, resulting in wide-ranging physical phenomena, bodily manifestations some of which may not be as a direct result of the Holy Spirit touching a person's life. It could be of human origin or of demonic origin. See page 146.

Four Kinds of Physical Phenomena:
1. That which is caused by God's presence on a person.
2. That which is partially Divine and partly emotional.
3. That which is wholly emotional or hysterical.
4. That which is from the devil – demonic manifestations. In the presence of God demons will either be 'playing up' to cause a scene or will be leaving! Read Mark 9:14-27.

Michael Harper writing about the twentieth century Pentecostal Revival wrote: 'There will always be sensuous people looking for cheap thrills and exciting experiences. There will always be those who specialise in the bizarre and unusual and who will be drawn to such a movement...when we move into the supernatural realm we are more likely to be deceived than before. Satan is very cunning, and can even disguise himself as an angel of light.'[1]

Unfortunately in many cases of physical phenomena we may be too quick to judge or presume we know that it is from God or the devil; someone seeking attention or a lack of restraint, but we can always see the *fruit* or *lack of it* within the person's life after the experience and more often that not, this will conclude a correct diagnosis because 'by their fruits you shall know them.' The Bible speaks much of godliness, personal character and putting to death the flesh life, the old man and walking in the newness of the Spirit.

With God's help we are called to discern and carefully distinguish between the flesh and the Spirit – we are called to exercise sober judgment. We are called to 'test the spirits' (is it of demonic origin?), not test the phenomena; we can also test the fruit in a person's life. Can they declare, "Jesus is Lord" (1 Cor. 12:13) and acknowledge that He came in the flesh? (1 John 4:1-2 and 2 John 7-11). See page 145.

It is all too easy to judge another, which we are commanded not to do (Matthew 7:1-5) and we may forget that it is the duty of the pastor or leader to exhort, correct and rebuke the flock (leading to edification via repentance and restoration) and *not us*. They are in spiritual authority and it is *they* who have to give an account to God for those under their care. No one is infallible, and mistakes will be made in areas of judgment especially in regards to physical phenomena, hearsay and half truths during times of revival and whenever the Holy Spirit turns up at a meeting.

We cannot judge a work of God by its phenomena nor by those who are in the flesh. Pastor John Kilpatrick said, "The surest way to stop judging manifestations is for it to happen to you!" Whilst Dave Roberts, editor of *Alpha* magazine wrote: 'Let those who are without carnal Christians somewhere in their congregation cast the first stone.'

Jonathan Edwards, the American revivalist and theologian rightly noted that 'although the Scripture is full of rules, both how we should judge our own state and also how we should conduct ourselves before others, there are no rules by which to judge emotions.'[2]

The revivals in Kentucky which began in 1800 during the pioneering days of America had perhaps the most 'wildest' (in a positive definition) physical phenomena on record, of shakings, jerking and loud cries, to name some, though undoubtedly, not all was as a direct result of the Holy Spirit touching lives as there is always a minority. See Appendix B.

Division and Divisiveness (See pages 160-161)
All revivals and accompanying phenomena are divisive to some Christians, but even Jesus, the Prince of Peace, stated that His ministry would cause division, as some members of a household would follow Him whilst others would not (Luke 12:51-53). Not everyone attributed Jesus' ministry as from

God (Mark 3:22-29), whilst others hated Him 'without a cause' (John 15:24-25). See John 7:40-43.

Stephen F. Olford speaking on 'The Price of Revival' said, "There is no mistaking it when God starts to work, for men and women are either antagonised by, or attracted to Christ, but never neutralised." Jonathan Edwards wrote: 'A work of God without stumbling blocks is never to be expected.'

To say that because something causes division it must be evil or wrong is an incorrect assumption; people were divided over Jesus' ministry, see John 9:16-34. The Nazarene 'sect' was 'spoken against everywhere...some were persuaded' and 'others disbelieved' (Acts 28:22-24). Imagine; revival comes to a church and is embraced by the leader, but the congregation are divided. Some want to stay with the status quo feeling safe with their familiar services or content in their traditions, whilst others embrace the Lord's will and some stand on the sideline, undecided. Is the leader of the church guilty of divisiveness because he has chosen to go God's way and allowed the Holy Spirit to do what He wants to do? No, the guilt of divisiveness lays on the other side, for those who do not want God to move and *oppose* His workings.

Jesus once said, "Glorify Your name" and a voice came from heaven. Those present were of divided opinion, some said it thundered and others said an angel spoke, but the sign happened for *their* sake (John 12:28-30).

On the Day of Pentecost thousands heard 'the wonderful works of God' in their own languages whilst others mocking said, "They are full of new wine" (Acts 2:1-15).

At Iconium, many Greeks believed the good news, but the 'unbelieving Jews stirred up the Gentiles and *poisoned their minds* against the brethren.' Even after staying there a long time where signs and wonders were performed, the 'city was divided' – to embrace them or stone them?! (Acts 14:1-5).

Who can Stand before God

Frequently in revival and times of refreshing, the human body will not be able to stand before the Holy presence of God. Over the centuries various revivalists and witnesses have described this as: 'stricken by God,' 'being overcome,' 'falling,' 'fainting,' 'struck down,' 'sank down,' 'fell over,' 'prostrated,' 'swooning,' 'deprived of their bodily strength,' 'slain in the Spirit' or 'resting in the Spirit.'

Eyewitnesses from different centuries in different countries have recorded these events as: 'swept down in a moment as if a battery of a thousand guns had been opened upon them,' 'cut like grains before a sickle,' 'they fell quicker than they could be cut down by a swordsman;' and 'it was like a field of battle those slain by the Spirit of the Lord.'

Daniel Powell Williams of Penygroes, in Carmarthen, South Wales, UK, was converted on Christmas Day 1904, in Loughor, the birthplace of the Welsh Revival (1904-1905). In reference to the revival he wrote: 'The manifestation of the power was beyond human management. Men and women were mowed down by the axe of God like a forest. The glory was resting for over two years in some localities.'[3]

These writers have also described these same people who have been overcome by the Spirit of God in involuntarily trembling as 'shaking,' 'jerking,' 'shivering,' 'convulsions,' 'agitation of body,' 'rolling around' and 'trembled.'

Sometimes people have been labelled as: Quakers, Jumpers, Ranters or Shakers because of the physical phenomena which characterised a movement. Throughout the Bible you will see these physical phenomena and many others scattered throughout the pages of the Holy Bible.[4]

Six Scriptural examples of Physical Phenomena:
- At the burning bush, 'Moses trembled and dared not look' (Acts 7:32 and Exodus 3:1-6).
- The Psalmist wrote: 'My flesh trembles in fear of You, and I am afraid of Your judgments' (Psalm 119:120).
- Jeremiah was heartbroken because of the false prophets, "All my bones shake. I am like a drunken man whom wine has overcome, because of the Lord, and because of His holy words" (Jeremiah 23:9).
- In the garden of Gethsemane, when Jesus responded to the soldiers, saying, "I am He," 'they drew back and fell to the ground' (John 18:5-6).
- At the resurrection of Jesus an angel of the Lord descended from heaven and rolled back the stone to

His tomb, 'the guards shook for fear of Him, and became like dead men' (Matthew 28:1-4).

- Peter preached on the Day of Pentecost and was interrupted by the convicted listeners who had been cut to the heart – "What shall we do?" (Acts 2:1-41).

Not a Sign, but Look for the Fruit

In times of revival, the focus should never be on the physical phenomena as a sign or proof of revival, but we should not be alarmed when we witness these events. There is nothing new under the sun and what has been will be. The main focus, within a person's life should be the person's lifestyle – do they bear fruit? Have they confessed and forsaken sin, do they have victory over sin, do they glorify Jesus more and is their life God exalting? Whilst Church history records that during times of revival physical phenomena will happen, to a lesser or greater degree, it is merely peripheral in the greater out-working of God, to be salt and light amidst a wicked and perverse generation.

Do not Dictate to God

Dr. James C. L. Carson, a prominent medical practitioner in Coleraine during the 1859 Irish Revival, speaking about the physical phenomena said, "Without doubt, there is a great physical agent, as well as a spiritual one, abroad. The one is, as it were, the hand-maid to the other. They are both specially from God, and are most admirably calculated to work out His great design.... It would be well for those parties who look on physical manifestations as an evil which should be avoided and repressed, to reconsider their ways. It is an awful thing to be found fighting against God. How dreadful is this presumption which will dare to dictate to the Almighty the way in which He should save sinners!"[5]

The Flesh, Excess and Attention-Seekers

Whilst the presence of God affects different people in different ways, we must be aware of foolish excess, attention-seekers and emotional manipulation – the flesh! But just as important; we are not to resist, quench or grieve the Holy Spirit by our refusal to submit to Him or by being an obstruction in the lives of others. Both outward and inward opposition to the things of God are very dangerous.

There will always be those who fall prey to the latest gimmick or fad and in times of revival or refreshing they may try to jump on the bandwagon and work it up in the flesh. This can be for several reasons: not wanting to be left out, believing it bolsters their spiritual level or plain scoffing or mocking the things of God by imitation. On the other hand, there will be those who will stubbornly resist God and what He is doing, believing it not to be from Him and these people are inversely fleshly as others are overtly carnal.

Others 'have a zeal for God, but not according to knowledge' (Romans 10:2) – this is also true of Christians who oppose revivals and the moving of the Holy Spirit, who think they are doing Him a favour, as did Saul the persecutor of the Church before his dramatic conversion.

Steve Hill speaking at the Brownsville Revival (1995-2000) and in the context of fleshly manifestations often said, "Bright lights attract bugs, and these people are probably from *your* church!" In an interview with *Charisma*, Steve stated that by his estimate five percent of what he saw during the revival was fleshly. He said, "You can go to any meeting anywhere and see flesh, if that's what you're looking for. I don't go to these meetings looking for flesh; I go looking for God." Steve concluded, "Am I going to concentrate on five percent? No. You deal with the important situations, but you let God control the revival."[6]

Helen Dyer in reference to the Mukti Revival (1905-1906) in India, wrote: 'The work went on rapidly…. Satan was also busy, and tried to counterfeit all he saw. Some who beheld the joy thought they could get it by imitating what they had seen the others do. Yet the work went on, and a spirit of prayer and supplication for a revival in India was poured out like a flood.'[7]

Exorcism – Deliverance from Demons

There will be those who demonically manifest, because when the Spirit of God comes down, the demons hate it. These demons need to be commanded to leave in the name of Jesus Christ and a deliverance session can take many hours, often over a period of time. Some people say that as

Jesus just spoke a word (which He did *on occasions*) and evil spirits fled, all we have to do is speak a word and they will leave. This has never been my case, instant deliverance; nor of John Wesley nor of most modern-day disciples who obey Jesus' command to preach the gospel and to cast out demons in His name (Mark 16:15-18), some of which can only come out by 'prayer and fasting' (Matthew 17:19-21 and Mark 9:18-29). This is covered alongside related topics of ministry in *Discipleship For Everyday Living: Christian Growth* by Mathew Backholer, chapters 35-50.

During the Argentine Revival (1982-1997), deliverance was *essential* for all new believers along with mass discipleship and being committed to a church of whatever denomination or style took the persons preference. Carlos Annacondia, during some of his campaigns would preach for two months every night and behind the platform there would be a 150-foot tent with yellow and white stripes, which was the "Spiritual intensive care unit" where mass deliverance sessions would be held. Trained workers, "stretcher bearers" would be on the lookout for people manifesting (under the influences of evil spirits / demons) and carry them to the tent where they would pray for them to be delivered. As time went on, mass deliverance sessions were commenced as the strong man was bound, Jesus' name invoked, curses were broken and people were delivered from the evil one.

Rebellion towards God and Quenching the Spirit

Remember, we can be just as carnal singing hymns or choruses in a restrained or reluctant manner as in jumping up and down trying to draw attention to ourselves. Resisting the Spirit of God and trying to work up something are both fleshly in nature and wrong. One is outwardly dishonouring to God, the other is inwardly dishonouring to God, both are sinful and neither glorifies the Lord.

Max Warren, in the context of worship during the East African Revival (1930s-1950s) wrote: 'Dancing rhythmic movements and repetitive singing in chorus are spontaneous African expressions of joy.... The appeal of these things in the separatist movement elsewhere should be a warning, lest the traditional sobriety of, for instance, Anglican worship and devotion, too rigidly interpreted, prove too constraining for the rejuvenate spirit of the African. If there is a danger in unrestrained ecstasy, there is also the dullness of decorum.'[8]

If we resist what the Holy Spirit is doing then we are carnal rebels and rebellion is as the sin of witchcraft (1 Samuel 15:23). We are commanded not to 'quench' nor 'grieve' the Holy Spirit (1 Thessalonians 5:19 and Ephesians 4:30) and 'resisting' Him is just as sinful (Acts 7:51), and if we do, then I fail to see how we can call Jesus our Lord, because as the saying goes: 'Either He is Lord of all or He is not Lord at all.'

To quench the Holy Spirit is like putting water on a fire, sticking to a routine of religion, our traditions and not allowing Him to do what He wants to. To grieve the Holy Spirit, is to go into the flesh, to sin, or *to attribute something which is of God as being from the evil one or to stop what the Holy Spirit is doing in a meeting. To quench or grieve the Holy Spirit both displace His rightful place within a meeting therefore disenabling Him to glorify Jesus. *This is the unpardonable sin which Jesus warned of, blaspheming the Holy Spirit (Matthew 12:24-31) when His anointing was attributed to beelzebub, the ruler of demons. To resist the Holy Spirit is being stiff-necked, rejecting Him and resisting what He wants to do in either our lives or the life of the Church; in effect we are saying, "We know better than God and our judgment is superior!"

Dr. Michael Brown was approached by a cynic who asked about the youth of the Brownsville Revival (1995-2000), whether or not 'it is possible that some of them are getting in the flesh?' His reply was, "I'm sure it's possible that some of them are getting in the flesh, just as I'm very sure it's probable that ninety-nine percent of people sitting in dead churches are in the flesh the whole time."[9]

Stephen F. Olford speaking on 'The Price of Revival' at Westminster Chapel, London, in September 1946, said, "It is really pathetic to enter some meeting places and sense the lifelessness and absence of joy among those who gather. It reminds one of the story of a brother who was a real personification of the lack of enthusiasm. He was standing one day outside a certain gospel hall, trying to invite folk into the meeting. He stopped one man and asked him to come in. "No thank you," replied the stranger, "I have enough troubles of my own!"[10]

Dr. Stanley Smith documented the story of the Ruanda Mission which was caught up in revival in 1937, which was the catalyst to the East Africa Revival (1930s-1950s). He wrote: 'They [the Africans] are convinced that the deadliest enemy to the cause of Christ is the nominal Christian and that every born again, blood-bought Christian must be characterised by burning zeal, by purity of life, and by standing as a witness to dying men of a life-giving Christ. Where such signs are missing, they seriously question the reality of the religious profession.'[11]

Leadership and Discernment
In the Old Testament, there was a man called Elkanah who had two wives, one was barren because the Lord had closed her womb. Hannah, was so desperate for a child and being provoked by Peninnah (Elkanah's other wife), she wept and refused to eat. In Shiloh 'she was in bitterness of soul, and prayed to the Lord and wept in anguish.' She made a vow to God, promising Him that if she gave birth to a son she would give him to the Lord all the days of her life. Hannah spoke only in her heart, her lips moved but no sound came out. Eli the priest thought she was drunk and rebuked her, saying, "How long will you be drunk? Put your wine away from you!" She responded gently, stating that she was not drunk, nor had she drunk any alcohol, but was in a sorrowful spirit and had prayed out of her anguish and grief. Eli was happy with the explanation and stated his desire for God to grant her request. The following year she gave birth to Samuel, who grew up in the house of the Lord and became a mighty prophet and leader of Israel (1 Samuel 1:10-20).

For those within leadership, to pastor a revival need a great level of humility, brokenness and discernment, especially when passing judgment on a situation. But when even the best leaders make mistakes, then how much more those who have lesser experience and maturity?

One worker during the Mukti Revival (1905-1906) in India, wrote: 'There is a very true work of God going on in our midst.... There is much one cannot understand at first, but one grows by His grace into the work and learns to distinguish by the outward signs as well as by the Spirit's inward teaching, the false from the true. Satan counterfeits all that the Lord does, and is working harder to hinder and spoil the work of God, but he is a conquered foe!'[12]

Pastor John Kilpatrick, of Brownsville AOG church, during the Brownsville Revival (1995-2000) in Pensacola, America, continually prayed, "Lord please give me wisdom to pastor this thing. Lord, I don't want to be so lenient that I let anything in, but Lord I don't want to be so hard either that I don't let what You're trying to do in – God please give me wisdom. Holy Spirit, help me to walk humbly before You. Holy Spirit, help me to keep my mind on the Lord and to keep my eyes on the Lord, and Holy Spirit, help me not to get distracted with things, where I begin to let the embers grow dim and cold in my life, and Lord, help me not to let the fire go out in this church; Lord, help me...."[13]

Do not Harden Your Heart

There is a grave danger when someone hardens their heart[14] against the things of God as did Pharaoh, or disbelieve, as according to their faith it will not be done unto them. See Matthew 9:27-29. This is the rule and not the exception. On occasions God overrides a person's will or intervenes in a dramatic way. Saul of Tarsus (later known as Paul) was struck by God and fell to the floor. He got converted against his will, after seeing the bright light as Jesus confronted him (Acts 9:1-9). Through his misplaced zeal, Saul, believing he was working for God was actually fighting against Him (see Acts 5:38-39 and Acts 23:9), persecuting those who loyally followed Jesus. Saul was persecuting Jesus Himself, but God still had mercy on him. Later on, Paul was persecuted for his faith in Christ and the revivals he saw were accompanied by opposition and riots.

Some aspects of God's activity seem harder to understand than others, but that is no excuse to reject what He is doing or to look down upon those who are having emotional responses, physical phenomena, because of His presence. To try to understand God is beyond comprehension as His ways are not our ways, and His plans are much higher than ours (Isaiah 55:8-9). 'There are many plans in a man's heart, nevertheless the Lord's counsel – that will stand' (Proverbs 19:21). 'The foolishness of a man twists his way, and his heart frets against the Lord' (Proverbs 19:3).[15]

Chapter Twenty-One

A Diversity of Views

Prone to make Mistakes

Some people incorrectly assume that because a person makes a mistake, or has a different theological viewpoint than them (on non essential doctrines) then they cannot be used of God. Thank God that despite our imperfections He can use us! We think of lying Abram, angry Moses, lustful David and sharp-tongued Peter and his denial. These men (despite their faults and character flaws) were set on doing the will of God with all their heart, mind, soul and strength.

The fifteenth century saw reformers such as John Wycliffe of England and John Hus of Bohemia (Czech Republic) whilst the Reformation of the sixteenth century was the most spiritual cataclysmic event that has happened in Europe during the last half a millennia, but all of the sixteenth century reformers had flawed personalities and some held extreme theological views, just like some of us, though naturally this does depend on what side of the fence you sit!

All of the leading reformers (except Erasmus) were distinctly opposed to foreign missions; 'reaching the heathen for Christ' was simply not on the agenda. They stated that the command to go and teach all nations had been carried out by the apostles, 1,500 years previously and therefore was no longer incumbent on them! This was regardless of the fact that vast sways of lands were filled with barbarous and simple tribes, and even in the twenty-first century there are still people groups who have never ever heard the name of Jesus Christ! – What are we doing about it?

Martin Luther, the German reformer was anti-Semitic, he wanted all Jews to be deported to Palestine and their synagogues and books burned, whilst to the day of his death he stood by the Roman Catholic doctrine of transubstantiation, that during communion the bread and the wine literally becomes the flesh and blood of Jesus Christ.

John Calvin gave great emphasis on God's predestined will, that for many who followed this line of thinking to the extreme, it literally relinquished them of any responsibility for their actions. Even John Wesley and George Whitefield, the godly Goliaths of the eighteenth century awakenings disagreed over predestination (Calvinism) versus man's free will (Arminianism) which caused a split in early Methodism and for many years greatly strained their relationship. See Appendix A. If Wesley and Whitefield, along with their respective supporters and followers had taken the advice of Henry Venn (1724-1797) then things may have been different. He was a preacher at Huddersfield, England, and refused to be drawn into an argument when the Calvinistic controversy broke out and discouraged such disputes. When once asked whether a certain minister was a Calvinist or Arminian he replied, "I really do not know, he is a sincere disciple of the Lord Jesus Christ, and that is of infinitely more importance than being a disciple of Calvin or Arminius."[1]

Huldrych Zwingli, the German speaking Swiss reformer, authorised the killing by drowning of Anabaptists (a Christian movement loosely organised, but who were not a cult) for those who participated in adult rebaptism. Also, Huldrych Zwingli and Martin Luther did not get along with each other.

John Knox, the Scottish reformer was all for the dispossession of a ruler, albeit a king or queen, by imprisonment, capital punishment or assassination, if the ruler went outside of the will of God by disobeying His commands, then he or she forfeited their right as God's governor and could be justifiably punished by the people!

All these men were giants in their time, and if you go to Geneva, Switzerland, you can see fifteen-foot (3m) stone statues of these reformers along with a large stone memorial to the entire Reformation era, but none of us would doubt that they all were men of God who came into the Kingdom for such a time as theirs, and the three essential reanimated biblical truths of the Reformation are still just as important then, as they are today within the Protestant Church: 1. The Holy Bible is the final authority on all matters of doctrine and dogma. 2. Justification by faith, salvation is only by faith in the atoning work of Jesus Christ; by grace and not of works. 3. The priesthood of all believers (1 Peter 2:5-9).

During the first few years of George Whitefield's ministry he was rash and impulsive, and was without financial savvy. He got into debt of £1,000 whilst financing an orphanage in Georgia, New England, and along with £200 of travelling expenses (debt) was nearly arrested in Britain because of it!

God moulds the person for the job, and He will take what He has got. We are flawed, but God is not. As a wise man once said, "It is an ungracious and ungrateful task to dwell on a man's weaknesses. It is more profitable and more pleasant to turn to the real good that they did." And it is to this that all those previously mentioned are truly remembered for.

Differences of Opinions

There is a big danger in building a lot on a little, especially when it is a man-made opinion, preconceived idea or an interpretation, and we must be aware of prejudices, such as personal, nationalistic, racial, denominational or theological, as these can all distort correct biblical doctrine. Even the best teachers will at times make mistakes. As the apostle James wrote: 'We *all stumble in many things.* If anyone does not stumble in word, he is a perfect man...' (James 3:2). Great men and women of God can be working towards the same end whilst using different means and methods; holding different theological views than their contemporaries (or from those in another century) and can still be used of God despite their differences or methods.

In mid seventeenth century England, George Fox founded the Society of Friends, the 'Quakers' and through his preaching of Scriptural truths, more than fifty thousand were converted back to the pure faith in forty years. Yet the Quakers, who used to be Christian, believed that baptism was not in accord with the mind of Christ. They believed that no outward form of baptism need be observed, but we could not doubt the commitment of George Fox and his followers towards the work of evangelisation during Puritan England.

Count Zinzendorf saw revival in his community at Herrnhut, (in modern-day Germany) in 1727, which sparked off the Moravian missionary movement. The Moravians greatly influenced John and Charles Wesley, though at the time, these ministers were unconverted. In England they held joint services, though within a few years the Moravians and the Wesley's soon parted company over doctrinal issues; and the Moravians who did not want to be associated with them published this fact in an English newspaper. When Zinzendorf visited America, the Tennents, who were used during the American Great Awakening (1735-1760), wrote tracts opposing him, alongside some other preachers. Yet they were all ministers of God, preached the pure gospel and all saw revival!

Jonathan Edwards and Charles Finney, two different revivalists from the eighteenth and nineteenth centuries respectively, both believed that the awakenings they were involved in could lead into the millennial reign; as have many revivalists since. They believed this, the imminent return of Jesus Christ because of what they were seeing as multitudes turned to Christ, year after year, as towns and communities were transformed to the glory of God.

In 1828, Dr. Edward D. Griffin, President of William's College, America, refers to the beginning of revival in 1792. We refer to it as the Second American Great Awakening. Dr. Griffin said, "In that year [1792] commenced that series of revivals in America, which has never been interrupted, night or day, and which never will be until the earth is full of the glory of the Lord as the waters cover the sea."[2]

Looking back, because the gospel had not been proclaimed in all the world (Matthew 24:14, coupled with Revelation 7:9, of every, tribe nation and tongue), it was impossible for the Lord to return, but Edwards and Finney were two of America's greatest ever preachers and Dr. Griffin saw his first revival in January 1792 in New Salem, New England.

William Miller was converted in 1815 and soon became known as a monomaniac by his friends, for constantly talking about the second coming of Christ, which he believed from the calculation in Daniel chapters 8-9 and Revelation chapters 10-12 would be in 1843. In August 1831, under conviction from the voice of God, "Go and tell the world!" William Miller began to preach when he was asked to, though he had resisted for some time. In Dresden, America, he was requested to remain and lecture during the week; and a revival began in which thirteen families except two people were converted. He saw revival in other places and within twenty years of ministry saw 6,000 converts, 700 of whom had been infidels. On 13 November 1833, there were signs in the heavens, a great display of falling meteors. From 2am until broad daylight, all over North America the whole heavens seemed to be in a fiery commotion.

In 1838, a minister named Josiah Linch united with William Miller and they became a mission team. Linch predicted from Revelation 9:10-15 that the Turkish government would surrender its independence on 11 August 1840. In 1839, the Turkish army was defeated by Mehemet Ali. England, Russia, Austria and Prussia, seeing the defeat of the Sultan of Turkey drew up an ultimatum which was placed in Mehemet's hands on 11 August 1840! Thus the Turkish Empire was defeated on the very day predicted by the prophecy. Jesus did not return in 1843, nor in 1844, which was the revised date, yet Linch was spot on with one prophecy whilst Miller and Linch were completely wrong in regards to the second coming. William Miller wrote: 'Were I to live my life over again with the same evidence that I then had, to be honest before God and man, I should have to do as I have done.... I still believe that the day of the Lord is near, even at the door; and I exhort you, my brethren, to be watchful, and not to let that day come upon you unawares.'[3]

Say the Wrong Things

On occasions we all say things that we did not mean to say (Luke 9:33), due to confusion, tiredness or a slip of the tongue etc., or we do not say what we intended to say. In haste or under duress we can speak foolishly (Mark 9:5-6). The Psalmist said, "I believe therefore I spoke...all men are liars" (Psalm 116:10-11) and there is a danger in being hasty with words (Proverbs 29:20). People can sincerely believe what they do, yet still be entirely wrong, see Jeremiah 23:16b, 25-26. A wise person will sift everything they hear or read to see whether it lines up with Scripture and will not major on the minors. Do not disregard or dismiss a person's teaching because you disagree with one sentence – take the best (of their Scriptural teaching) and leave the rest (the fleshly comments), that's maturity. The revivalists through the ages had differing views and theological stances, yet God still used them despite their differences or failings.

Revivalist, John Berridge (1716-1793) of Everton, England, oftentimes over indulged in his humour and declared, "I was born with a fool's cap on." In a letter he wrote: 'Odd things break forth from me as abruptly as croaking from a raven.'

Opinions may Change

Over time people may change their opinions and views on certain issues. If this happens in the normal run of everyday life, should it be considered inconsistent when after receiving greater understanding or due to unexpected events a spiritual view should change? Should we be stubborn like a mule and stick to our principles, even when we realise that our views however honest and sincere at the time were flawed in the view of today's light? Whilst the Bible declares that 'a double-minded man, [is] unstable in all his ways' (James 1:8) it is good, right and proper that we listen to our conscience under the light of the Holy Spirit who will guide us 'into all truth' (John 16:13). It is better to admit that we were wrong than to live in the realm of stubborn pride.

John Wesley disdained the idea of lay-preachers, it was repugnant to him and his dislike of them was only overruled by the advice of the one whose counsel he never neglected, his mother, the saintly Susanna Wesley. John Wesley also thought that it was wrong to preach outside of a church building, until he found the doors of many churches closed to him! On Saturday, 31 March 1739, John Wesley met George Whitefield in Bristol, England, because he had been invited by his friend to take over the successful preaching to the tens of thousands of colliers at Kingswood. The next day Wesley stood in his friend's congregation in the open fields with conflicting feelings. He wrote: 'I could scarce reconcile myself at first to this strange way of preaching in the fields, of which he set an example on Sunday; having been all my life (till very lately) so tenacious of every point relating to decency and order, that I should have thought the saving of souls almost a sin if it had not been done in a church.'[4]

One author from the nineteenth century, writing about the eighteenth century Evangelical Revival (1739-1791) wrote: 'So far was Wesley from being obstinately wedded to his own opinions that he laid himself fairly open to the charge of inconsistency by so frequently modifying them.'[5]

George Whitefield disagreed with the physical prostrations that happened under John Wesley's preaching, but he changed his mind when it happened during his sermons! Wesley, on 7 July 1739, spoke to Whitefield 'of those outward signs which had so often accompanied the inward work of God. I found his objections were chiefly grounded on gross mis-representations of matter of fact,' wrote Wesley in his *Journal*, 'but the next day he had opportunity of informing himself better, for no sooner had he begun to invite all sinners to believe in Christ, than four persons sunk down close to him, almost in the same moment. One of them lay without sense or motion. A second trembled exceedingly. The third had strong convulsions all over his body, but made no noise, unless by groans. The fourth equally convulsed, called upon God, with strong cries and tears. From this time on I trust, we shall all suffer God to carry on His work in the way that pleaseth Him.'[6]

In 1852, evangelist William Booth met Catherine who shared his views on social reforms but not over the role of women preachers; they married in June 1855. In 1860, Catherine Booth started to preach as she felt compelled by the Spirit of God and could not stay silent any longer, her husband was so impressed by her anointing that his views on women preachers changed. The following year revival broke out in Hayle, Cornwall, where 7,000 Cornishmen were converted in just eighteen months during 1861-1862.

John Wesley, ordained by the Church of England never wanted to start a new denomination, though as the decades rolled on it was inevitable that it would happen, but not in his lifetime. When his Societies were formed he made sure that the meetings never clashed with the parish church timetable and he enjoyed celebrating the Feasts Days which are part of the Church of England's calendar. But John Wesley set apart Dr. Thomas Coke (who did not become a Methodist until 1776) as 'a superintendent' which could be construed as consecrating himself to be a bishop, thus informally beginning the extended framework of a new denomination.

It is always easier to consider the failures of others and to denounce "their heresies" and ministries. It makes it more palatable to hide from our own failings and flaws and diverts our attention from the work God has called us to do!

Controversy and Contentions

Controversy for the sake of controversy is not a good thing, because 'a brother offended is harder to win than a strong city, and contentions are like the bars of a castle' (Proverbs 18:19). The Holy Bible informs us of many things which we should not discuss because of the negative effects that can be provoked and manifested within ignorant, unsanctified or stubborn lives. If we desire to see revival in our lives, our church and our country then we must stop being controversial just for the sake of it. We should be generous in our acceptance of others and we must be aware of the tone of our voice as it may be more inclined to aggravate than to consolidate. But the denunciation of sin and a clarion call to "repent," whilst preaching Christ and Him crucified is always controversial for lukewarm Christians as it rocks the boat of complacency and challenges them to forsake sin and to flee to Christ from the wrath to come.

We should not build our biblical knowledge or faith on one truth only to neglect other truths which are equally important. We can overemphasise or give more prominence to some issues and neglect or underemphasise others. If you take just one part of truth and do not consider the other parts then you will reach a wrong conclusion. Truth out of balance becomes error. There is truth, half truth or error. Truth is found in having firm grounding in the Word of God. Half truth and error can be because of ignorance (Acts 18:24-26), deception (2 Timothy 3:13) or being under the influence of deceiving spirits (1 Timothy 4:1-2). J. Edwin Orr wrote: 'Half the heresies are due to an overemphasis of real truth without the balance of other doctrines in proportion.'

If we know what someone believes and our opinion is contrary to theirs, then why do we keep bringing the same subject to the fore? Why do we want to discuss certain subjects? Is it to learn, to inform or to force our beliefs onto another? Remember: 'A fool has no delight in understanding, but in expressing his own heart' (Proverbs 18:2).

It is also possible for the same event to be seen or interpreted differently than others. When the Lord appeared to Saul, his companions all saw the light and were afraid, but none except Saul heard Him speak (Acts 22:16-19).

Chapter Twenty-Two

Disunity Within the Body

Doctrine, Discussions and Misunderstandings

We are called to come together in the 'unity of the faith' (Ephesians 4:11-13), not the unity of *our* doctrine as nonorthodox doctrines vary, whilst the fundamentals of orthodox Christianity are unchanging. Therefore we should not stand aloof because of denominational nonessentials. Some truths are fundamental whilst others are not as central as we might believe. We should have love one for another so that all men will know that we are His disciples (John 13:34-35). Revival can touch a congregation, yet pass by others in the same village when tradition or denominational doctrines become more important than the unity of the faith; one in Christ.

It is possible to believe that some Christians are *wholly* wrong who nevertheless are pleasing to God and would be to us, if we understood them. Under the command of God, Moses summoned the seventy elders of Israel and the Lord descended in a cloud. He took of the Spirit that was on Moses and placed the same Spirit upon the elders and they began to prophesy. Two elders, Elad and Medad remained in the camp, but the Spirit of God came upon them and they prophesied. Joshua, Moses' assistant said, "Moses, my lord, forbid them!" But he replied, "Oh, that all the Lord's people were prophets and that the Lord would put His Spirit on them" (Joshua 11:16-30).

After the land of Canaan had been taken, two and a half tribes of Israel who had chosen not to settle in the Promised Land, set up an altar of witness on the other side of the Jordan River. This was seen as an act of unfaithfulness, following after another god and the tribes of Israel wanted to punish them. Ten tribal rulers spoke to the alleged offenders and when the innocence of the altar was revealed, (a grave misunderstanding) all the twelve tribes of Israel were able to rejoice together as war was averted (Joshua 22:11-34).

It is possible for Christians to get confused in regards to false doctrine, heresy and heretics, which can lead to contentions because their senses have not been exercised 'to discern good and evil' (Hebrews 5:14). Some hold allegiance to a particular leader, "I am of Paul" or "I am of Apollos" whilst rejecting others (1 Corinthians 1:12-13, 30-31). This inevitably causes friction and even division, but our allegiance should always be to Christ and His doctrine.

During the 1859 revival in Wales, unity was manifested amongst several denominations, particularly the non-conformists bodies. 'This unity arose from two main sources; the one, an agreement as to the basic truths of the gospel, and the other, a common, fervent desire for a visitation of the Holy Spirit to glorify Christ as Saviour and Lord. Inasmuch as each denomination based its faith and practice at that time upon God's revealed truth, as found in Holy Scripture, their unity did not involve the violation of any of their distinctive principles, nor the surrender of any essential belief, as these were all common to all. Consequently, their prayer meetings and joint services were eminently useful in furthering the work of the revival, being soundly based on essential, Divinely-revealed truth.'[1]

One of the keys to revival is unity amongst the brethren, albeit only a small group of believers may be praying for a spiritual awakening, but it is impossible to be in unity when we keep having discussions on non-important issues which only cause division, suspicion or estrangement. The Bible warns us not to discuss certain things as they are unprofitable; unedifying and are divisive, see Appendix D.

James Hervey (1714-1758), a minister during the British Great Awakening in reference to disputes of doubtful disputation wrote: 'If they happen to be started in conversation, I always endeavour to divert the discourse to some more edifying topic. I have often observed them to breed animosity and division, but never knew them to be productive of love and unanimity.'

Revival – Unites and Upsets (see pages 15-16)

There is a paradox within revival in that it unites, but it also upsets some and repels others, but Jesus stated that even family members would be divided over Him and His ministry

(Matthew 10:34) but blessed are the unoffended ones (Matthew 11:6), so let us not be alarmed. See page 142.

James Burns from the early twentieth century wrote: 'To the Church, a revival means humiliation, a bitter knowledge of unworthiness.... It is not the easy glorious thing many think it be.... It comes to scorch before it heals; it comes to condemn ministers and people for their unfaithful witness, for their selfish living, for their neglect of the cross.... That is why a revival has ever been unpopular with large numbers within the Church.'

Dr. Martyn Lloyd-Jones saw a localised revival in his church at Sandfields, Aberavon, near Swansea, South Wales, UK, in 1930, though he himself was reluctant to call it revival. As minister of Westminster Chapel, London, he said, "...There has never been anything that has so promoted spiritual unity as revival. But a revival also invariably has another effect, and that is that it creates a new and fresh division. And why does it do so? It does so for this reason, those who have experienced the blessing and the power of God are naturally one and they come together; there are others who dislike it all and who criticise it all and who condemn it all and who are outside it all and the division comes in."

Slander and False Testimony

There is a growing problem with the body of Christ of those who thrive on negativity whilst some pass on erroneous information via email, social media or word of mouth without checking out the facts for themselves. Some go so far as to post articles on websites, for non-Christians to laugh and mock thus repulsing them from the Christ of Christianity.

There is a difference between truth and gossip and much of what we call passing on truth, God calls gossip. Many misrepresenting, misquoting or half truths are perpetuated on the evidence of hearsay and can cause untold harm, and ruin reputations and ministries. Many people are gullible as 'the simple believes every word' (Proverbs 14:15), whereas 'the sons of this world are more shrewd...than the sons of light' (Luke 16:8). When the Lord visited Abraham; after hearing the outcry against Sodom and Gomorrah He *went down to see for Himself* (Genesis 18:21). Leaders should 'inquire, search out and ask diligently' when accusations are brought against others (Deuteronomy 13:4, 17:4 and 19:18).

If you have started a rumour, even unintentionally by passing on erroneous information then you need to retract it. Inform those to whom you passed it on or entrusted it to and try to counteract the negative. You must also ask forgiveness to the one wronged. The circle of apology extends to the circle of offence, but a public maligning needs a public retraction, a public apology and may even need a public asking of one's forgiveness, which will lead to public reconciliation. In Pyongyang, in modern-day North Korea, an elder's public repentance, confessions and reconciliation led to beginning of the Pyongyang Great Revival (1907-1910) in which 50,000 were converted in its first year!

Smoke and Fire

Some believers assume the worst about those whom they have never met and speak against events or meetings of which they have not attended. This is very sad. Some people have the philosophy based on the adage that, 'where there's smoke there's fire,' but it was this mentality that led to the stoning of Stephen, the first Christian martyr (Acts 6:19-14 and Acts 7:54-59). A similar incident happened more than nine hundred and thirty years prior to Stephen's martyrdom, in the days of Elijah. Naboth the Jezreelite refused to sell his vineyard to King Ahab and began to sulk. Ahab's wife, Jezebel, hatched a plan; she wrote letters in her husband's name, used his seal and sent them to the elders. Naboth was invited to a fast amongst the elders and nobles of the city, but was seated between two scoundrels who bore false witness against him. Those present stoned him to death, yet he was innocent of all accusations (1 Kings 21:1-13).

Many inflammatory statements and lies were levied against John the Baptist, the so called man with 'a demon' (Matthew 11:18). Jesus was accused of being a glutton, winebibber, Samaritan (a cultural insult, see 2 Kings 17:29 and John 4:9), a madman with a demon (Matthew 11:19, John 8:48-49 and John 10:19-20) who worked miracles by His close association with demons (Matthew 9:32-34). Other biblical figures were accused of various things that were completely untrue and had no foundation in fact: Joseph was accused of adultery with Potiphar's wife, Moses was accused of lording it over the Israelites, Nehemiah was accused of trying to rebel against the king, Jeremiah was accused of trying to defect to the Chaldeans, whilst Daniel was thrown into the lions' den as King Darius had been duped by his advisers into passing a vain law which brought Daniel's allegiance into question. Even the apostle Paul was slanderously reported as saying, "Let us do evil that good may come!" (Romans 3:8).

On numerous occasions, religious leaders watched Jesus closely and tried to trap Him by His words or actions, or sent spies so as to accuse, entrap and discredit Him, see Matthew 21:23-27, Mark 3:1-6, Mark 12:1-17, Luke 13:10-17 and Luke 20:20-25. The apostle John stated that because of the pride of Diotrephes, he refused to look after the brethren and talks nonsense of them 'with malicious words' (3 John 10). Whilst 'some indeed preached Christ' so wrote the apostle Paul, out of 'envy and strife' because of 'selfish ambition' and desired to 'add affliction' to his chains (Philippians 1:15-16).

William Miller saw revival in Dresden, America, in 1831 and other revivals. But because of his lectures on the second coming (see pages 154-155), he was greatly maligned and much untruth was published and spread abroad against him. The editor of the *Gazette and Advertiser* of Williamsburg, Long Island, referred to an interview with William Miller: 'Our curiosity was recently gratified by an introduction to this gentleman, who has probably been an object of more abuse, ridicule and blackguardism, than any other man living.... When our interview closed, we were left wondering at the cause of the malignant spirit of slander and falsehood with which a man has been assailed, who has spent his time and substance in a course of unceasing toils to persuade men to 'flee from the wrath to come.' '[2]

Howell Harris visited John Wesley in Bristol, England, UK, on 18 June 1739. Initially, Harris had been quite reluctant to meet Wesley due to the many evil reports that had been given to him, but said after hearing him preach, "As soon as I heard you preach, I quickly found what spirit you were of.

And before you were done, I was so over powered with joy and love that I had much ado [trouble] to walk home."[3]

The Press and Media

It is to the advantage of the press and media to make a story sensational and they will often twist, bend or even fabricate a story so as to increase sales. If unbelievers write maliciously about their own, then how more critically will they write about the family of God and their ministries? See Psalm 56:5, John 15:19 and 2 Timothy 3:12.

With 24 hour news, media sound bites, webcasts and video related internet sites, many leaders and their meetings (where excess has occurred) have been edited so as to portray the ministry or its teaching in the worst possible light. But let us all be sensible in our own sphere of work and be wise in all that we do and say. Charles Stanley said, "Be aware of confusion; what we thought we taught we didn't teach, and what we didn't mean to teach we taught!"

Heresy Hunters, Revival Police and Judging

If you follow God there will always be opposition and those who do not appreciate your work in the Lord, and 'if you do not run with them' then they may 'speak evil of you' (1 Peter 4:4). But solace can be found because Jesus said, "Woe to you when *all* men speak well of you..." (Luke 6:26), therefore if you have no opposition can your ministry be of God?

There are a minority of Christians who believe it is *their* ministry to criticise other Christian ministries. Heresy hunters or revival police as they are known, go in search of the negative whilst dismissing the positive. The spirit in which error is pointed out is not done in a spirit of love, to inform and correct but to denounce and condemn. It is also unhelpful when their premise is that the one at fault is a wolf, even when the accused confesses Jesus Christ as Lord and adheres to the fundamental doctrines of orthodox Christianity. Francis Frangipane wrote: 'When an attack site fails to list even one good thing about a ministry, you tend to believe their goal is not to discern, but to destroy.'

In Acts eighteen there was a certain Jew named Apollos, a preacher of Jesus Christ who knew the Scriptures well, the Old Testament. He was fervent in his proclamation of the good news and 'taught accurately the things of the Lord though he knew only the baptism of John.' When Aquila and Priscilla heard, 'they took him aside and explained to him the way of God more accurately' (Acts 18:24-26). Notice that Aquila and Priscilla did not condemn him or label him a heretic for not teaching the whole truth, but privately, 'took him aside' and explained to him the truth 'more accurately.'

Some Christians have condemned Christian workers because of what they did prior to conversion and this is very wrong. If the blood of Christ has cleansed us from *all* sin (1 John 1:9); if God has cast confessed sin into the depths of the sea (Micah 7:19) and it is as far as the east is from the west (Psalm 103:12) and is not remembered by God (Isaiah 43:25) then it should not be repeated or posted on websites.

Some Christian leaders (or ministries) have retracted statements or beliefs once held, yet some Christians *still* perpetrate these old beliefs or sayings and keep repeating that which has been dealt with. This is also unbiblical.

Is it possible that many who level accusations against Christian ministries have never built a work that edifies others and are simply envious? See Acts 13:45. Is it also possible that some Christians try to hide their own deficiencies or vent their own frustrations and hurts by pulling down others? Perhaps they do not understand Psalm 133, 'the unity of the brethren' or Jesus' word, "That they may be one just as We are One" (John 17:22). Christian leaders often find that when these people, members of their own congregation are approached in love and gentleness, they often espouse their poor spiritual state and seem lost in a haze, and live under shadows of oppression.

Individual Christians and even those in leadership make mistakes and on occasions fall into or commit sin. The objective for any fallen brother or sister in the Lord should be for their restoration (after repentance) and not condemnation or gloating (Galatians 6:1-5). Let us be thankful that the early Church did not condemn denying Peter, doubting Thomas and Saul the persecutor. Could it be that there go I, bar the grace of God? If a brother or sister has erred and committed sin, then it is the Church's duty to try and bring the offender to a place of repentance and restoration which is the spirit of Christ, going in search of the lost or straying sheep.

The standard truth for anybody who is guilty must be on the testimony of two or three witnesses (Deuteronomy 19:15-19, 2 Corinthians 13:1 and 1 Timothy 5:19). People need to be treated fairly and graciously and are innocent until proven guilty and not the other way around. Christians should always begin with the bias towards believing the best as love 'thinks no evil' and love 'rejoices in the truth; bears all things, believes all things, hopes all things...love never fails' (1 Corinthians 13:5-8). See page 229.

According to the New Testament the best qualified to pass judgment on individuals, are those in leadership; like the apostle Paul who wanted to warn the churches he had founded – his flock(s). To name an offender is unwise unless we have the heart of compassion like Jesus and the sanctification and anointing of the apostle Paul. He was at liberty to warn the churches of individuals and to inform about those who had fallen away, as he had pastoral oversight. When Paul had to rebuke individuals or churches, he wrote in spirit of love, 'weeping,' (2 Corinthians 2:4).

James aptly pointed out: 'We all stumble in many things' (James 3:2), so none of us are perfect, yet many point out an issue not in a spirit of love which leads to correction, but in a spirit of condemnation which leads nowhere. Let us never forget that 'mercy triumphs over judgment' (James 2:13) and 'whatever you want men to do to you, do also to them' (Matthew 7:12). Jesus warns us about judging and with the measure we use it will be measured back to us (Matthew 7:1-6). We are told 'to speak evil of no one, to be peaceable, gentle, showing all humility to all men. For we ourselves were once also foolish...living in malice and envy, hateful and hating one another' (Titus 3:2-3). James confirms these words: 'Do not speak evil of one another, brethren' (James 4:11), whilst the apostle Paul set a higher standard in that love 'thinks no evil' (1 Corinthians 13:5), and Jude openly wrote that false teachers 'speak evil of whatever they do not know' (Jude 1:10), whilst the prophet Amos pronounced a warning for those who desired the Day of the Lord; as it will be a day of judgment for those looking for others to be punished, who had not examined themselves, 'it will be darkness and not light...as though a man fled from a lion and a bear met him' (Amos 5:18-20).

Chapter Twenty-Three

False and Spurious Converts

Saved or Not?

The Holy Bible plainly declares that 'whoever calls upon the name of the Lord will be saved' (Acts 2:21 and Romans 10:13), but those who confess with their mouths are also called to profess by their changed lives; that is, 'show forth fruits worthy of repentance' (Matthew 3:8). Genuine disciples of Christ can be differentiated from those who come in sheep's clothing, yet inwardly are ravenous wolves because 'by their fruit you will know them,' and a 'good tree cannot bear bad fruit' (Matthew 7:15-20). *If* we abide in God's Word, then we are His disciples and we shall know the truth and it will set us free (John 8:31-32). Also, people will know that we are Jesus' disciples, '*if* we have love for one another' (John 13:34-35) and if we 'walk worthy of the Lord, *fully* pleasing Him' and increase in the knowledge of Him which qualifies us to be 'partakers of the inheritance' (Colossians 1:10-12). By the Word of God and His grace we are able to receive the inheritance, but only 'those who are sanctified' (Acts 20:32). See page 179.

Jesus said that not everyone who calls Him "Lord" will enter the Kingdom of heaven, even though they may have done many miraculous signs and wonders in His name, but He will openly declare, "I never knew you; depart from Me you who practice lawlessness" (Matthew 7:21-23). See Luke 6:46-49.

Charles H. Spurgeon, preaching on the subject of calling (salvation) in March 1859, said, "[Jesus] who hath saved us and called us with a holy calling (2 Timothy 1:9) – many are called, but few are chosen.... It is 'a holy calling, not according to our works, but according to His own purpose and grace which was given us in Christ Jesus before the world began.' This calling forbids all trust in our own doings and conducts us to Christ alone for salvation, but it afterwards purges us from dead works to serve the living and true God. If you are living in sin, you are not called; if you can still continue as you were before your pretended conversion, then it is no conversion at all; that man who is called in his drunkenness will forsake his drunkenness; men may be called in the midst of sin, but they will not continue in it any longer.... Now, by this shall ye know whether ye be called of God or not. If ye continue in sin, if ye walk according to the course of this world, according to the spirit that worketh in the children of disobedience, then ye are still dead in your trespasses and your sins; but as He that hath called you is holy, so must ye be holy. Can ye say, 'Lord, Thou knowest all things, Thou knowest that I desire to keep all Thy commandments and to walk blamelessly in Thy sight. I know my obedience cannot save me, but I long to obey. There is nothing that pains me so much as sin; I desire to be quit and rid of it — Lord help me to be holy?' Is that the panting of thy heart? Is that the tenor of thy life towards God and towards His law? Then, beloved, I have reason to hope that Thou hast been called of God, for it is a holy calling wherewith God doth call His people."[1]

Tares and Imitators

There are those who are tares, that is supposed and alleged Christians who act the part, sound the part and will blend in very well at any church meeting, but it is not until the harvest that they are truly exposed for what they are — tares and not wheat and they will be burned whilst the wheat will be gathered into God's barn (Matthew 13:24-30). See *Tares and Weeds in Your Church* by R. B. Watchman, and page 121. Jude notes false teachers who were so well disguised that they even participated in the 'love feasts,' but only ministered for their own financial gain, being 'clouds without rain, carried about by the winds; late autumn trees, twice dead, pulled up by the roots; raging waves of the sea, foaming up their shame; wandering stars for whom is reserved the blackness of darkness for ever' (Jude 12-13).

Some so-called Christians know all about doctrine, but nothing about devotion, they may be living concordances of the Word of God, yet not know the Word who came in the flesh. They may know virtually everything about Christ and religion, yet not know Him in a personal relationship. The road to destruction is very broad, but narrow is the gate that leads to eternal life and 'there are few who find it' (Matthew 7:13-14), and 'if the righteous one is scarcely saved' what about the ungodly and habitual sinners? (1 Peter 4:18). Whilst we cannot be plucked out of God's hand (John 10:28) is it possible that we may wander from the path of righteousness and be so entangled in a web of sin that we are unable to break free and thus disinherit ourselves from the family of God? Whilst others are taken captive by the devil to do his will (2 Timothy 2:26) and for some their very conscience has been 'seared with a hot iron,' as they give 'heed to deceiving spirits and doctrines of demons' (1 Timothy 4:1-3). Thus rendering them unable to discern between the holy and the unholy, the clean and the unclean (Leviticus 10:10) and more often than not they will call 'evil good and good evil; who put darkness for light and light for darkness' and 'put bitter for sweet and sweet for bitter' and woe unto them! (Isaiah 5:20). 'If we sin wilfully after we have received the knowledge of the truth, there no longer remains a sacrifice for sins...' (Hebrews 10:26). '...As they crucify again for themselves the Son of God' (Hebrews 6:6-8).

Evangelism, Statistics and Those who Fall Away

Jesus gave the parable of the sower; the seed that was scattered being the Word of God. Some fell on the wayside and was trampled underfoot or eaten by birds; some fell on stony ground and sprang up, yet withered because of a lack of soil and moisture; some fell among thorns, it grew, but was choked by the thorns and withered, whilst other seed fell onto good ground, grew and produced a harvest (Matthew 13:1-23, Mark 4:1-34 and Luke 8:4-15).

Therefore, according to Jesus, much sowing is needed in sharing the good news and should we be surprised if three quarters of confessions never produce a real harvest? But this does not mean that we sit back on our laurels as we are called to make *disciples*, not favourable statistics or church-goers with the nickname Christian.

In evangelistic campaigns the fall-away rate is very high and only a minute fraction of those who profess Christ become part of a church and are still standing within a few months, let alone years, but in revival this is not the case. Many are not truly born again and have not passed from death to life. Most are not *truly* repentant. They are without Jesus Christ and many serve themselves and Satan's will.

Evangelist and Christian TV presenter, Ray Comfort, founder of Way of the Master, in his book, *Revival's Golden Key* cited eighteen examples from across the globe of crusade and denominational conversion statistics. He wrote: 'These statistics of an eighty-four to ninety-seven percent fall away rate are not confined to crusades, but are general throughout local church evangelism.'[2]

During revival the vast majority of converts stay true to the faith, though there are those who come under conviction of sin, yet for whatever reason they never come to the faith. During the Lewis Revival (1949-1952) in the Outer Hebrides of Scotland, Duncan Campbell stated that seventy-five percent were converted outside of a church building on the moorland, at home and by the side of the road as God's Spirit arrested them!

J. Edwin Orr wrote: 'Those who profess to decide [for Christ] in revival atmosphere show a convincing degree of assurance, for in revival, the Holy Spirit of God does His work unhampered by the usual hindrances of Christians.'[3]

Retired missionary and Bible teacher, Paris Reidhead in *Finding the Reality of God* noted the ministry of Charles Finney. He wrote: 'Finney was in Rochester, New York, where a blue-ribbon committee of outstanding citizens was appointed by Henry Ward Beecher to study the converts who, a decade earlier [in 1830], had come to Christ under Finney's preaching. It was found that eighty-five percent of those who had made professions under Finney's preaching were still faithfully living for Christ.

'In contrast, it is being reported that only one-half of one percent of those who make decisions for Christ in our evangelistic meetings today will be living as Christians two years from now. This is how far we've strayed from the Word of God.'[4]

Many are invited to the Great Supper at the end of the age and we are to 'go into the highways and hedges [byways] and compel them to come in' that God's 'house may be filled,' but many will make lame excuses (Luke 14:15-24).

John George Govan, revivalist and founder of The Faith Mission, Scotland, said, "About all work for God, one feels that the all-essential thing is the approval and cooperation of God by the mighty workings of His Spirit. Without that all the plans of man and the varieties of work engaged in will be an utter failure. But if it be in the power of His Spirit, God will use many means and methods for the advancement of His Kingdom."[5]

The British Weekly made an inquiry into the permanent results of the Torrey-Alexander missions, assisted by Kennedy MacLeans report. Reuben A. Torrey quietly pointed out that almost every minister who stated that he got nothing out of the missions *put nothing into them* or *opposed them*.[6]

Revivals and False Converts

Even during times of revival there are those who pretend to turn to Christ having been under conviction of sin, but do not pass from 'death to life' (1 John 3:14) experiencing the new birth, being 'born again' (John 3:3-21). Some are self-deceived and their conversion is only done in pretence; they go through the motions, but are still unregenerate. In Jeremiah's day, Judah ignored Israel's example of what happened to a backsliding nation. The Lord spoke through the prophet Jeremiah saying, "Judah has not turned to Me with *her whole heart, but in pretence*" (Jeremiah 3:10).

There are also those who are 'obstinate children' (Isaiah 30:1, NIV) who take no counsel from God, but carry on in their own sinful lifestyle and these are not converted.

It is possible for people to make an intellectual 'head' decision to follow Christ or for Christians to make a fuller commitment to Him, as in full surrender, yet not understand what they have promised, and therefore they are unable to walk into the reality of such a commitment. If we look back to the world with longing eyes we are not fit for the Kingdom (Exodus 16:2-3, Numbers 11:4-5 and Luke 9:57-62), but if we turn back to the world, the latter is worse than the beginning (Hebrews 10:36-38 and 2 Peter 2:20-22). We should not be deceived by disobedience, but we are called to enter into the rest of God (Hebrews 3:7-19 and Hebrews 4:1-6, 11). Have we? Trusting and resting in Jesus Christ.

Many of us, especially those within Christian ministry would have seen people going through the motions of Christianity without knowing the Christ of Christianity. They can look the part, say all the right things, but they are not "born again" and they have not repented and forsaken their sins and do not live for Jesus. Then there are those whose emotions have been stimulated and have had an emotional conversion. Those who during an appeal, put their hand up, maybe even come to the front and repeat a prayer, believe that they are saved and then *carry on as normal*. They may faithfully turn up for the Sunday service, even attend the church socials and still be unregenerate. Let us not forget that even John Wesley, ordained by the Church of England went to America to convert the Indians and came back realising that he himself was not converted! There were also quite a few Church of England vicars who got converted during the Evangelical Revival (1739-1791), such as John Berridge of Everton, England, and Daniel Rowland of Llangeitho, Wales, whilst William Haslam of Cornwall, England, was an unconverted vicar for nine years, until he saw the light in Oct. 1851. All of these men had been trained in theological studies and ordained by bishops! They looked the part, talked the part yet had not passed from 'death into life' (John 5:24). After conversion, they all saw revival.

Simon, a former sorcerer *believed* the message of salvation and was baptised during the Samaria Revival. He 'continued with Philip' the evangelist, being amazed by the signs and wonders that he saw, yet was only found out when he tried to buy the impartation of the Holy Spirit (Acts 8:5-23) and that is how we got the word simony.

The Cost of Discipleship and False Followers
In the second year of Jesus' ministry, He spoke on the cost of discipleship, that we have to be drawn by the Father to Him and then *committed* to His way. Jesus being the Bread of Life of which we have to eat, *if* we are to partake of eternal life (John chapter 6). It was during this time, the height of His popularity that Jesus revealed the different motives as to why the multitudes followed Him. There is also a parallel between the motives of those who followed Jesus then and now and those who travel to places of revival. Some followed

Jesus for the excitement; 'a great multitude followed Him, because they saw His signs which He performed on those who were diseased' (John 6:2). Others followed Him for what they could get from Him, 'you seek Me, not because you saw the signs, but because you ate the loaves and were filled' (John 6:26). But Jesus challenged His followers to identify with Him, 'whoever eats My flesh and drinks My blood has eternal life, and I will raise him up at the last day' (John 6:54). But it was 'from that time many of His disciples went back and walked with Him no more' (John 6:66) though the genuine and true disciples stayed loyal to Jesus.

There are many people who are 'in it' for what *they* can get out of it. Those who love to hear what God is doing; missionary stories, stories of deliverances, healings and miracles – they love to be entertained by the workings of God in and through people's lives, 'their mouth shows much love, but their hearts pursue their own gain' wrote Ezekiel. 'Indeed you are to them as a very lovely song of one who has a pleasant voice and can play well on an instrument.' The stories excite their emotions, but when you challenge them to a greater commitment or full surrender to God (Romans 12:1, Galatians 2:20 and 2 Cor. 5:15), 'they hear your words, but they do not do them' (Ezekiel 33:31-33).

Rev. James Robe saw the Kilsyth Revival (1742) in Scotland. Within his parish not everyone who was awakened to their sinfulness and their need of the Saviour came to a saving knowledge of Jesus Christ and were not born again. He wrote: 'Some of these [having been awakened to their sin] were many weeks, if not months under great terror and distress. Some of those who lost their impressions came to no saving issue, by being engaged too much in worldly affairs. "The cares of this life choked the word, and they became unfruitful." Some through ignorance, and not being diligent to learn the way of salvation through Jesus Christ [a blasé attitude]; some through the influence of evil company, and consulting with flesh and blood ['what is your opinion?']; some through the outcry raised by the Seceders [those who had withdrawn from the established Church], that all their convictions were but delusions and from the devil, one way or another they resisted the Holy Spirit, and provoked Him to withdraw His influences, and so the work of the Spirit upon them ceased, and came to no saving issue.'[7]

William C. Burns, deferred his missionary call to China, as he saw revival during 1839-1841, from Dundee to Kilsyth in Scotland. In China he saw the Peh-Chuia Awakening (c.1854). On 6 September 1840, he was preaching from Matthew 25 (the ten virgins) at the Moulin Parish Church in Scotland. He said, "We are very thankful when we see a lamp burning brightly for one year, but how many of those that have been lighted are blown out. At Kilsyth [1839], for instance, there are few who, for some months promised fair haven, but the light is extinguished. It reminds us of a nursery of plants. The first year, when they are all lying close together in the plantation, they seem to thrive and are allowed to grow up together; but the second year they must be thinned, and only the choice plants can be given a place in the ground; in successive years they are thinned again, and what a small, small number of the original seedlings remain in the dark forest of a hundred years. It is just so, in the spiritual world, especially when there has been a great awakening. At first, there are numbers of professors, the crowd follows Jesus. There is no shame, no reproach, and it is easy to follow Him when there is no cross on the way. But in a short time, when religion is no longer the fashion of the day, when the crowd forsakes Him, then too many of those whose lamps for a time seemed to burn the brightest, turn back and walk no more with Jesus.

"Some go further than this, their lamps remain lighted for a longer time, and while all goes on smoothly and they remain in the society of their great friends, they find that after all, it is a rather comfortable thing to serve God; but when they have to sacrifice something that is peculiarly dear to them, or else to give up Christ, it is found that they have been hypocrites all along.... None can tell in this world, how many once promising professors, have been ruined by the example and influence of the ungodly. I daresay those of you who are old enough, remember examples of this at Moulin [probably referring to the Moulin Parish Revival (1799-1805) of Perthshire, a Gaelic speaking district at the time]. One man married an ungodly wife, and that cost him his soul; some woman married an ungodly husband, and that cost her, her soul. Some fell in the time of reproach on account of the word, and alas! Too many, have continued in the sunshine of worldly prosperity so long, that the riches of this world and the cares of this life, have sprung up and choked the word."[8]

Thomas Phillips documented the 1859 Welsh Revival. In his rebuttal to the objections that the new converts will backslide, betray religion and bring disgrace on the whole movement, he wrote: 'Suppose this would be found true in part, where would be the marvel? Is not the Kingdom of heaven compared to ten virgins, of whom five were foolish? And to a net cast into the sea, which gathered of every kind? And is not the Christian Church a field in which wheat and tares grow together until harvest? We must be prepared for disappointments – a Judas will appear here – a Demas there – Simon the sorcerer, Diotrephes, and men of kindred spirit will "arise" again. It has been so in former revivals and have we right to expect that the present will be an exception!?'[9]

False Repentance and Double-Mindedness

There is a state of true and false repentance. True repentance is confessing (Leviticus 5:5) and forsaking one's sin (Proverbs 28:13) before God and asking His forgiveness for those sins. Ephesians 4:31 tells us 'to put away' bitterness, wrath, anger, clamour, evil speaking and malice. Colossians 3:5 tells us to 'put to death' fleshly passions, fornication, evil desire and covetousness. Whilst Galatians 6:19-21 lists a whole host of sins, 'the works of the flesh' and that 'those who practice such things will not inherit the Kingdom of God.' The following two verses list the fruit of the Spirit, nine of, which are manifested through love, which exemplifies all true Christians and states 'those who are Christ's have crucified the flesh with its passion and desires. If we live in the Spirit, let us also walk in the Spirit' (Galatians 5:22-25). We are also called to be 'salt and light' (Matthew 5:15-16) which follows after The Beatitudes.

False repentance is getting emotionally charged, often shedding "crocodile" tears (because we have been caught, found-out or are under conviction of sin) yet still carry on how we were before. Esau despised and sold his birthright, yet he later sought repentance with tears but he could not find it (Hebrews 12:15-17). Esau was not truly repentant, but grieved because he lost out on that which should have been his; a large inheritance. The rich young ruler, who obeyed the commandments and desired to inherit eternal life became sorrowful, not because he could not inherit it, but because he did not want to give away his own inheritance to the poor and truly follow Jesus. It was this "one thing" which stopped him from having treasure in heaven (Lk. 18:18-27).

The Samaritans 'feared the Lord yet served their own gods' (2 Kings 17:32-33). The people of Judah 'worship and swear oaths by the Lord, but who also swear by Milcom' (Zephaniah 1:5). In Jesus' day, 'even among the rulers, many believed in Him, but because of the Pharisees they did not confess Him...for they loved the praise of men more than the praise of God' (John 12:42-43). James noted: 'A double-minded man, [is] unstable in all his ways' (James 1:8).

From 1927 to 1937, revival swept across China, but especially in the Northern Provinces. Rev. Olav Espegren, president of the Norwegian Lutheran Mission who ministered in south-western Honan and north Hupeh wrote a report for the year 1933. It is dated 24 January 1934. He emphasised the great need for pastoral care of those who have "come through," but also noted that defections were among such as had simulated repentance, but had not really come through. Otherwise his impression was that very few of the newly saved fell away.[10]

Christian sociologist, George Barna, founder and president of Barna Research Group wrote: 'Most Christians have plentiful exposure to God's truth and exhortations, but few have actually been pierced by the truth, principles, and meaning of the Christian faith.'[11]

In 1743, in the midst of the American Great Awakening (1735-1760) Jonathan Edwards published the *Treatise Concerning the Religious Affections*. The second chapter is about 'false signs of true religious affections.' He noted:

- That enthusiasm can quickly end, just like the Israelites deliverance through the Red Sea, who habitually complained in the wilderness.
- People have been enlightened as in Hebrews 6:4-5, but are unacquainted with the better things that 'accompany salvation' (verse 9).

- A counterfeit love of which the apostle Paul alludes to in Ephesians 6:24, 'grace be with all those that love our Lord Jesus Christ in *sincerity*. Amen.'
- Godly sorrow without a change of character, such as: Pharaoh and the ten plagues, "I have sinned," yet carried on defying God (Exodus 9:27); King Saul who wept before David whom he tried to kill at least three times (1 Samuel 24:16-17, 26:21); King Ahab humbled himself (1 Kings 21:27) but carried on in sin and the dogs licked up his blood (1 Kings 22:37-38); the children of Israel in the wilderness who tested God ten times and still doubted Him (Numbers chapter 14, especially verse 22).

Eight Categories of Deceived Christians

1. A Non-Christian: One who thinks that he or she is a Christian, yet have never put their faith in Jesus Christ's atoning death for the forgiveness of their sins. At the end times, unrighteous people will follow the deceptions of the devil (2 Thessalonians 2:7-12).
2. A Premature Christian: One who does not live the life, who constantly, deliberately and habitually sins (John 14:15, 21, Hebrews 6:1-6 and Heb. 10:26-31).
3. A Young Christian: One who gets led astray. Simon (who had previously practised sorcery) wanted to buy the power of the impartation of the Holy Spirit. Peter denounced him and called him to repent as his heart was not right in the sight of God, being poisoned by bitterness and bound by iniquity (Acts 8:9-13, 18-23).
4. A Naïve Christian: One who has been taken captive by the devil to do his will (2 Timothy 2:26), or one who has been deceived by another (2 Timothy 3:1-6).
5. A Religious Christian: One who outwardly appears right before God, but in their heart they are looking for the praise and adoration of man. The Pharisees were full of hypocrisy and lawlessness (Matthew 23:1-7, 13-15, Matthew 23:23-33 and Luke 11:42-44).
6. A Traditional Christian: One who believes that their devotion to their tradition is more important than their relationship to God (Matthew 23:16-22 and Mark 7:6-13). Often doctrine comes before devotion.

7. An Apostate Christian: One who upon seeing lawlessness abound, allows their love for Christ to grow cold (Matthew 24:10-12 and 2 Thess. 2:3-4).
8. A "Manipulated" Christian: The elect who after seeing deceiving signs and wonders follow after a false Christ or false prophet (Matthew 24:23-26).

Prevention of Deception

The question is posed: "How can I prevent myself from being deceived?" Jesus said, "Take heed that you do not be deceived..." (Luke 21:8). I think we would all agree that prevention is always better than cure. See also chapter fifteen, The Dangers of Revival (beware of deceivers and warnings from Scripture) and chapter twenty-six, Warnings and Wisdom.

We should dig deep from the Word of God and have firm solid foundations in sound biblical doctrine. Most people do not decide to be deceived (or to deceive others), but it is a process that happens over time, a gradual process, rather than a sudden single event. We must all take heed as to who or what we are listening to, and who or what is influencing our knowledge of God and Christianity. We are all called to intelligently judge the message we hear and the person who brings it. For Christians, only the Holy Bible (God's objective Word) can truly judge our personal experiences (subjective feelings), thoughts, attitudes, doctrine and interpretation of Scripture, along with any preconceived ideas.

It is a sad fact that people will frequently believe what they want to believe, that which they are comfortable with. Those who look for teachers to teach them what they want to hear or not to teach on that which they do not want to hear! And that is why several cults were founded two centuries ago with their aversion to hell and eternal torment.

Some captains of the army asked the prophet Jeremiah for a word from the Lord, but when it came they rejected it. They stated that Jeremiah had spoken falsely (Jeremiah chapters 42-43). Some hear what they want to hear and will follow their own deceptive heart (2 Timothy 4:3-4). Jesus preached on total commitment, however hard the cost, but many turned back and followed Him no more (John 6:44-66).

Chapter Twenty-Four

Counterfeit Conversion

Genuine Conversion or Impostors

The tragedy of the twenty-first century is that there are many people who attend church who genuinely believe they are saved and part of God's family (John 1:12), yet they are not. They have had a counterfeit conversion – thus meaning that they are not converted at all, though they sincerely believe they are saved, and even in times of revival a small minority of counterfeit conversions can rise to the surface.

Repentance, a renouncing and turning away from the works of darkness with faith in the death and resurrection of Jesus Christ is the foundation of salvation. Are you saved – saved from what? From the wrath to come, the lusts of the flesh? Saved from selfishness, greed, impure thoughts, a deceitful heart – saved from what? Jesus said, "Therefore by their fruits you will know them" (Matthew 7:20) because without holiness no man shall see the Lord (Hebrews 12:4) and we are commanded to be holy because He is holy (1 Pet. 1:16).

The righteous one is scarcely saved (1 Peter 4:18) and those who do not do the will of God are not part of Jesus' family (Matthew 7:21 and Mark 3:35). Jesus declared that we are justified and condemned by our words (Matthew 12:37) and our confession of faith in Christ (Romans 10:9-10) is the crux of our faith. If the Lord will say to some, "I never knew you" – to those who even did miracles and cast out demons in His name (Matthew 7:21-23), can you really say you are saved? Jesus said, "Narrow is the gate and difficult is the way which leads to life and there are few who find it" (Matthew 7:14). See page 167.

God knows who His chosen ones are and if we are not wearing the right clothes at the wedding feast we will be caught out and cast out (Matthew 22:11-14). We must accept and live by the Word of God and make Jesus not only our Saviour, but our Lord and Master. Have you?

Counterfeit Conversion

Steve Hill was the evangelist from the Brownsville Revival (1995-2000). Preaching on 'Counterfeit Conversion' he said, "This nation is sick of counterfeit conversion and counterfeit Christianity.... Now, a counterfeit is made as an imitation of something else with the intent to deceive. It is an inferior imitation or copy. It is a sham, something that is likely to be confused with the genuine article.... Unfortunately there are churches and ministries around the world that crank out counterfeit conversions.... We have substituted low-cost fakes for high-cost truth. Too many of us have fallen for religion because it satisfied the little craving we had inside. However, once you experience and taste the real thing in a genuine revival meeting, you will feel almost like you have been ripped off."[1]

Andy Banton, General Secretary of The Open-Air Mission wrote: 'In the work of evangelism today there is an awful lot of shallowness. It seems to be a common assumption that if people simply hear about Jesus and then make a commitment to Him, they are saved. The feeling a person experiences which bring them to that commitment are rarely asked about, let alone examined. So what does the Word of God say about what a person should experience in their coming to a saving knowledge of Jesus Christ? In Acts 2:37 we are provided with the answer. Peter had been addressing a huge crowd in Jerusalem on the day of Pentecost. Luke records that as he spoke, many were 'cut to the heart.' What does this phrase mean? In the very depths of their beings, many of Peter's hearers were convicted of their sin. They actually felt a sense of their moral dirtiness before a holy God. They were now aware of what God had already been aware of – their responsibility for the death of the Lord Jesus. This was something that was laid bare before their eyes. They not only saw it but felt a sense of horror of it. In fact the people now felt something of the enormity of their rejection of the One who had claimed to be the Messiah. Like a repentant King David they knew what it was to have hearts that were broken and contrite (Psalm 51:17).[2]

Jesus said, "That which is born of the flesh is flesh and that which born of the Spirit is spirit" (John 3:6). If we work in the flesh our fruit will correspond and souls [will] be brought into false experience.... If our lives do not convict of sin there is something wrong.[3]

Steve Hill wrote: 'How do you know if you are a counterfeit convert? Number one, *if you serve God for what you can get out of Him*.... Ask not what Jesus can do for you, but ask what you can do for Jesus.... [Number two], he *only does what he has to do, even though it's not what he really wants to do*.... True Christianity is rooted in a "want to" motivation. You *want* to serve God because He first loved you!... We need to live the same way at home as we do at church.... [Number three] his basic motivation is fear, not love...his fear of hell and punishment keeps him outwardly moral, but his brand of self-made obedience is formal, heartless, loveless, and completely worthless.... Counterfeit Christians don't know the Lord; they only know *about* Him.'[4]

'Examine yourselves as to whether you are in the faith. Prove yourselves. Do you not know yourselves that Jesus Christ is in you? – Unless indeed you are disqualified' (2 Corinthians 13:5).

A. W. Tozer said, "The fact is that we are not producing saints. We are making converts to an effete type of Christianity that bears little resemblance to that of the New Testament. The average so-called Bible Christian of our times is but a shallow display of true sainthood. Yet, we put millions of dollars behind "movements" to perpetuate this lower form of religion and attack the man who dares to challenge the wisdom of it." See pages 169-170.

The False Doctrine of 'Simply Believism'
Rev. Duncan Campbell gave the following address at a meeting for ministers, at Oxford and Manchester in the early 1950s, "There is a growing conviction everywhere, and especially among thoughtful people, that unless revival comes, other forces will take the field, that will sink us still deeper into the mire of humanism and materialism.

"...It has been said that "the Kingdom of God is not going to be advanced by our churches becoming filled with men, but by men in our churches becoming filled with God." Today, we have a Christianity made easy as an accommodation to an age that is unwilling to face the implications of Calvary, and the gospel of "simply believism" has produced a harvest of professions which have done untold harm to the cause of Christ."[5]

The False Doctrine of 'Only-Believism'
Rev. Duncan Campbell preaching during the Lewis Revival (1949-1952) said, "When a soul is born again, created within that soul are aspirations after God. Just as a lamb runs after the mother and not the mother after the lamb, the truly regenerate soul will seek after pastures where he can be fed. This is something we need to emphasise these days when there is so much unreality among those who respond to appeals made. The doctrine of 'only-believism' has, I fear produced a harvest of sceptics! What is the difference between the imitation rose, man-made, and the real? One lacks life and perfume; the other fills the room with its fragrance. There may be a strong resemblance, but the difference is fundamental."[6]

To Follow Christ
Evangelist Billy Graham, speaking to J. Edwin Orr during the Hollywood for Christ Campaign of September 1951, said, "In the past, evangelists have not always seemed willing to face the fact that the so-called 'converts' passing through their enquiry rooms are not all converts.... Furthermore, many evangelists, including myself, used to spend ninety-five percent of their efforts in persuading men to *decide* for Christ. Now I am convinced that it takes ninety-five percent of evangelistic effort [follow-up] to get men to *follow* Christ, as compared with five percent necessary for decision.'[7]

No Transformation and Cheap Grace
Revivalist and evangelist for more than thirty years, James A. Stewart wrote: 'The appeals which win men without transforming them, which joins them to the Church without bringing them into fellowship with Christ, are fatal to a pure Christianity, and in the end must put the very existence of the Church in jeopardy.'[8]

Dietrich Bonhoeffer died under the Nazi regime for his faith in Christ. In his book, *The Cost of Discipleship* he wrote: 'Cheap grace means grace sold on the market like cheapjack's wares. The sacraments, the forgiveness of sin, and the consolations of religion are thrown away at cut prices. Grace is represented as the Church's inexhaustible treasury from which she showers blessings with generous hands, without asking questions or fixing limits! Grace without price! Grace without cost! The essence of grace, we suppose, is that the account has been paid in advance; and, because it has been paid, everything can be had for nothing.'

Flimsy and False Conversions
Oswald J. Smith wrote: 'Where there is genuine conviction of sin it is not necessary to urge, coax or press in the energy of the flesh; sinners will come without being forced; they will come because they must...in our twentieth century evangelism...men are urged to be saved before they know they are lost, to believe without being convicted of their need. The fruit is picked before it is ripe, and of course the work is bound to come undone. If we are to get Holy Spirit fruit, God must prepare the ground; the Holy Spirit must convict of sin before men can truly believe...There is another gospel, too popular in the present day, which seems to exclude conviction of sin and repentance from the scheme of salvation; which demands from the sinner a mere intellectual assent to the facts of his guilt and sinfulness, and a like intellectual assent to the fact and sufficiency of Christ's atonement; and such assent yielded, tells him to go in peace, and to be happy in the assurance that the Lord Jesus has made all right between his soul and God; thus crying, "Peace, peace," when there is no peace...It is one thing to hold up the hand and sign a decision card, but it is quite another thing to get saved...it is one thing to have hundreds of professed converts during the excitement of the campaign, but it is another thing to come back in five years after and find them still there.'[9]

'Flimsy and false conversions of this sort may be one reason why so many who assume the Christian profession dishonour God and bring reproach on the church by their inconsistent lives, and by their ultimate relapse into worldliness and sin. 'By the law is knowledge of sin.' Sin must be felt before it can be mourned. Sinners must sorrow before they can be comforted.... True conversions are the want of our times.' – J. H. Lord.[10]

Evangelist John R. Rice, preaching on 'Spectators in the Heavenly Grandstand' said, "God forgive us – we fat preachers, we oil-tongued preachers, peace-at-any-price preachers, preachers who do not hit sin, who cannot lose a friend for Jesus, preachers who never make anybody mad, we preachers that do not know anything about hell and judgment and repentance; I think sometimes Paul says, 'Lord, take him out! Lord, take him out! I have marks on my body where they stoned me and left me for dead! They had to let me over the city wall of Damascus in a basket at night with ropes; I have been in chains over at Rome. Lord, take him out! He has no tears, no broken heart and no power of the Spirit. Take him out, Lord, and get somebody who can preach, somebody who means business.' "[11]

Marie Monsen – Do Not Pick Unripe Fruit!

Marie Monsen was a Norwegian missionary who arrived in China in 1901. She saw revival across China from 1927-1932, in every mission station she visited (of differing denominations) in numerous provinces. In November 1931, she arrived at Chenping, one of the mission stations of the Norwegian Lutheran Mission in Honan, and saw revival. In the second week she spoke at the Chenping annual three day conference. At the end of the day, as her custom was, she would take her stand at the door and as the people left, she pointedly asked, "Are you saved?" The next day, as the people left, with her incredible discernment, she asked, "Are you still on the road to destruction?"

Her co-worker wrote: 'Many came to see her and confess their sins, but she sent them away, some as often as three to four times. They were not in a condition of real need. "Pray that God's Spirit may enlighten you concerning your sins," was the admonition they received to take away with them. She never tired of admonishing us, "Do not gather unripe fruit." '[12]

Chapter Twenty-Five

Preach the Pure Gospel

Who is to Blame?

In the previous two chapters we looked at false and spurious converts and counterfeit conversion, not just a minority in times of revival, but the majority outside of revival! Those who make a profession of faith at an evangelistic event or church meeting, but do not live their confession; that is their public confession of faith, because they deny Jesus by their deeds and tongue, whereas Jesus should be proclaimed by their lifestyle and public witness of Him. They call Jesus their Saviour, but it is obvious that He is not their Lord. But who is to blame? The counterfeit converts for being sold down the river under false pretences and promises or the eager evangelist or preacher who needs more 'scores' on the tally card to appease the committee or church?

You may not be an evangelist, but we are all called to evangelise and if Jesus has changed you, then He can change anyone! We should be preaching the gospel in season and out of season, Christ and Him crucified, a blood bought atonement which purchased salvation for mankind at the extreme and ultimate cost. We should always be prepared to share our testimony and preach the unsearchable riches of Christ Jesus. The apostle Paul was not ashamed of the gospel, knowing it is the power of God to salvation (Romans 1:16). Outside of Jesus Christ there is no other name by which we must be saved (Acts 4:12), and those who reject Jesus Christ stand condemned (John 3:18).

'Deliver those who are drawn towards death, and hold back those stumbling to slaughter. If you say, "Surely we did not know this," does not He who weighs the heart consider it? He who keeps your soul, does He not know it? And will He not render to each man according to his deeds?' (Proverbs 24:11-12).

Principal of Emmanuel Bible School, Birkenhead, England, John D. Drysdale, wrote: 'Call men to repentance and restitution, call them to break off their sins by righteousness – call them to leave the world with all its shady tricks in business, and often unfaithfulness in home life and you will soon find out in the first instance that there is something in the heart of man which fights the revelation and makes him determined to have his own way. Are we willing to preach and pay the price for a heaven-born revival? Are we cast upon God enough to release His glorious power against all the power of the enemy?...dare we preach this soul-emancipating salvation? When we do, I believe we shall see our land once more in the glory of a God-given revival.'[1]

Rev. Duncan Campbell preaching during the Lewis Revival (1949-1952), quoting Dr. J. Jowett said, "If Christ is not real and dynamic in our lives, we shall be like common people in a common market, babbling about common wares." Rev. Campbell continued, "We are today living in the midst of very shallow thinking, producing shallow experiences.... Let me point out what we do not take seriously to heart today – that there is a difference between Christ being revealed *to* me and Christ being revealed *in* me. It is possible to have Christ revealed *to* me in the pages of the Word, in the lives of His people, and yet not have Christ revealed *in* me."[2]

Law and Grace – Not Pick and Mix

The apostle Paul did not shun to declare the whole counsel of God. We must preach: Jesus Christ and Him crucified for our sins; the cross, the blood, repentance, new life in Christ, the judgment to come, hell and the lake of burning fire for those who refuse to depart from iniquity, and for those who reject Jesus Christ as their Lord and Saviour.

The law (the Ten Commandments) is our schoolmaster that brings us to Christ, because we can see with greater clarity how we have transgressed the moral law. If you have lied you are a liar, if you have stolen, you are a thief etc., it brings conviction of sin by the Holy Spirit and our conscience condemns us. We are guilty before a holy and just God who demands an account of that which is past. Once we preach the law it makes the judgment (hell) seem reasonable, and just (as for every action there is a consequence – sowing and reaping) – if I break the law of the land, I will be punished for it, how much more when I break God's perfect law of liberty? After the law which prepares the heart then we can preach grace. The wages of sin is death, but the gift of God is eternal life in Christ Jesus (Romans 6:23).

It was John Wesley who stated that he used to preach the law, to bring awareness of sin and then sprinkle it with grace. The reformer, Martin Luther, said of the law, "In its true and proper work and purpose it humbles a man and prepares him – if he uses the law correctly – to yearn and seek for grace." Charles Finney said, "Evermore the law must prepare the way for the gospel..."

Never forget that a Christ-less, cross-less, blood-less message will result in spine-less, defence-less and power-less church goers with the nickname Christian. For too long, premature Christians (what the Scriptures call: tares, goats or accursed children) have been birthed who have no real knowledge of salvation or of God and soon become entangled by the cares of this life, the deceitfulness of riches, or they fall away under trials and tribulations. Other writers call them 'spurious Christians,' 'dummy Christians' or 'adulterous' or 'false converts.' Jonathan Goforth of China, called those with a 'give me' attitude 'rice Christians' as some people are offered inducements to come to Jesus.

A. W. Tozer wrote: 'It is in my opinion that tens of thousands of people, if not millions, have been brought into some kind of religious experience by accepting Christ, and they have not been saved!'

Preach the Gospel – Not a False Message

We should not preach a false gospel message of 'easy believism,' 'self-improvement,' 'self-centredness' and 'self-indulgence,' or 'come to Jesus and all your problems will go away,' or 'come to Jesus and receive financial benefits from God.' Whilst there are many benefits in Christ Jesus (of peace and joy, acceptance in Christ, having a lighter yoke etc.), we should preach the entire gospel, not just a 'pick and mix' gospel and declare that each individual has to take up their own cross daily and follow Him, and that those who live godly in Christ Jesus will suffer persecution.

Far too many people who call themselves Christians do not live up to His name. If following Jesus had legal requirements, many Christians would be charged and fined under The Trade Description Act; they are not Christ-like, godly, nor anointed. If Christianity was a crime, would there be enough evidence to convict you?[3]

A successful preacher was listening to the silver-tongued orator from Tennessee, Dr. Robert G. Lee, but soon felt bad about his own sermon delivery. He spoke to Oswald J. Smith and asked him if he wrote out and memorised his sermons, would they be improved? Smith replied, "Listen! You don't need to be eloquent to be a successful evangelist. You want to be as forceful as you can, speaking as if you believed in your own message. Now, if you can do that, why worry about being eloquent?"[4]

William C. Burns saw revival across Scotland, during 1839-1841 and in 1847 became a missionary in China, where he also saw revival. Preaching on Ezekiel 37 (the valley of dry bones) at St Leonard's Church on 11 March during the Perth Revival (1840) he said, "Ah, here is the strength of the minister of the gospel. He prays for the Spirit of the Lord, that it would come down and bless the Word, causing the seed to spring up and bear fruit; and when the Spirit does accompany the words, how marvellous are its effects. It breathes on the slain, they live, and 'stand on their feet, an exceeding great army.' It is sad when ministers do not come from the secret place to the pulpit, for then they do not come with the fullness of the Spirit. Pray much for us, that all who preach the gospel be much burdened in prayer, yea, live in prayer for the descent of the Spirit, and the blessing of the Holy Ghost, or else we may as well not preach to you at all."[5]

Whilst we are called to give honour to whom honour is due, there are those who idolise revivalists, yet choose not to live up to the message that those same revivalists brought. That which is found in the Holy Bible: repentance, faith in Christ, forsaking all known sin, holiness, purity of heart and being endued with the Spirit of God. But all virtue, power and glory belong to God and to Him alone through the ministries of fully surrendered vessels that became known (and are known) as revivalists.

Chapter Twenty-Six

Warnings and Wisdom

The Two Kingdom's Clash

Physical phenomena, bodily manifestations should not be sought, but whenever the Holy Spirit comes, they will be seen, to a lesser or greater degree. When the Holy Spirit comes there will be a clash between the Kingdom of God and the kingdom of darkness. Physical phenomena can be from God, the devil or of the flesh when over excited humans work it up. This can be attention seeking or trying to be part of the crowd, not wanting to be the odd one out, as some believe that if they imitate phenomena, what they see around them, then they too will receive a touch from God, not realising that the phenomena is a result of God touching people and not the other way round. Bishop Thomas Birch Freeman during the Gold Coast Revival (1875-1878) in Ghana (and beyond) held 'conventions with his leaders advising them how to act during the various phases of the revival in progress. Lest the people should come to view that loud cries and tremblings as a necessary part, or as adjuncts to conversion, he exhorted them to guard against all unnecessary excitement.'[1]

There is also a combination of the flesh and the devil which can be hard to distinguish. A manifestation may be demonic in its origin but flow into the flesh, whereas at other times it begins in the flesh and then becomes demonic. If a person is under the influence of demons / evil spirits then they need deliverance. If someone is trying to 'work up' a blessing then they should be taken to one side and gently spoken to out of a pastor's heart of love and compassion.

God's presence affects people differently and if they have demons or are under the influence of the evil one then the demons will manifest. This is true not only in times of revival, but in a church meeting or a Christian conference, demons may play up, cause a scene, or will try to get out of God's presence as fast as they can – with or without their human host! In any move of God there will be a minority who willingly or unwillingly attempt to bring the work of God into contempt. More often than not it is because these people are under the influence of the evil one and have been taken captive by him to do his will.

Christians cannot be possessed, that is completely taken over like Legion from Gadarenes (Mark 5:1-20), yet many Christians still need deliverance, because at the point of conversion we are not always automatically delivered. Many Christians have weak spots, areas which they have never allowed God to touch or have chosen not to fully surrender to Him. Even Spirit-filled Christians may still have demons / evil spirits. These demons may have come in prior to conversion or after conversion, through an entry point of habitual sin, an open doorway which gave the enemy a legal entry point into their life or during a time of fear or trauma. *Discipleship For Everyday Living,* chapters 40 and 48 covers this subject.

The Audience and Mystical Experiences

In any Christian meeting there can be too much emphasis on some things and not on others. Naturally if we attend a conference on healing, then the focus will be on healing. But within revival, the focus must always be on Christ, the cross, repentance, getting the sin out of our lives, worshiping the Lord, holiness and everything else should be subservient.

In any Christian meeting, there will be a wide variety of people and it is unwise to constantly share one's deep spiritual or mystical experiences. Some present are just babes in Christ, probably the majority, who have not grasped or applied the basic biblical truths. By constantly sharing these experiences these young Christians may think that the central emphasis of Christianity is on experiences and encounters, but from Scripture we know that it is becoming Christ-like; hence why the focus must always come back to Christ and the cross and not a person and their experiences. Would we teach at PhD level to those who are still in middle school? The apostle Paul in a letter to the Corinthian Church made reference to one who was caught up to the third heaven – a vision of paradise (2 Corinthians 12:1-5), but he didn't dwell on his experience or elaborate, but moved on.

John Piper wrote: 'Oh, Lord, forbid that we should lose our biblical bearings; forbid that we become trendy or faddish and begin to substitute the sand of experience for the rock of revealed truth. Show us the fullness of the power of the gospel, Lord, and keep us from preoccupation with secondary things, no matter how spectacular.'[2]

An Experience, Personalities and Spiritual Gifts

There is a difference between those who come to seek an experience at a meeting and those who come to seek the Lord and it is to the latter category that we should belong. We are to bring our sacrifices of praise and our very lives as an offering to God – we should not go to a meeting as receivers, but givers – givers of ourselves. We should all prepare ourselves before we come to the house of the Lord, but especially before we partake of the Lord's Supper, lest we be found unworthy and bring judgment on ourselves.

There are some Christians who come to a meeting or conference only to seek a personality or for an impartation or anointing; rather than looking for Christ and the benefits of the teaching. An anointing can only come by personal sacrifice and paying the cost, spiritually speaking. God does not fill dirty vessels and an impure impartation can be transferred through the laying on of hands if the imparter has evil spirits, because areas of their lives have not been dealt with. A speaker may have the gift of knowledge but can also be influenced or moved by a spirit of divination or a familiar spirit; the latter two can be just as accurate as the first, though the source is demonic and not of the Spirit of God.

God cannot be bought and we cannot purchase His blessing, a healing, a prophetic word or an anointing – this is simony, the sin which Simon the former sorcerer fell into and he had been converted and baptised in the revival at Samaria, see Acts 8. There are personalities who prostitute their gifts whilst some specialise in fortune telling and divination under the guise of words of knowledge, words of wisdom or prophetic utterances. Some false preachers, teachers and apostles bring in just enough truth so as not to arouse suspicion, whilst some genuine Christian workers have a mixture in their gifting which are contaminated and polluted by the enemy. This makes it more difficult to discern the wheat from the chaff, the precious from the vile and the clean from the unclean. Appearances can be deceptive.

We may have begun to run the race well, but let us beware of being tripped up or stumbling near the finish line, otherwise we will not receive our full reward. Let us be careful and cautious as we are our own worst enemy.

Andrew Strom wrote: 'Deep repentance, daring faith and 'agonising,' spirit-filled prayer have always been the keys to genuine revival in any age and this of course applies to everybody, not just to those in ministry.'

'...The difference between revivals that are true and those that are false [are]: One is centred around the cross and deep repentance and holiness and death to self, as well as forgiveness, cleansing and infilling of the Holy Spirit – who is the Spirit of holiness. The other is centred around excitement and soulishness and the seeking after 'experiences' for their own sake – often with selfish agendas – "Bless me God," or "Give me more," rather than a focus on getting right with God.'[3]

Caught up in the Atmosphere

In any Christian meeting or conference we must be aware of being caught up in the atmosphere where emotions can override our level of discernment, or where peer pressure or manipulation can lead us to participate in things which we feel uncomfortable with, as we disregard the small still voice of the Holy Spirit. There are a minority who use techniques and methods, which whilst they should not be used, are used to stimulate and move emotions so that we do something or are more prone to do something than if these techniques and methods were not in operation. This is very applicable in regards to soliciting finances, "Give now, hurry!" "Write that cheque (check) and bring it to the front!" These appeals may go direct towards the heartstrings, "If you don't give, the ministry will go under..." and / or end in coercion which is plain manipulation, "...You will be responsible!" These appeals often bypass our intelligence which prompts us to be led of our emotions (or out of fear) rather than of the Spirit.

We should be generous givers, but let us be wise givers who sow into fertile soil being led of the Spirit. Let us allow

God to guide us so that we make the right choices when we invest into His Kingdom, building on solid foundations with Christ at the centre, with ministers of truth and integrity.

What Message do we Give Out?
Millions of churches around the globe are full of people who diligently and faithfully attend Sunday worship and yet are not part of the family of God. They are church-goers with the nickname Christian and they are unregenerate – in heart and lifestyle. But, is it any wonder that thrill seekers turn up at meetings or conferences to have an experience which can tickle their emotions and raise the hairs on the back of their neck? Should we blame these people for their spurious conversions when we have not been preaching the gospel in truth and purity, with Christ, the cross, His shed blood and full surrender at the core of the message?

If we preach Christ and Him crucified; the law and grace, the judgment and mercy of God, repentance, sacrifice and full surrender then we will not end up wealthy or popular. Those in Christian ministry who live like Hollywood stars or Premier League footballers should look at their message – is it New Testament Christianity as revealed by John the Baptist, Jesus, Peter & the apostle Paul or another gospel?

The Bible tells us to 'test the spirits' and warns us of: tares, wolves, accursed children, hirelings and false: prophets, teachers and apostles. From this we can deduct that not all those who profess the name of Jesus Christ are genuine and loyal to the King and His cause and have a variety of motives for teaching or preaching about Him and His message whilst cloaking their sermons in Christian verbiage.

Some teachers, preachers, apostles or prophets are just out and out false, whilst others are lopsided in their teaching, focusing more on some aspects rather than others which are equally or if not more important. The apostle Paul wrote: "The Lord knows those who are His" (2 Timothy 2:19), but often we don't. Life does not consist in the abundance of our possessions (Luke 12:15), but of our wealth in Christ, the unsearchable riches of Christ. Let us keep focused on Christ and be like the Bereans who didn't believe something just because a preacher said so, but 'searched the Scriptures daily to find out whether these things were so' (Acts 17:11).

The Upheaval of Revival

Revival is not the romantic ideal which many Christians make it out to be. Just as Jesus came as a babe, He will return as a Judge with a sword in His hand, and if we are not living right before a holy and just God, when the Refiner comes, the Holy Spirit, He will scorch / chastise before the floods will be poured out. See pages 15-16, 72, 142 and 160.

Revival can be traumatic for Christians within the Church as it really rocks the boat and sifts and shakes. The blessing of revival is to cut free and deliver, for the cleansing, purging, sifting, shaking and restoration of the Church. Judgment always begins at the house of the Lord (1 Peter 4:17) and if we are not living right, then look out!

Revival can be a solemn commotion and a Divine disorder all at the same time; with some rejoicing that the Holy Spirit has come whilst others are on their faces before a holy God, weeping and confessing their sins, looking to the cross and pleading for pardon in fear of the wrath to come.

Leonard Ravenhill wrote: 'Revivals shatter the status quo. We can no more have a Spirit-born revival without a moral and spiritual upheaval than we can have an earthquake without destruction.'[4]

Charles H. Spurgeon said, "A dead calm is our enemy, a storm may prove our helper. Controversy may arouse thought, and through thought may come the Divine change."[5]

Dr. John White in *When the Spirit Comes With Power* wrote: 'My main theme has to do with the Church's panicky flight at the approach of revival, and the failure to recognise it when God sends it. Revival has dangers. But our fear may lead us to reject what God sends. We must not neglect power because it has dangers.

'The greatest fear in some quarters is that what appears to be the power of God may be nothing more than a massive hoax by the enemy. It is a fear that is paralysing whole segments of the Church, a dread that debilitates, that causes our hands to hang slack and our feet to lag, at a time when the trumpet calls for advance and attack.'[6]

Chapter Twenty-Seven

Hindrances to Revival

The Greatest Enemy

Many Christians are happy with the status quo and attending church is just a ritual. There are also many church-goers with the nickname Christian, those who have never been born again, let alone, fully surrendered, nor matured in the Lord and thus are not disciples which Jesus commanded all those who followed Him to make, "Go therefore and make disciples..." (Matthew 28:19). Jesus declared in the preceding verse, "All authority has been given to Me," yet all too often many who have made a profession of faith, live and act as if He has no authority and thus by their lack of witness and inaction deny Him. They are Christians 'who are at ease in Zion' (Amos 6:1), the 'complacent ones' (Isaiah 32:9-15). Like the tribes of Gilead, Dan and Asher the 'curse' of 'Meroz' is pronounced against them by the Lord 'because they did not come to the help of the Lord...' in the work He has now delegated to the Church (Judges 5:17, 23).

It has been said that the greatest enemy to each individual is self – self that has not surrendered to God – we have not offered our bodies as 'living sacrifices' which is merely our reasonable service (Romans 12:1), nor taken up our cross daily and followed the Master. All too often it is not Thy will be done, but *my will* be done. Self must be crucified and dethroned. If we truly desire to see our lives changed in personal revival – which always precedes local or national revival, then we must die to self.

Oh, God, "Send revival, and start the work in me," should be our cry to our heavenly Father, whose will should be done on earth, as it is in heaven. "I must decrease and He must increase," should also be our declaration, repeating the words of John the Baptist – the revivalist (John 3:30).

Evan Roberts who was used in the 1904-1905 Welsh Revival, in his later years wrote: 'The baptism of the Holy

Spirit is the essence of revival, for revival comes from knowledge of the Holy Spirit and the way of co-working with Him which enables Him to work in revival power. The primary condition of revival is therefore that believers should individually know the baptism of the Holy Ghost.'[1]

God does not give the Spirit by measure (John 3:34) and has promised to give the Holy Spirit to those that ask Him (Luke 11:13). It is the responsibility of each and every believer to be endued with power from on high (Acts 1:8), but He only gives the Holy Spirit to those who obey Him (Acts 5:32). Do you obey God? Have you been endued with power from on high? See *Holy Spirit Power* by Paul Backholer (2013). I was once asked if I had received the Holy Spirit which I answered in the affirmative. I was then immediately asked, "Does the Holy Spirit have you?" which I had to answer in the negative – and that got me thinking.

Putting Sin Away
In March 1962, Rev. Geoffrey R. King gave the presidential address at the Annual Assembly of the London Baptist Association. He said, "There can be no quickening of the power of the Holy Spirit in church, home or individual life unless and until we deal faithfully with sin. In the New Testament the Church was separated from the world and was thus able to reach the world. Vain the lifeboat when the sea gets into it. Only in separation can it be a means of saving. Consider what I say."[2]

Nicky Cruz wrote: 'For too long Christians have conformed to the world. We have allowed the world not only to *affect* us but to completely *infect* us. To take over our hearts and minds and keep us in bondage to sin, even though we convince ourselves that we're free.'[3]

Octavius Winslow wrote: 'If a child of God restrains prayer, he opens the door to the departure of every grace and to the admission of every sin…. It should be remembered by every professing man, that there is a great difference between prayer and praying; we mean, between the formal observance of the duty and the spiritual character of the observance.'[4]

Beware of the gradual decay of grace in your own life which catches you unaware. You may appear outwardly vitalised, but inwardly you are decaying. Octavius Winslow wrote: '...No child of God ever receded into a state of inward declension and outward backsliding, but by slow and gradual steps and...that a process of spiritual decay may be going forward within the secret recesses of the soul....'[5]

Oswald J. Smith wrote: 'No sooner have I dealt with sin than I am compelled to deal with self. And so must you. God insists on having first place. Where then do you stand in relation to His will? Have you really surrendered all to Jesus Christ? Do you recognise Him alone as your Lord and Master? Are you willing to go, where He wants you to go, to do what He wants you to do, and to be what He wants you to be? Have you still a will of your own, or is God's will yours and is it your supreme delight to please Him? Who holds the reins of your life? Who controls your actions? In your choices and decisions, is God the *dictator? Or are you?'[6] *The one who dictates, not a tyrannical leader.

Why No Revival?
There could be hundreds of reasons as to why there is no revival, but the responsibility lies with us, individuals, members of the body of Christ, the Church, those who choose not to forsake sin, nor press in and plead for God to come and heal our land. Revival is first and foremost for the Church so that it can be revived and reflect Christ. As someone once said, "The hindrances to revivals are the sins of the individuals." See also chapter twenty-eight, Why Revivals Cease. An evangelist once asked his friend, "Do you know of any great hindrances to revival?" the person replied, "Yes. I know of *one* very great hindrance – myself!"

J. Edwin Orr wrote: 'If we are not *positively* channels through which the Spirit pours revival blessing on others, then we are hindrances to the work of God. There is no neutral position. Let us face the question squarely. Let there be no evasion.'[7]

Leonard Ravenhill in his book, *Sodom had no Bible* wrote: 'I offer it as my considered judgment that the main reason why we do not have heaven-born, Spirit-operated revival in our day is that we are content to live without it.'

Stephen F. Olford speaking on 'The Price of Revival' at Westminster Chapel, London, in September 1946, said, "We must face up to the dishonesties of life. Think, for a moment of the dishonesties of lying – that is, any species of designed deception. How many times a day do we lie, in thought, word or deed? Then there is the dishonesty of hypocrisy, pretending to be what we are not, in our prayers, confessions, messages and the like. Another serious dishonesty is that of thieving, or robbing God, by misspent money and squandered hours, which God gave us to serve Him in the winning of souls…. Also, am I out of place, or out of adjustment to the will of God – in relation to my personal life? Family life? Church life? Social life? Business life? Recreative life?…If we are out of adjustment at any one point, let the Christ of Gethsemane teach us to pray, 'Thy will be done.' These are heavy demands, but they constitute what is entailed in seeing revival. Indeed this is the price of revival!"[8]

John D. Drysdale wrote: 'The greatest hindrance to deep, permanent, and spreading revival are carnality and worldliness in ministers and church members…There are many others in our churches who are a decided hindrance to revival; the great army of non-effectives; the well-behaved, do-nothing people, who take up pew room on Sundays (at least once a day) but are never seen at a prayer meeting, or the open-air meeting; nor are they particularly interested in the evangelisation of the heathen. Such people weigh heavily upon the heart of spiritual ministers; they are the devil's instruments of discouragement.'[9]

Rev. Douglas Brown was used in the East Anglia Revival (1921-1922) in England and the Fishermen's Revival (1922) in Scotland. He said, "If you have men in your pulpits who doubt the Bible, the deity of Christ, the atonement, the great fundamentals of your faith, you can't get revival."[10]

Charles G. Finney was the great American revivalist of the 1820s-1860s. His greatest work was his *Lectures on Revival* (also known as *Revival of Religion*) which was written from experience and practical observation during revivals. Finney knew that the way to help promote revival was to break up one's 'fallow ground for it is time to seek the Lord, till He comes and rains righteousness on you' (Hosea 10:12).

Hindrances to Seeing Revival – by Charles Finney
- Ingratitude, want of love towards God, neglect of the Bible, unbelief, neglect of prayer, neglect of the means of grace (silly and futile excuses as to why you cannot attend religious meetings).
- Performing Christian duties, such as prayer and Bible reading in a worldly frame of mind, in such carelessness that you can not remember what you prayed or read.
- A lack of love for fellow believers and no concern for the unconverted.
- Neglect of family duties (setting a bad example before them, not reading the Bible to your children, or praying with and for them).
- Neglect of watchfulness over your own life, sinning before the world, the church and before God!
- Neglect to watch over the brethren, unconcerned for their state of soul, not reproving them in love over their lukewarm attitude or blatant sin.
- Neglect of self denial in any areas especially in regards to serving the Lord.
- Worldly mindedness, pride, slander, envy, censoriousness (a bitter spirit), levity (lack of respect for God). Lying, cheating, hypocrisy or bad temper. Finney's definition of lying was: any calculated deceit; if you try to convey an impression contrary to the truth, you lie.
- Robbing God, in time, money (tithes and offerings), misapplying your talents and power of mind, wasting your precious resources (on smoking etc.).
- Hindering others from being useful, wasting their time (especially the minister), destroying fellow believers confidence, playing into Satan's hand – repent and confess immediately.

- Taking sides against another Christian when a non-believer bad mouths / speaks evil of them.
- Neglecting the claims of world mission; being focussed only on their own field of labour, their own church, their own circle of ministry.
- A dishonouring of the Sabbath and or fighting against the Temperance Reformation – a group who were against alcohol consumption.

During the Ruanda Revival (1937-1950s), at one mission station; two missionaries had been for a long time estranged from one another. During the 1937 Easter Convention, the Holy Spirit showed one of the missionaries her guilt and she went and apologised to her fellow labourer. The two were immediately reconciled and went straight away to a meeting which was attended by a large number of village evangelists. They testified of what God had done for them. A. C. Stanley Smith wrote: 'It seemed as though their simple but costly testimony opened the floodgates of Divine power.... The striking fact was not how much missionaries can help the work of God, but how much they can hinder it.'[11]

Rev. Duncan Campbell in the conclusion to his narrative about the Lewis Revival (1949-1952) wrote: 'One who though mightily used of God, did not escape the bitter opposition of leaders in the Church: "I verily believe revival would have come to – [unnamed village or town] at that time if prayerful sympathy, instead of carnal criticism had been shown. If only those who opposed had gone to hear for themselves, how different the story might have been today!'[12]

The Wisdom of J. Edwin Orr
J. Edwin Orr was one of just a handful of revivalists who saw revival across the decades and on different continents. Edwin Orr had a varied ministry, including teaching and preaching on revival across half a century. He wrote: 'The greatest hindrance to revival is *sin*...There are sins of the flesh – impurity of thought, impurity of words, impurity of deed. There are sins of that unruly member, the tongue – lying, deceit, spiteful talk. How many fall into pride; and then hypocrisy. Sometimes there is a heavy burden upon our

consciences, some deceit, some theft; some disgrace....
There is lack of love...prayerlessness.... And now to deal
with the greatest hindrance of all. We may have sinned in a
hundred ways, and we may confess our sins; but lack of faith
can rob us of victory...unbelief – what a terrible snare....
Unbelief is sin, (Hebrews 3:12 and Romans 4:20)...Faith is
the victory. Unbelief is defeat.... Are you praying for revival?
Are you revived?... Lord send a revival, but begin now in
me.'[13]

J. Edwin Orr was asked by a Danish newspaper editor,
"What in your opinion is the greatest hindrance to world-
revival?" To which he responded, "...the indifference of
believers themselves. Revival will come to us – only by the
way of *obedience* to the Word, of living faith, and of
unceasing *prayer* – when as Paul wrote in Romans 12:1, we
present our bodies as a living, holy, and God-acceptable
sacrifice."[14]

J. Edwin Orr, in response to the question, "Why is it that God
does not hear our prayers for revival?" wrote: 'Because of
your inconsistencies.... Is the Almighty (I ask it reverently)
deaf to His pleading people? Or are God's people deaf to a
pleading God? Which? – I know which. Hypocrisy and
humbug make the so-called prayers for revival so much hot
air.... Stop and think a moment. The lack of revival in *your*
district, in *your* church, in *your own* life is due not to God's
failure, but to yours. Dare you tell me that God denies revival
to a heart that is willing to pay the price?'[15]

Commenting on his ministry in South Africa during 1936, J.
Edwin Orr wrote: 'One thing I know – in my own campaigns,
there was revival in varying degrees always in proportion to
the willingness of the Christians to pay the price. Where
there was little blessing, there were hindrances: where there
was much blessing, there was eagerness.'[16]

J. Edwin Orr wrote: 'Too often there is the desire for
denominational revival, a selfish desire which has no
fulfilment. It is when we want to see the body of Christ

receive a time of refreshing from the presence of the Lord that our hopes have a prospect of fulfilment.'[17]

Unconditional Surrender

If you confess that Jesus Christ is Lord then you must allow Him to be in control. Full and unconditional surrender to the will of God; putting to death the old man and exchanging your life for His; a giving of yourself to be entirely at His disposal and to hate the things of the world so that they have no hold over you (1 John 2:15-17); so that you can live entirely for the glory of God and to be led of the Holy Spirit.

G. D. Watson (1845-1924) was a Wesleyan Methodist minister and evangelist. He wrote: 'If God has called you to be truly like Jesus in all your spirit, He will draw you into a life of crucifixion and humility. He will put on you such demands of obedience that you will not be allowed to follow other Christians. In many ways, He seems to let other good people do things which He will not let you do. Others who seem to be very religious and useful may push themselves, pull wires, and scheme to carry out their plans, but you cannot. If you attempt it, you will meet with such failure and rebuke from the Lord as to make you sorely penitent.

'Others can brag about themselves, their work, their successes, their writings, but the Holy Spirit will not allow you to do any such thing. If you begin to do so, He will lead you into some deep mortification that will make you despise yourself and all your good works.

'Others will be allowed to succeed in making great sums of money, or having a legacy left to them, or in having luxuries, but God may supply you only on a day-to-day basis, because He wants you to have something far better than gold, a helpless dependence on Him and His unseen treasury.

'The Lord may let others be honoured and put forward while keeping you hidden in obscurity because He wants to produce some choice, fragrant fruit for His coming glory, which can only be produced in the shade. God may let others be great, but keep you small. He will let others do a work for Him and get the credit, but He will make you work and toil on without knowing how much you are doing. Then, to make your work still more precious, He will let others get the credit for the work which you have done; this is to teach you the message of the cross, humility, and something of the value of being cloaked with His nature.

'The Holy Spirit will put a strict watch on you, and with a jealous love rebuke you for careless words and feelings, or for wasting your time which other Christians never seem distressed over. So make up your mind that God is an infinite Sovereign and has a right to do as He pleases with His own, and that He may not explain to you a thousand things which may puzzle your reason in His dealings with you.

'God will take you at your word; if you absolutely sell yourself to be His slave, He will wrap you up in a jealous love and let other people say and do many things that you cannot. Settle it forever; you are to deal directly with the Holy Spirit, He is to have the privilege of tying your tongue or chaining your hand or closing your eyes in ways which others are not dealt with. However, know this great secret of the Kingdom: When you are so completely possessed with the Living God that you are, in your secret heart, pleased and delighted over this peculiar, personal, private, jealous guardianship and management of the Holy Spirit over your life, you will have found the vestibule of heaven, the high calling of God.'[18]

That is Victory

Albert D. Helser became a missionary in 1923 and worked in the Sudan for seventeen years. He wrote: 'When you are forgotten or neglected, or purposely set at naught and you smile inwardly glorying in the insult or the oversight, because thereby you are counted worthy to suffer for Christ – that is victory. When your good is evil spoken of, when your wishes are crossed, your taste offended, your advice disregarded, your opinions ridiculed and you take it all in patient loving silence – that is victory.

'When you are content with any food, any raiment, any climate, any society, any solitude and any interruption by the will of God – that is victory. When you lovingly and patiently bear with any disorder, irregularity, any unpunctuality, or any annoyance – that is victory.

'When you never care to refer to yourself in conversation or to record your own good works, or to itch after commendation; when you can truly love to be unknown – that is victory. When you can stand face to face with waste, folly, extravagance, spiritual insensitivity and endure it all as Jesus endured it – that is victory.

'When like Paul, you can throw all your suffering on Jesus, thus converting it into a means of knowing His overcoming grace and can say from a surrendered heart, "Most gladly, therefore, do I take pleasure in infirmities, in reproaches, in necessities, in persecutions for Christ's sake" – that is victory (2 Corinthians 12:7, 11).

'To love equally as much the grace that comes through being 'instructed how to be hungry' and how to suffer, as you love the faith required to know how to be 'full' and to abound in health – that is victory.

'When death and life are both alike to you through Christ, and to do His perfect will, you delight not more in one than in the other – that is victory; for, through Him you may be able to say, "Christ shall be magnified in my body, whether it be by life or by death" (Philippians 1:20 and 1 Cor. 15:54).

'The perfect victory is to 'put on the Lord Jesus Christ' and thus triumph over one's self (Romans 13:14). 'In all these things we are more than conquerors through Him who loved us' (Romans 8:37). He knows, He loves, He cares – nothing this truth can dim; He gives the very best to those who leave the choice with Him.'[19]

Rev. Duncan Campbell preaching during the Lewis Revival (1949-1952) said, "One of the facts that we have to face in the life of the Spirit is this; that public sentiment is against God, and if we are to follow the Saviour and walk in His footsteps, we must set our face against public sentiments."[20]

One preacher said, "The great hindrance to God pouring out His Spirit in Pentecostal power on many a convention of God's people is simply a refusal on their part to be broken."

Bible teacher, Derek Prince, speaking on Isaiah 40:3-4 (preparing the way of the Lord) in the context of God reviving the Church said, "You and I are going to have to determine whether we will be channels for His glory or mountains that hold it out?"

Chapter Twenty-Eight

Why Revivals Cease

A Time for Everything
Ecclesiastes chapter three reveals that 'to everything there is a season, a time for every purpose under heaven.' Just like the tide that ebbs and flows in relation to the moon's position, so too revival has its seasons. This is not to say that at regular intervals revival will appear, but merely that it has its season to end, just as there is 'a time to be born and a time to die, a time to plant and a time to pluck what is planted' (Ecclesiastes 3:2). There is a time for revival and a time when each individual revival wanes or ceases. The Church is either how it should be (for a period of time) or sin has grieved the Holy Spirit and He departs.

Why do Revivals Cease?
Why do revivals cease? Hundreds of reasons could be given but they can be listed under three categories:
1. Sin – Members of the Church, but especially leaders committing sins of commission or sins of omission. Doing things which should not be done: lying, stealing, cheating, boasting, committing adultery etc. and neglecting things which ought to be done: Bible reading, prayer, evangelism, missions, tithing, assisting the poor, orphans & widows etc.
2. Breaking physical laws – Neglecting the needs of the body, especially the leadership or those on the frontline who have additional responsibilities or pressures and are under constant spiritual attack. A lack of rest, sleep deprivation, not eating a balanced diet (or eating at irregular hours), lack of exercise and fresh air can lead to a physical breakdown, a heart attack, illness or burnout. Nobody is invincible and spiritual adrenaline or spiritual hyperactivity will only last so long before something gives. See pages 57, 109 and 206.
3. A revival has run its course – The Church is now revived and the subnormal Church is now the normal Church.

Common Causes for Revival to Cease

The most probable reason why any revival will cease is when those involved become complacent and prideful in action and attitude and thus take the revival for granted. Never be foolish enough to boast and brag about the sparks that you have kindled, and walk in the light of your own fire! (Isaiah 50:11). If you neglect the One who is a Consuming Fire then the work of God will soon fizzle out, because the Spirit will be grieved. Never trust in your own works rather than the Spirit of Grace and Supplication, the Baptiser in fire!

To keep a revival burning and blazing hot it must be continually fed and stoked by prayer, humility, abiding fellowship and the observance of the commandments of God. It is possible to be so caught up in the things of God that apathy sets in, and the wrong mindset comes over us, "No need to pray, God is here to stay." He won't stay where He is taken for granted, neglected, grieved or not wanted.

There is also a big danger in being led of our emotions rather than of the Spirit of God. Revival and any move of the Holy Spirit are time consuming events – time just flies, but there is a danger in neglecting essential aspects of the human body, such as food and rest. Though man can not live on bread alone, but by every Word of God (Luke 4:4), without nourishment, he will surely deteriorate.

Most people even in the midst of revival will have family to care for and a job to hold down. Let us not become so spiritual that we become of no earthly good. A tired man is an unhappy man and it is difficult to be a light in the world if we stay up all night. We must learn to pace ourselves, whilst running the race so that we can obtain the prize and enjoy it!

Diluting the precious Word of God will also stop a revival; sin needs to be called sin and truth needs to be thundered from the pulpit as well as the streets. Revival rocks the boat and often upsets it, but vain is the lifeboat which is filled with the seas of worldliness. Any unworthy boat or ship that is unable to contain the precious holy cargo will sink.

There will be opposition and bad press, levelled not only at revival, but especially the revivalist or leaders at the fore. If they begin to move in the flesh, revival can stop. If you're part of 'a great work' like Nehemiah; don't waste your time with opponents. 'Why should the work cease...?' (Nehemiah

6:3-4) and reply graciously (if at all) like George Whitefield did to one of his accusers: 'I thank you heartily for your letter. As for what you and my other enemies are saying against me, I know worse things about myself than you will ever say about me. With love in Christ, George Whitefield.'

Why a Revival Would Cease by Charles Finney

- When the church thinks revival will cease, it will. It does not matter what enemies say or believe, but if the church loses its faith, it will lose the revival.
- When Christians consent that it will cease, it will. But if they see the danger, which drives them to their knees in agony and concern, it can be avoided.
- When the church stops to speculate and argue about abstract doctrines that have no bearing upon practice.
- When anything distracts the attention of the church, even the appearance of an angel.
- The church taking wrong ground on some great moral question such as slavery [homosexuality, abortion etc. – author's note].
- Ecclesiastical difficulties, the revivalist is called away from the work [or not permitted to return] to answer charges before his [or her] superiors regarding the use of new methods etc.
- When Christians become proud of their 'great revival' in what they have done!
- When Christians begin to proselytise to their denomination, stirring up sectarian difficulties, promoting this or that denomination.
- The Spirit may be grieved by boasting of the revival, to puff up the church; the pastor foolishly writing to the local newspapers [or emailing everyone / social media, having impure motives].
- Some, under pretence of publishing things to the glory of God, have (often unknowingly) exalted themselves or their denomination.
- When Christians lack brotherly and sisterly love, one for another.

- Christians of all denominations should lay aside all prejudices. Prejudices hinder the person so that they cannot come to a correct understanding on the subject and are unable to correctly pray in this state of mind.
- A protracted meeting should be conducted throughout by the same minister (or evangelist) if possible. Sometimes through courtesy, visiting ministers are invited to speak and there has been no blessing as they did not come in a state of mind which was right for such a work. [This was evident on some nights in the Lakeland Outpouring, 2008].
- When Christians become mechanical in their attempts to promote revival and prayer begins to wane, praying without emotion as before.
- When the minister does not pour out fire (arousing passionate preaching) upon the hearers, when he is behind the pulpit.
- When the church becomes exhausted by the labour, neglect to eat and sleep at the proper hours and let the excitement runaway with them so that they become exhausted and their bodies or mind give way and breakdown. [This is what happened to Evan Roberts of the Welsh Revival, 1904-1905].
- When Christians do not feel their dependence on the Holy Spirit, believing they can do the work in their own strength, or promoting themselves or their ministry instead of the Lord.
- A revival will decline and cease, unless Christians are frequently revived – frequently convicted and humbled and broken down before God.
- Revivals can be put down by the continued opposition of the old school, combined with a bad spirit in the new school. When those who are for or against a revival battle it out, with a bad spirit, printing articles and rebuttals in the papers for public viewing. Those who are engaged in revival should keep to the work [Nehemiah 6:3] and mind their own business when they or the work are slandered, as it is God who vindicates.

Chapter Twenty-Nine

Revival Merchandise and Memorabilia

Merchandise, Memorabilia and Christian Workers

It was during the Brownsville Revival (1995-2000) that the author was first made aware of revival merchandise and memorabilia. At the time, some websites and individuals questioned the commercial motives of the Brownsville Church and some of the revivalists themselves.

There are some people who believe that if merchandise or memorabilia is for sale within a church building or is connected in any way to a revival, then they assume that it is not a move of God, but merely a money making venture, but this is largely unfounded and untrue.

There are those who strongly object to Christians making money, especially during times of revival, via books, DVDs or music CDs etc., but is it not fair to say that a worker is worthy of his wage? Does not the school teacher as well as the shelf stacker get a wage for the hours they have worked?

Large types of revival merchandise such as Christian: books, music, DVDs etc., edify and build up the body of Christ which is an aim of Christian ministry; after conversion, to make strong and healthy disciples, to bring to a full stature and knowledge of Christ. Also, if a lay worker is in secular employment in order to pay the bills and feed the family, is it so wrong that a Christian worker (like the apostle Paul) supplements or earns an income in order to survive? Those within Christian ministry have bills to be paid, just like the next person; mouths to feed, children to clothe and others who need assistance. Let us not forget that not all Christian workers get a guaranteed salary, or even a wage. Jesus had a team of faithful supporters to meet His and the disciples needs (Luke 8:1-3). The apostle Paul on occasions reverted to his trade as a tent maker in order to live (Acts 18:1-3) because he never wanted to be a financial burden to anyone. Did he sell the tents, or give them away for free? It could be asked, was tent making the most effective use of the apostle Paul's time? If he had had more support would he have planted more churches and written more letters?

In the early days of the Argentine Revival (1982-1997) it was the poor and the destitute that filled the plots of land and later the stadiums which were brightly illuminated and pleasing to the eye, a crowd drawer for the evangelistic campaigns. There were no seats which gave the people freedom to move around so that they did not become restless and there were food stalls to satisfy the natural appetites of man. Some may say that it sounds more like a fairground than an evangelistic crusade (which flowed into revival), but we all have to eat and why not in aesthetic surroundings? If Christians do no take the initiative to *supply a demand* then others will, and even Jesus fed His listeners!

Revival Merchandise

The author had always believed that revival merchandise was a recent invention; that was until November 2006 when he revisited Moriah Chapel in Loughor, South Wales, the site where the Welsh Revival (1904-1905) broke out on 31 October. He was looking in a cabinet which had been displayed for the Centenary Celebrations. Inside the cabinet were revival postcards of Evan Roberts, his brother and some of the lady helpers, which had been published at the time by the *Western Mail* newspaper, alongside other revival related items of memorabilia including books and porcelain.

On 4 November 1904, Evan Roberts wrote to the editor of the *Sunday Companion* asking for a quotation for a visible representation of his visions on printed postcards which would give the message wider circulation. On an internet auction website the *starting* bids for these revival related postcards generally range from £3-20 ($4-26) with an exchange rate of £1 = $1.3 U.S. dollars (August 2021).

The revival curators at Moriah Chapel have done a superb job in accumulating and displaying the 1904-1905 revival merchandise in the school room (where the revival broke out), including: books (some of which are rare), postcards, paper cuttings or photocopies and revival hymn books etc. But what most surprised the author, was a white mug with Evan Roberts face and shoulders emblazoned on it. It had been bought in an antique shop in Mumbles (ten miles away), it was produced in and around the time of the revival and was in the cabinet display. Also, cotton handkerchiefs with the face of Evan Roberts were manufactured as was a Staffordshire figurine similar to the busts of other revivalists.

With a little searching on the internet the author found a considerable market in revival memorabilia with many items appearing on internet auction sites. He was informed by a proprietor of a Christian shop that a single Jonathan Edwards signature sold for $25,000 (£16,660)!

In the summer of 2007, whilst searching on one site, the author came across a white cup and saucer with a black transfer of Evan Roberts on each item; just as he had seen at Moriah. The porcelain was the product of A. B. Jones and Sons, Grafton Works, (Grafton China), Longton, Staffordshire, the Grafton back-stamp was used between 1900 and 1913 which could date the cup and saucer to around 1905 or 1906, so during or just after the revival. The seller wrote: 'The condition is good with no chips, cracks, restoration or discoloration; there is some age wear to the gold lustre rims....' The cup measures 2.5" (6.5cm) high with a rim diameter of 3" (7.5cm), the saucer has a diameter of 5.5" (14cm).' The starting price for this set was £47 (approximately $94) – 2007 summer exchange rate.

For the centenary of the Welsh Revival, special porcelain plates were commissioned and famous anniversary dates connected with popular Christians such as missionary explorer David Livingstone, as well as Christian institutions like the Baptist Missionary Society and the British and Foreign Bible Society, all have their own memorabilia, including medallions, porcelain, postcards and posters.

Revival Memorabilia Collectors

There are also revival memorabilia collectors who specialise in accumulating everything in connection with a particular revival or revivalist. At the end of September 2007, the Christian Broadcasting Network (CBN) reported on the 150th anniversary of the Fulton Street Revival (1857-1859) which led to America's last great awakening. They spoke to Pastor Ted Lavigne of Kissimme, Florida, who owns the world's largest collection of memorabilia from the 1857 revival, including rare photos, studio viewer and portrait of Jeremiah Lanphier. In the collection, Pastor Ted Lavigne had a studio viewer (stereoscope) where you look at studio cards (stereographic cards) which make the object or person on the card appear in 3D. On a studio card he had Jeremiah Lanphier sat at a desk inside the lecture room of the old North Dutch Church (on the corner of Fulton and William Street, New York), where the noon-day prayer meeting began in September 1857 – the birthplace of the revival.

The studio viewer is like a diver's face mask coupled with binoculars (the viewfinder) which has a base attached (from 30-40cm long) with a sliding holder to which the studio card is placed. You look through the viewfinder and adjust the sliding holder until the picture comes into focus.

What the author found fascinating was that this revival memorabilia was incorporated into the technology of the day. Whilst studio cards are of a similar size to standard postcards, they have two identical images printed side by side, so that when they are viewed through the studio viewer, it gives a 3D image. In a similar sense, using the latest technology, it would be like having a holographic projection of a revivalist, though this would be very costly!

Methodist Memorabilia

During and after the Evangelical Revival (1739-1791) which is also known as the British Great Awakening or the Methodist Revival, on anniversary dates connected with John and Charles Wesley's birth, conversion, death, year of the awakening and the foundation of the Methodist Society; memorabilia was produced, such as: complete figurines, busts, statuettes, mugs, saucers, plates and medallions etc. some of which are more than two centuries old.

In the summer of 1839, the Centenary Jubilee was celebrated on both sides of the Atlantic, as one author wrote: 'In a spirit worthy of the memories it recalled.' In May 2007, the author visited the first Methodist Chapel in the world, The New Room founded in 1739 in Bristol, England. It is also known as John Wesley's Chapel. In the preacher's rooms upstairs, where Methodist preachers were lodged, (the stables are outside); apart from seeing Wesley's cassock, the bed that he slept in when visiting, his chair, the desk that he wrote at, a lock of his hair, numerous paintings and Methodist history etc., there was a plethora of revival memorabilia from the eighteenth and nineteenth centuries. In the nineteenth century there were at least sixty potters in Staffordshire who made porcelain figures and busts of John Wesley of various sizes – about twenty were on show in The New Room. They were from four to twelve inches in height. The reason there were so many manufactures at the time is because the demand was so great. On display there were also minted medals, medallions, handkerchiefs and many other Wesley revival memorabilia (Wesley-mania), items all manufactured in the nineteenth century. In the early twentieth century, one cigarette manufacturer even had Wesley cigarette cards! The manufacturer obviously did not realise that smoking and Christianity are at odds with each other, as the harmful effects of smoking were unknown.

In August 2007, the author visited Wesley's Cottage at Trewint, Altarnun, Cornwall, England. It is believed to be the smallest Methodist Chapel in the world and is the first place in Cornwall to accept Methodism when John Nelson and John Downes arrived on 29 August 1743 and were taken into the cottage of Digory and Elizabeth Isbell's for refreshment.

As you open the door you walk upon Cornish grey slate which had been worn smooth over the centuries. Downstairs is a fireplace, a low pulpit and chair with brass candle holders on display over the mantelpiece; an antique collecting box, ink pot and hourglass. You can also purchase your own modern reproduced John Wesley thimble, bone china plate or mug. On display there was a wooden cross which was made from wood from the home where Susanna Wesley (the mother of John and Charles) was born in 1669!

Up the flight of wooden stairs is the second floor with eleven wooden seats and two glass-fronted cabinets. The roof was only six feet four inches high and you could see the floor below through the old wooden floorboards. In 1950, the Isbell's House and Wesley Rooms, which had fallen into ruin had been restored. There were many items of revival merchandise on display which had been contributed from around the globe; including a small doll-sized effigy of John Nelson behind a pulpit encapsulated in a glass dome ornamental case; this type of merchandise the author had never seen before or since.

Behind two glass cabinets were plates (including an octagon shaped plate), porcelain figurine of Wesley in a pulpit, busts of John Wesley (the rarest Wesley busts can sell for £1000s), a teapot, large drinking cup, milk jug, John Wesley's first edition *Journal* (1769) and John Nelson's first edition *Journal* (1767), hymn books and other interesting items, all connected to John Wesley and Methodism. Also on display, in a jewellery type ring box, cushioned with cotton wool was a coin which was given to William Chenhalls by John Wesley when he was a boy – he never spent it!

On Saturday, 26 March 1785, Easter weekend, John Wesley, stayed at Ambrose Foley's house at Quinton, (twenty miles from Northampton), England. In gratitude to his hosts and their warm hospitality, Wesley presented to Mr and Mrs Foley, a tea-service. The 1890 edition of *Wesley His Own Biography, Selections From The Journals* with 450 illustrations shows that the teacups and saucers had an oriental design (Chinese), but the teapot on its side depict the face and shoulders of John Wesley (who was centred) with the inscription 'The Rev. John Wesley A.M.' with fifteen other Methodist preachers (and their surnames) encircling him with biblical scenes in the background, including two stone tablets with Roman numerals on them (Ten Commandments), the cross and an angel. Thus John Wesley, had no qualms with revival memorabilia.[1]

In the summer of 2007, the author was on an auction website where he saw a John Wesley Pulpit Figure which was dated to around 1875. It was a Staffordshire pulpit chimney breast ornament of the monumental type, having an imitation clock below a figure of John Wesley. The seller wrote: 'The manufacturer is believed to be Sampson Smith of Longton.... The figure of Wesley and the clock are in very good condition, but the other extremities of the item have suffered.... The unusual feature of this item is that the clock shows the time as being 9.35am, not 11.30am which is most common. The item had a height of 11" (28cm) and was priced at £40 (approximately $80 – mid 2007 exchange rate).

In October 2007, an internet auction website sold a John Wesley Staffordshire figurine, preaching from an open book, dated c.1850-1899 for $365 (approximately £179). It had a height of about 6.75" (16.5cm) with a base diameter of 3" (7.5cm) with 'John Wesley' inscribed on the base. The figurine had a chip and had early restoration to its hands.

In November of the same year, a John Wesley 'Rule of Conduct' Halcyon Days enamel pot sold for £77 (approximately $144). It was described as in excellent condition, size: 2.3" (5.5cm) long and 1.1" (2.5cm) tall; date of manufacture unknown; with 'John Wesley (1703-1791) Rule of Conduct' inscribed on the inside lid. The external decorated lid reads: 'Do all the good you can, by all the means you can, in all the ways you can, in all the places you can, at all the times you can, to all the people you can as long as you ever can.'

In October 2008, a Staffordshire mug commemorating the fiftieth anniversary of the death of John Wesley (1791-1841) sold for £127 (approximately $216) and was in fine original condition. It was printed in grey tones on an off-white ground with a portrait of Wesley, Centenary Hall, London, and the date and birth of Wesley around an open Bible.

In July 2008 the author was at the Moffat Mission in Kuruman, South Africa. Inside the Moffat Homestead amongst various Moffat artefacts was a 3" (7.6cm) statuette of John Wesley from 1839; (Centenary Celebration of the Evangelical Revival), the year in which Robert Moffat, a missionary to Africa for fifty-three years was in England. The accompanying display card incorrectly stated that the statuette was 'produced for the 50th anniversary celebrations in 1839' (it was the centenary) but did note that: 'Moffat was greatly influenced by the movement and was on leave in England at that time.' Thus Moffat who saw revival in 1829 at the mission, probably purchased this very item.

Billy Bray Memorabilia

In the summer of 2007, the author visited Three Eyes Chapel, Kerley Downs, near Truro, in the parish of Kea, Cornwall, England. It had been built by the revivalist Billy Bray in around 1835 and at a later date was enlarged. Its walls are adorned with Billy Bray (1794-1868) memorabilia, photos and achievements from his life including a Centenary Celebration poster of his life, 1794-1894, which had been originally collated (before being printed as a poster) from photographs and a few postcards which were evidently produced.

On sale were Billy Bray mugs, thimbles, bookmarks, a postcard of his grave (at Baldhu Church, less than one mile away), books about his life and even printed tea-towels. There were six visitor books on display which dated back to 1959, thus proving the popularity of the former drunkard turned lay-preacher's church, long after he passed into glory.

Why Revival Memorabilia?

If we did not have revival merchandise, most notably books (see chapter thirty, Why Revivals are Chronicled), then several generations down the line our ancestors may not be able to fully understand what happened in the past when God came down in revival power.

In a similar sense; talking of unknown facts, nobody knows the burial plot where Billy Bray's wife, Joey, is buried. She is interred at Baldhu Church graveyard and Billy who died four years later in 1868 possibly lay beside her – though the monument erected to the memory of Billy Bray does not state this. Everyone connected with Joey knew the burial plot at the time and therefore did not deem it necessary to put facts to paper. Whilst this issue is ever so minor, it proves the point that facts are lost when not put into print.

What Purpose Does Revival Memorabilia Serve?

There are many and varied reasons as to why some revivalists, those who are involved in the revival, the church, its members or associated ministries (and even entrepreneurs) produce revival memorabilia. It could be books (see chapter thirty), porcelain (the least common now), printed or recorded sermons; teaching tapes and CDs, videos or DVDs of the services (the most popular), or even bumper stickers, badges, greeting cards and T-shirts.

In the past, churches which have experienced revival have sold their Christian merchandise during these times of blessing within the location of the revival, such as the church foyer. Since the mid 1990s, but especially in the subsequent decade, ministry websites became very popular outlets for worldwide customers to purchase revival memorabilia.

- Books, tapes, CDs and DVDs (documented services) provide a faithful account of what has happened and can be passed on for posterity. See page 223.
- People want to know about moves of God; how it started, who was involved etc., and where there is a demand the need should be met. See page 222.
- If the revivalist does not write about their work then someone will. A book is sometimes written by the revivalist to explain fact from fiction and to address misunderstandings. See pages 220-221.
- There is always a demand for a revivalist to retell their experiences, years or even decades after the event. They cannot be in two places at once and so to meet the demand, a book is often written. Rev. David Davies from the Congo Revival (1953-1957) was still being asked to share his revival experiences six decades after the event!
- Books and DVDs etc. help fire-up those who are not yet on fire and praying for revival. A person on the other side of the world could be given the book or DVD and their life could be transformed as they read or see the wonderful workings of God. See page 220.
- Revival books and DVDs add fuel to the flames of those who are already passionate for revival and increase one's faith. They help spiritually stimulate a person to press in deeper for the things of God.
- The profits of items sold if directed back into the church where revival has broken out, will assist in paying additional staff wages, increased utility bills (drinking fountain, toilet flushes, electricity or gas for heating, air-conditioning and lighting) that inevitably occur when multitudes descend on your church building; prematurely ageing carpets and seating etc.
- If people travel halfway round the world to a revival location (which is not cheap), then they want to have physical mementoes (which are cheap in comparison to their plane ticket and accommodation) which they can share with their friends, family and local church.
- Christian T-shirts are living evangelism. At the Brownsville Revival (1995-2000) there was a stall in

the car park where you could buy Christian T-shirts, two of which had printed on them, 'Run to the Mercy Seat' and the 'Pensacola Outpouring,' which was run by a Christian entrepreneur. Inside the church foyer and semi-circular hallway, the Brownsville Church and ministries relating to the team sold books, videos of every service, tapes, music CDs, badges and a red bumper sticker, 'Yes Lord We Will Ride With You.' With the Lakeland Outpouring (2008), Christian T-shirts, 'Come and Get Some' were on sale within two months. A Christian artist who had been inspired by a specific Lakeland meeting in connection with Israel was selling hand painted greeting cards on an internet auction website.

A Western Phenomenon

Not having found any evidence to the contrary, I believe that revival merchandise is only associated with the West. This is because the majority of Western Christians have surplus money, disposable income, even though revival memorabilia began in the eighteenth century when money was very tight and poverty abounded. In the West, we like to collect items, have hobbies and we have a fascination with ornaments and mementoes from places we have visited, often displaying these items around our homes, on the traditional mantelpiece or keeping them safe in a drawer full of past memories.

When most of us go on holiday we think nothing of buying souvenirs which are often thrown out within a few years. Many of us have pictures or home videos of our family and friends, so does it seem so strange to buy a memento which is connected to the person or ministry in which we were saved, healed, revived, delivered or called into Christian ministry? People want to remember the good times and milestones in their lives and this includes: reliving the revival experiences through reading books, watching the services or listening to the worship or teaching CDs.

Let us not be upset over Christian products that are sold during times of revival (or from ministries outside of revival) as they can encourage, build up and stimulate us in the most holy faith and that investment can last a lifetime.

Chapter Thirty

Why Revivals are Chronicled

Imagine if nobody ever chronicled a revival – the volumes of Church history would be greatly diminished and a large portion of God's blessing and the heritage of the Church would be unknown to future generations. Many valuable and important lessons would be lost, yet known only in eternity. Little detail is known about the Shotts Revival (1630) in Scotland, under John Livingston because it was never documented at the time. The omission of our forefathers to transmit a full and circumstantial account of the revival is not only our generation's loss, but all generations.

What if Doctor Luke had not chronicled the book of Acts? We would have lost eighteen accounts of revival from Church history. The history of the Christian Church would be incomplete and it would have taken a completely different course. Doctor Luke wrote: 'It seemed good to me also, having perfect understanding of all things from the very first, to write to you an orderly account, most excellent Theophilus that you may know the certainty of those things in which you were instructed' (Luke 1:3-4).

The apostle Paul wrote to the church at Corinth: 'All these things [from the Old Testament] happened to them as examples, and they were written for our admonition...' (1 Corinthians 10:11). The psalmists wrote: 'This will be written for the generation to come, that a people yet to be created may praise the Lord' (Psalm 102:18) and 'One generation shall praise Your works to another and shall declare Your mighty acts' (Psalm 145:4).

Why Revivalists Write
- There is a demand to know about revivals and not everyone is able to travel to a revival. Where there is a need for the story to be told, it will be met by one person or another. If the revivalist does not write

about their work then somebody else will. I think it is better that those who have paid the price, profit from it than those who are just out to make a profit!

- Royalties from the sale of books if directed back into the church or mission organisation connected to the revival, assists in paying the bills and wages of people. It can also finance more labourers to go into the harvest field and fulfil the Great Commission.
- A book is frequently written to explain fact from fiction as rumours can circulate. A book by the revivalist is the wheat that distinguishes it from the verbal chaff.
- Books written by eye-witness or faithful researchers provide a faithful account which is beneficial not only for the present, but for future generations.
- Revival books add fuel to the flames of those who are already passionate to see revival in their nation.

Spread the Facts – Promote Revival
In May 1905, evangelist / journalist, Frank Bartleman, who would become the chronicler of the Azusa Street Revival (1906-1909) was given the book *The Great Revival In Wales* by S. B. Shaw. The Welsh Revival began on 31 October 1904, so within seven months a book had already been printed. After reading it, Bartleman who was already involved in active Christian work resolved to give up his secular employment and became a channel in which the burden for revival could come upon him. After receiving 5,000 copies of the pamphlet, *The Revival in Wales* by G. Campbell Morgan, he began to distribute them. He wrote: '[It] spread the fire in the churches wonderfully' and 'they had a wonderful quickening influence.' He also began to sell S. B. Shaw's book amongst the churches that he spoke at and 'God wonderfully used it to promote faith for a revival spirit.'[1]

Reluctant Authors
Some revival authors like Rev. Duncan Campbell reluctantly wrote about the Lewis Revival (1949-1952) because others had written about it with greatly exaggerated reports. Rev. Campbell wrote fact; to distinguish it from the verbal fiction, which at the time was flying around, and to bring balance to some inaccurate newspaper reports which

over exaggerated the move of God. He also made reference to this in some of his sermons which were recorded for posterity and can be heard online.

Veteran missionary and revival author, Eva Stuart Watt published the events of the Imbai Revival of 1935 and 1936, in the North East Belgian Congo, after being asked to write the account by Norman P. Grubb, the Honorary Home Secretary of Worldwide Evangelization Crusade (WEC). Eva got the information from two WEC missionaries, Lily and Jack Roberts (siblings) and wrote: 'It was never their wish that the story should be published. Indeed they had carefully refrained from passing it on, even to their colleagues on the field, any details of the wonderful things God was doing, in case the Holy Spirit should be grieved and the movement curbed.'

Norman Grubb in the foreword to *Floods On Dry Ground* wrote: 'So many of us seek for revival and ask how it may be found...the telling of the story [of the Imbai Revivals of 1935 and 1936] revealed the secrets and findings as well as giving the results. I felt so sure that blessing and revelation in the ways of the Spirit would come to many if they could hear it, that I asked Miss Eva Stuart Watt...wherever she could find time to put it into book form. After waiting on God her consent was given.... If any read this story who have lost their first love, I pray that it may be used to show them the way back to blessing and usefulness; and to others who feel the pressure and power of Satan in their field of labour, and the barrenness of the soil, the Holy Spirit may use it to reveal the secrets of 'floods upon the dry ground.' '

To Educate and Inform

The phrase 'Toronto Blessing' was coined by a journalist. After this move of the Holy Spirit broke out in January 1994, at the Airport Vineyard Church in Toronto, Canada, it touched the United Kingdom in late May 1994 and by October had touched an estimated two thousand churches.

Dave Roberts, editor of *Alpha* magazine authored *The Toronto Blessing* which was published in October 1994. In the preface he wrote: 'As you read on I hope you will find a report that is 'warm, but thoughtful.' This book is no means a definite document. Other writers are even now working on books that will look in-depth at the theological, historical and pastoral aspect of this 'time of refreshing.' This is an A-Z map. Others will compile the Ordnance Survey, with its fine detail and extended analysis.

'This book aims to enquire, inform and perhaps inspire. As controversy inevitably surrounds such events, it has as one of its primary aims a desire to get beyond the immediate surface impressions we sometimes gain and help generate light rather than heat by what it reveals.'

To Know and Understand the Facts

William Newton Blair was used in the Pyongyang Great Revival (1907-1910) in Korea. In *The Korean Pentecost* he wrote: 'During my year of furlough, I have found everywhere the greatest interest in the progress of the gospel in Korea, and particularly a desire to know and understand the facts concerning this revival of 1907. To meet this desire, I have put into writing my own recollections of the revival.'

The Most Qualified

In 1860, Thomas Phillips reluctantly published the accounts of the 1859 Welsh Revival. In the preface he wrote: 'The writer of the following pages, while sympathising most heartily with the revival in Wales, feels some difficulty in becoming its historian. He must confess that, since the meeting in the Mansion House in November last, when the revival in Ireland was made the leading topic, both in the address and the prayers, he has often thought and said, "Oh that some would tell the story of the Welsh Revival to these and other dear Christian friends!"

'Soon after this, he was asked by his esteemed friend and neighbour...to give his people an 'Address on the Revival in Wales' – a request with which he gladly complied and many of the facts given in the present publication were related on that occasion.

'Again and again he has been urged by many highly valued friends, both in England and Wales, to give a sketch of this remarkable religious movement. He pleaded constant occupation in the service of one of the leading public societies, as a reason why he should decline the task. At the same time he has felt the force of the remarks made by many friends – "You have travelled the length and breadth of the land; you know and speak the language of the people; you are from your office, necessarily acquainted with the leading ministers and members of the various sections of the Christian Church in Wales; you have recently visited the scenes of revival and therefore well qualified to give us some account of it." All this may be true and as the writer cannot say that he is required to make 'brick' without 'straw,' he has at length resolved to do what lay in his power to meet the wishes thus expressed.'

To Preserve for Posterity
In the spring of 1934, Dr. Gustav Carlberg sent a circular letter to about two hundred missionaries across China who were experiencing revival. Also, a Chinese translation was sent to more than three hundred Christian workers! In part of the letter he wrote: 'For some time it has been in my mind to make a collection of material showing the progress so far, in order that some kind of record may be preserved in permanent form [see page 225]. It is felt that such a record of God's work in China at the present time would serve as a great stimulus, as well as an inspiration, to the churches of the homelands, aside from the value of such a record from a historical point of view.' Dr. Gustav Carlberg's findings were published the following year in *China in Revival*.

Called of the Lord to Write
Norwegian born Marie Monsen, more than three decades after she saw revival across China from 1927-1932, authored *The Awakening – Revival in China 1927-1937*. In the preface she wrote: 'Because I saw only the first workings of revival in China which began in 1927 I never intended to write about it. A strong inward urge to write, however, which has been with me for a year or two, has been intensified lately through the unexpected visits of several missionaries who have seen the fruits of revival. Courage to write was given through the Word: 'They rehearsed all that God had done with them' Acts 14:27. They found listeners sufficiently spiritually-minded to understand them. It is readers of like mind, whom I believe God wishes to reach through the testimony He Himself has caused to be written.'

In his early twenties, J. Edwin Orr, an unknown Irish preacher, prior to his first tour of Europe in the early 1930s agreed on a seven book deal with Marshall, Morgan & Scott. On his world tours he was nicknamed 'the boy preacher' as he looked so young. Edwin Orr was a man of vision and had agreed to write of his travels and ministry, without knowing that he would be used in so many localised revivals which he saw in different countries of Europe, the USSR, North America and on the Australian and African continents during 1934-1936 and in Brazil during 1951-1952.

I had to Write – To Give Glory to God

It is very interesting to note that at the height of the Mukti Revival (1905-1906) in India, a request came from Bombay to Pandita Ramabai, founder of the Mukti Mission and leader of the revival, to write about this move of the Holy Spirit. She declined fearing it would 'hinder the work of the Spirit, but shortly after the Spirit of power decreased and there were evident signs that the revival was waning.'

After prayer regarding the source of decline, Ramabai concluded that she had made a grave mistake in not giving God the glory for what He was doing throughout India and the world, and said, "The depression had come because we refused to give God the glory by not allowing the account to be published." An article was written and published in the *Bombay Guardian*, a Christian weekly paper, edited by Mr Dyer and from there it went around the world and the revival fires were rekindled.

Newsworthy Facts

For the last century it has been common for those who have been used in revival or have seen it in the ministry of others to document the facts. Such newsworthy features have been published in newspaper and magazines, but more commonly bound in a book; but since 1995, have also found themselves reported on media websites and social networks.

Jonathan Goforth of China and Manchuria, Paget Wilkes of Japan, Duncan Campbell of Scotland and John Kilpatrick of America, to name but a few, all wrote about the revivals they were involved in. In the eighteenth century, revivalists such as Rev. James Robe of Scotland, Jonathan Edwards of

America, John and Charles Wesley of Great Britain, George Whitefield of Great Britain and America and John Nelson of England, wrote journals or documented accounts about the revivals which they were involved in (including revival sermons) which were published in their lifetime and beyond.

John Wesley, founder of Methodism wrote an unbroken journal for more than fifty years. It is the most accurate documentation of social history of Great Britain from 1739-1791 for that time period. He preached on a circuit, never staying in one place for more than two weeks and more often than not, travelling every day to a new preaching location. Year after year he visited the same places (and some new ones) and the contrasts of the people's nature and social condition between the years and decades revealed the social transformation of the nation as one quarter of the population during Britain's Great Awakening (1739-1791) also known as the Evangelical Revival were converted![2]

In 1742, Rev. James Robe desired to 'publish about a sheet once a week or a fortnight' on the account of the Kilsyth and Cambuslang Revivals (1742) '…to serve the truth and the interest of religion and to satisfy the longing curiosity of those who are giving Zion's King no rest until He makes His Jerusalem a praise in the midst of the earth…' These sheets were collated and later published under the title *When the Wind Blows*.

Rev. James Robe continued: 'Praise to our God, for these His mighty acts are not to be confined to the present generation, wherein they appear. Posterity shall reap the benefit of them and it is our duty to transmit the history of them to posterity, that they may reap the greater benefit by them and praise the Lord more distinctly for them. It would be a contempt of these wonderful works which God hath made to be had in remembrance, if they should be buried in oblivion, so as not to be known by those who live in after ages. One generation shall praise His works together and declare His mighty acts.'[3]

Revival Royalties

There are some who object to revivalists writing accounts of revivals; or more to the point, profiting from their literary work. But why should the person who has spent time and effort not be rewarded for their work? Is not a labourer worthy of his wages? The revivalist would have made tremendous sacrifices to see revival. Would we expect a Christian builder, teacher, bus driver or architect to sacrifice months of their time and skills and not be reimbursed?

Royalties can help support the author who is often the pastor or evangelist from within the church where revival has broken out – some of whom are without a regular wage. Large amounts of royalties can assist towards the church mortgage or help pay for the church supplies, assists in employing new staff, supporting missionaries and evangelists who have been sent out from the church, building Bible schools and training colleges, sponsoring Bible students, feeding the poor and supporting orphans etc.

All of John Wesley's and the vast majority of Dwight L. Moody and Ira Sankey's royalties were invested into the Kingdom of God. But when Moody and Sankey came to Britain in 1877, the press said Sankey had come to sell his organs and Moody his hymn-books! Wesley wrote around two hundred books and pamphlets, whilst the Moody and Sankey songs books sold an estimated fifty million copies in their lifetime! The following example is not a revivalist, but nonetheless is worth noting, the great missionary explorer David Livingstone, used the proceeds (£6,000) of his first book, *Missionary Travels* (1857) to fund the construction of a paddle steamer which was used in Africa, and to support his wife and children back in Britain.

J. Edwin Orr lived 'as close to voluntary poverty as his hosts would let him' and made 'his own decision in the mid 1930s not to touch the royalties [which had begun to come in after his fourth book] for personal needs, but to give them to missionary causes.' He wrote: 'It may interest critics to know that the author does not touch the royalties for personal purposes, but instead supports a number of different missionaries in different parts of the world.'[4]

There are some Christian workers and founders of ministries who are successful authors (or artists) and do not draw a wage even though they work full-time; thus the wage which they are entitled too can be directed towards other Christian causes. Whatever our occupation, do we have excess income which can be invested into God's Kingdom?

Chapter Thirty-One

Evaluating the Past and Looking Forward

Revival is wonderful, it is glorious, but like everything, there are those who disagree. Just like any church service there will be positive and negative aspects, not only in the elements of the service (our preferred length of sermon, the subject, style of worship, the preacher's personality and even those who sit next to us, in front of us or behind us and how they act or react), but in the type and maturity level of those who are present. We cannot dismiss revival because of its small negative aspects no more than we would dismiss a Sunday service where negative apathy is often present. We take the best and leave the rest and should never throw out the baby with the bath water; rejecting the majority because of a negative minority is not maturity. "Bright lights attract bugs," said Steve Hill frequently during the Brownsville Revival (1995-2000) in Pensacola, America, "And they probably come from *your* church" was his witty reply!

Don't blame God for the devil's hindrances or be annoyed with God when people scream out or roll on the floor under conviction of sin! Let God be God; He does things His way because He knows best. The presence of God always testifies to the world that its works are evil (John 7:7 & 16:8) and non-Christians and lukewarm believers will be offended!

In regards to revival let us not be like the fool who has no delight in understanding, but in expressing his own heart (Proverbs 18:2); nor like the man who answers a matter before he hears it, as it is folly and shame to him (Proverbs 18:13), but let us pray that the Lord will give us understanding in all things (2 Timothy 2:7).

The problem with analysing revivals and it is something that needs to be done, is that it is often better understood by a future generation. Revival can only be lived in the present and is best understood when looking back. We are all too prone to subconsciously view past revivals through rose-coloured glasses, yet tend to put contemporary revivals under a high powered microscope! Dr. Michael Brown, the resident theologian from the Brownsville Revival said, "We tend to sanitise past revivals and demonise present revivals."[1] The revivalist James A. Stewart, thirty-three years after he saw his first revival in Latvia in 1931 wrote: 'Oh, beloved, it is only when revival is a matter of history that it may gain the subject of applause.'[2]

The controversial Lakeland Outpouring (2008) was a revival of healing under the ministry of Fresh Fire headed by Todd Bentley. The meetings were beamed across the world via God TV who received more than 45,000 emails in regards to the broadcasts and internet web-casts – deemed by some as a media revival. Putting aside the sad circumstances of the outpouring's demise through the personal failings of individuals, the outpouring brought blessing and encourage-ment amongst the body of Christ, but also friction and division. The evangelical community was divided into camps of opposing forces with their battle swords of words drawn and delivered over the internet. One book in reference to Lakeland, Todd Bentley and the Prophetic Movement, was published within forty-one days, though it was largely written prior to Lakeland and utilised the present spiritual climate.[3]

Due to Lakeland's exposure, many 'revival police' and 'heresy hunters' came to the fore because of this mass televised move of God which was unprecedented in history. This was followed by The Bay of The Holy Spirit Revival (2010) under Nathan Morris and John Kilpatrick. At Lakeland, there was a mixture of the flesh and sometimes the demonic, as demons manifested through people, which on occasions were incorrectly attributed as an anointing, or from the Holy Spirit. There were various personalities involved, of varying maturity and of different ages (some of whom were young in the Lord) of both genders. No two consecutive nights were the same and there were many different speakers and guests over the three months when Todd was at the fore. There was too much emphasis on some things and less on others and several high profile personalities have said, "I would have done things differently," but each move of God has lessons that we can learn, if only we take the time to evaluate.

Lakeland exposed to the body of Christ, its hunger for the reality of New Testament Christianity. Many Christians were healed, blessed and refreshed, hundreds were saved, whilst other brethren were revived, refreshed and invigorated whilst thousands were trained and encouraged to be witnesses in the highways and byways of their towns, at different meetings connected with Lakeland, at Ignite Church.

As with any evaluation of recent moves of God, it is best to start with a bias of believing the best (1 Corinthians 13:7) and treating the leader(s) as a brother or sister in the Lord rather than wolves or tares. This is not to say we leave our brains at the door or disregard the warnings in Scripture, but we must not jump to rash conclusions or be only basing our conclusion on the opinions of others. See page 166.

Let us not be like Professor Bob, a fictional, satirical character, who was frequently mentioned during the Brownsville Revival (1995-2000) – he had not had a touch from the Lord in forty years! He represented those who were quick to pass on their negative opinions without ever investigating the facts for themselves; those who believe that the gifts of the Holy Spirit have ceased (see page 101) and those who only want God to turn up at church on *their* terms.

In revival, in the midst of the presence of God, there can be a mixture of the flesh or the demonic and any combination, working in and through those who are not fully sanctified and surrendered to the Lord; be it the leader at the fore, assistants, elders and deacons, church members and especially those who have come in off the street, as they have heard that something is happening. As in any group of people there will be mixed ages of maturity in the Lord, from babes in Christ to those who take solid foods (1 Corinthians 3:2) as well as the curious, seekers, fad-lovers and those who turn up for mischief! When God touches someone's life, we often do not know their circumstances or whether they are even converted at all. To judge hastily would be unwise as the measure we use; it will be measured back to us (Matthew 7:2). The Kingdom of God and the kingdom of the devil are at conflict with each other and during moves of God there are power clashes and manifestations.

When God comes and descends on a meeting, in church or on a community, He comes to revive and transform and for many it can be a truly emotional experience of jubilation and joy; or terror and fear for others – the Refiner has to do His sifting and shaking first, sometimes quite literally! An old acquaintance of the author went to the Toronto meetings in Canada, back in the mid 1990s; in his heart he scoffed at some of the physical phenomena as he saw people jump, jerk and even bounce around. By his own confession, God got a hold of him and he began bouncing around the auditorium like a pogo stick, hands stuck to his side, unable to stop or resist, but as he informed the author, it was a humbling experience and God shook the pride from him and thus fruit was born in his life. It sounded just like the Kentucky Revival in the early 1800s! See Appendix B.

Max Warren wrote: 'One of the uses of history is to present a mirror in which we can recognise ourselves not in outward lineaments of those things which are peculiar to the fashion of our age, but in those fundamentals of our human nature which do not change. In this sense any revival movement which looks at history only to shrink from its lessons, is like the man in the Epistle of St, James who, seeing himself in a glass, goes away and at once forgets what he looked like, and so in a very true sense of the word loses himself.'[4]

As in all moves of God, there will be prominent leaders who if not already, will rise through the ranks and be seen as the spokesperson(s) during times of revival. No revivalist would have ever called themselves perfect or sinless, but would have been the first to acknowledge their imperfections; that they stood and ministered by the grace and mercy of God. Revivals are led by people that are not perfect, some are vulnerable and may have weak areas, whilst with others, their spiritual gifts are far greater than the character of Christ formed in them, as sanctification is an ongoing work. But let him who is without sin cast the first stone at any brother or sister who has been tripped up and fallen from grace. May they be helped and brought to a place of repentance and restoration. Peter denied the Lord, Thomas doubted Him and Saul persecuted Him, yet all were forgiven and used to advance the Kingdom of God. Imagine if the early Church had cast them aside? – And nowhere is it recorded that the

Church reminded them of their past sins! God does not look on the outward appearance and judge, but He is very interested in the heart which should be entirely given over to Him. King David greatly sinned, in adultery and murder but he was a man after God's own heart and was restored.

Duncan Campbell retelling his experiences of a prayer meeting during the Lewis Revival (1949-1952) said, "When God stepped down, suddenly, men and women all over the parish were gripped by the fear of God – God are my hands clean? Is my heart pure?" After a man prayed and told God that His honour was at stake, "A power was let loose in Barvas that shook the whole of Lewis.... The Holy Spirit began to move among the people." The minister writing about what happened on the following morning said, "You met God on meadow and moorland, in the homes of the people, God seemed to be everywhere." ...An awareness of God that gripped the whole community.... There was a dance in progress that night and while this young man was praying in the aisle, the power of God moved into that dance, and the young people, over a hundred of them fled from the dance, as though fleeing from a plague and made for the church.... When I went into the pulpit, I found a young woman...lying on the floor [repeatedly] crying, "Is there mercy for me?" – God was at work. Well that meeting continued until four o'clock in the morning." Then Mr Campbell was informed that at the police station, between 200-300 people had turned up from the neighbouring village which was five or six miles away. They were "so moved by the power of God," said Campbell and desired to see the constable who was "a God-fearing and well-saved man." Mr Campbell saw young men kneeling by the roadside, one group was about half a dozen, with one man under the influence of drink and his old mother kneeling beside him, saying, "Oh Willie, Willie, are you coming at last?" Willie became the parish minister and from the group of men who sought the Lord that night, nine went into the ministry!

The author's hope is that by reading this book, we may be more aware of the happenings during times of revival: What we might see, (from God, the devil – an imitator and infiltrator, and over-excited people), without denouncing a genuine move of God as counterfeit. That we handle the negative in a spirit of love and grace, but especially towards those who disagree with us and who may have valid points.

As was stated at the beginning of this book, there is always a danger that a minority of those who have actively sought for and prayed for a revival will reject it when it comes – what a tragedy; because the effects and results were different than what they had anticipated and like the religious Pharisees and Sadducees, missed the day of visitation and got upset with those who embraced it! (Luke 19:42-44).

We all need to be careful that we do not miss the day of visitation, when the showers of blessing fall, the former and the latter rain, and let us not be too hesitant to move into the River of God. Some at first may appear paralysed, unable to roll up their trouser legs and paddle, let alone wade, but like in Ezekiel's day, the river flows from the temple and only in steps may we walk into the river, up to our ankles, then our knees, and up to our waist until we are immersed in the River of God which is life giving, refreshing and reviving and brings healing to the nations (Ezekiel 47 and Revelation 22:1-5).

Let us not read about the past and allow spiritual nostalgia to take over so that we become passive. Let us be active in our prayers for revival, for our church and nation and let us not forget that "prayer is the blood-bought way to the throne of grace" as stated a evangelist from the Shantung Revival (1930-1932) in north China. We are commanded to be holy, to live holy, to offer our bodies as living sacrifice and let us not have "too much emphasis on charisma and not enough on character" as the Anglican vicar Mark Stibbe often says.

To see revival we must first get our own lives in order. Then with clean hands and a pure heart we can plead God's covenant promises so that the Spirit will be poured out on those who are thirsty, the Church will be revived and He will come and heal our land as floods are poured out – God will be glorified amongst the nations; Jesus will be lifted high, drawing all men to Himself, the Holy Spirit will have His way in the Church and the desert will bloom once again.

'O Lord, though our iniquities testify against us, do it for Your name's sake; for our backslidings are many, we have sinned against You' (Jeremiah 14:7).

Appendices A-D

Appendix A – Controversy and Contentions Within The Evangelical Revival (1739-1791)

The Evangelical Revival (1739-1791), spanning seven decades and two generations inevitably had varying views and opinions on a variety of subjects, which included personality clashes between the numerous revivalists themselves who came from different denominations and were at varying levels of sanctification.

Archibald W. Harrison in his book *The Evangelical Revival And Christian Reunion* wrote: 'The Revival was singularly rich in men and women of strong character, whose temperament did not always blend harmoniously. Even the wisest and best may sometimes be difficult. The leaders of the Revival suffered much from detraction and misrepresentation – even from scurrilous detraction and misrepresentations in their lifetime, but when the mist of controversy had passed away their fine qualities appeared.'[1]

The main blight on the history of the Evangelical Revival was the doctrines of 'Election' (Calvinism) as preached by Whitefield, versus 'Free Grace' (Arminianism) as preached by the Wesley's. This led to two camps being birthed within Methodism. The ironic thing is that these men of God were striving for the same goal, to preach Christ and to see men turn back to God, and regardless of their theology, God brought about revival wherever they went.

At the end of March 1741, Wesley went to hear Whitefield preach, having heard much of his unkind behaviour since his return from Georgia, New England, though this debate had been going on in private between the Wesley's, Whitefield, the Moravians and their close associates for over a year. Wesley in his *Journal* wrote: 'He told me, he and I preach two different gospels; and therefore, he not only would not join with, or give me the right hand of fellowship, but was resolved to publicly preach against me and my brother, wheresoever he preached at all.'

George Whitefield then wrote a letter to John Wesley which had been printed without either party consenting and was distributed in great numbers. The Methodists foolishly decided to embrace one and denounce the other, so the Societies were divided. Whitefield then printed a letter that he had written in answer to John Wesley's *Sermon on Free Grace*. Wesley in his *Journal* wrote: 'It was quite imprudent to publish it at all, being only the putting of weapons into their hands who loved neither the one nor the other.' Wesley stated that if Whitefield wanted to write anything then he should not have called his name into question. Wesley continued, 'He has said enough of what wholly foreign to the question, to make an open (and probable, irreparable) breach between him and me; seeing "for a treacherous wound, and for the bewraying [betraying] of secrets, every friend will depart." ' Though they both met again in May 1742 when they were summoned before the Archbishop of Canterbury and the Bishop of London.[2]

In August 1743, John Wesley tried to arrange a conference, where he and his brother would be present along with George Whitefield and the Moravians. He was even prepared to make concessions for the sake of peace; but as Whitefield and the Moravians refused to take part, the conference was not held.[3]

Within a decade the friendship between Wesley and Whitefield had been healed, as Wesley on 28 January 1750 wrote in his *Journal:* 'I read prayers and Mr Whitefield preached. How wise is God in giving different talents to different preachers.'[4] Whitefield died on 30 September 1770, in America. John Wesley was informed on 10 Nov. and preached a memorial sermon in London on 18 Nov. by the request of the executors of Whitefield's will.[5]

John Wesley with his strong affirmations led him to separate from the Moravians and Calvinists because what he saw clearly he proclaimed freely. He was never willing to surrender a truth of tested validity and he tested religious experience consistently by the standard of the New Testament. John Wesley often attacked principles, though not necessarily the person who held or promoted them. The controversy of 'Election' and 'Free Grace' was at the infancy of the revival, and thus its labourers lacked the wisdom of which only years can bring. They were also more prone to strong rebuttals of that which they held dear to themselves as important truths and gave harsh denunciations for those who disagreed and tried to undermine them.[6]

August Toplady (1740-1778) is best known for his hymn writing, most notably, *Rock Of Ages* which was first published in 1776 in London's *Gospel Magazine* where it was calculating the 'National Debt' in terms of sin. In a pamphlet entitled *An Old Fox Tarred and Feathered,* he calls John Wesley 'a low and puny tadpole in divinity' and in his *More Work for Mr. John Wesley,* he rakes up every possible and impossible slander against the veteran, who was in his seventieth year and old enough to be Toplady's father! Wesley's response was, "Mr Toplady I know well; but I do not fight with chimney sweepers" and left others to defend him such as Sellon, Olivers and Fletcher. The ironic thing is that Toplady was converted in Ireland under a Methodist preacher![7]

See also point 2 of chapter 16 in Sources and Notes, page 242.

Appendix B

Kentucky 1800s and Ireland 1859 – Physical Phenomena

The revivals in Kentucky, America, began in 1800 during the frontier days as settlers pushed further West and had some of the most 'wildest' (in a positive definition) physical phenomena on record. Undoubtedly not all was as a direct result of God's presence, the Holy Spirit touching lives, as there is always a minority who are under demonic activity. The author disagrees with the manifestation of involuntary barking, believing it to be of demonic origin even though the author from 1808 stated that it was a humbling process. In the Bible, dogs are unclean and disdained.

Barton Stone was the protégé of James McGreedy and both were Presbyterian ministers. Both were used during the Red River Revival (1800) in Kentucky. In May 1801, Barton Stone, who had been preaching at the Cane Ridge Meeting House in Bourbon County, Kentucky, called for a camp meeting at Cane Ridge. In August he called another and 20,000 people turned up for what had been billed as a six day camp and thus sprang the Cane Ridge Revival (1801).

James B. Finley, a convert of Cane Ridge who later became a Methodist circuit rider wrote: 'The noise was like the roar of Niagra. The vast sea of human beings seemed to be agitated as if by a storm. I counted seven ministers all preaching at one time, some on stumps, others in wagons and one standing in a tree.... Some of the people were singing, others praying, some crying for mercy...while others were shouting most vociferously. While witnessing these scenes, a peculiarly-strange sensation such as I had never felt before came over me. My heart beat tumultuously, my knees trembled, my lips quivered and I felt as though I must fall to the ground. A strange supernatural power seemed to pervade the entire mass of minds there collected.' Finley got on a log for a better view 'of the surging sea of humanity...it was indescribable. At one time I saw at least five hundred swept down in a moment as if a battery of a thousand guns had been opened upon them and then immediately followed shrieks and shouts that rent the heaven.'[1]

Peter Cartwright, a Methodist circuit rider, estimated that he had preached 14,600 sermons and received into the Church at least 10,000 adults and baptised nearly as many children. In his *Autobiography* he noted the 'jerks' that came as he preached on those who heard the Word of the Lord or as they sang, 'convulsive jerking all over, which they could not by any possibility avoid and the more they resisted the more they jerked.... I have seen more than five hundred persons at one time jerking in my large congregation.' In regard to the *proud* gentlemen and young ladies present, Cartwright noted for the ladies that as the jerks began, 'their fine bonnets, caps and combs fly; and so sudden would be the jerking of the head that their long hair would crack almost as loud as a wagoner's whip.'[2] This phenomena produced no injuries.

Peter Cartwright wrote: 'I always looked upon the jerks as a judgment sent from God, first, to bring sinners to repentance, and secondly, to show professors that God can work with or without means and that He could work over and above means and do whatsoever seemeth [to] Him good, to the glory of His grace and the salvation of the world.'[3]

William Gibson who documented the Ulster Revival of 1859 in Ireland, received a letter from the Bishop of Down and Conner, Ireland, from the Bishop M'Ilvaine of Ohio, America. In the letter there was reference to the case of 'striking' [people being struck to the ground under the power of God]. Bishop M'Ilvaine wrote: 'I was conversing the other day with the grandson of a very intelligent and prominent man among the early settlers of Ohio, who said that when those accounts from Ireland were first read among his friends, they exclaimed, 'Why, that is exactly what occurred among the Scotch-Irish in Kentucky, in 1804!'[4]

Richard M'Nemar of Union Village, Ohio, America, published a series of articles in 1808. In *No 10 New Lights and Schismatics* he wrote: 'The principal thing that distinguished the Schismatic worship from that of the New-Lights was their taking the privilege of exhibiting by a bold faith, what others were moved to by blind impulse. This they considered a great improvement, growth and advancement in the spirit of the revival. Upon this principle, the voluntary exercise of dancing was introduced as the worship of God, by Br. [Brother] Thompson and some others who were forward in prompting the grand schism....'

'At the spring sacrament at Turtlecreek in 1804, Br. [Brother] Thompson had been constrained just at the close of the meeting to go dancing and for an hour or more to dance in a regular manner round the stand, all the while repeating in a low tone of voice, "This is the Holy Spirit, Glory!" But it was not till the ensuing fall that the Schismatics began to encourage one another to praise God in the dance and unite in that exercise; just believing it was their privilege to rejoice before the Lord and go forth in the dances of them that make merry.

'However, the Schismatics aimed at that worship which should be expressive of uniform and continual joy, yet they were far from obtaining it and at least the one half of their exercise were of contrary nature; some of voluntary and others of an involuntary kind.'

Richard M'Nemar went on to write about the rolling exercise, the jerks and the barks all of which were part of a humbling or rebuking process for disobedience. He wrote: 'The rolling exercise which consisted of being cast down in a violent manner, doubled with head and feet together and rolled over and over like a wheel, or stretched in a prostrate manner, turned swiftly over and over like a log. This was considered very debasing and mortifying, especially if the person was taken in this manner through the mud and sullied therewith from head to foot.

'Still more demeaning and mortifying were the jerks.' Richard M'Nemar goes on to recount similar examples as Peter Cartwright, but also noted that the more people resisted, the worse the jerks came and what began in the head movements went on to affect the entire body. 'He must necessarily go as he was stimulated, whether with a violent dash on the ground and bounce from place to place like a football, or hop round with head, limbs and trunk, twitching and jolting in every direction, as if they must inevitably fly asunder. How such could escape without injury was no small wonder to spectators.'

Richard M'Nemar noted that those who resisted and refused the voluntary dance 'had to bear these afflicting operation from month to month and from year to year....'

'Although these strange convulsions served to overawe the heaven-daring spirit of the wicked, and stimulate the halting Schismatics to the performances of many duties disagreeable to the carnal mind, yet in all this, their design was not fully comprehended.'

Richard M'Nemar went on to mention that the Schismatics 'were not a little alleviated by the many extraordinary signs and gifts of the Spirit through which they were encouraged to look for brighter days. Among these innumerable signs and gifts, may be ranked prophecy; being caught up or carried away in this spirit...dreams ...seeing visions, hearing unspeakable words, the fragrant smell and delightful singing.'[5]

Appendix C

Opposition and Attempted Assassinations

On one Saturday, after a Ladies Meeting, Brenda Kilpatrick, wife of John Kilpatrick was verbally harassed by a man. She boldly proclaimed the name of Jesus and claimed the victory – this was during the Brownsville Revival (1995-2000).

The young Canadian evangelist, Oswald J. Smith, in the summer of 1913, was on his way to preach at Hog's Hollow, Kentucky, when conspirators set an ambush, pulled out their guns and fired, thankfully nobody was hurt. He went on to see revival in the Russian Mission Fields of Europe in 1929 and beyond and became the famed pastor of Toronto People's Church, Canada, a church which supported more missionaries than any other in the world.

In 1949, Billy Graham, an evangelist for Youth For Christ was preaching in downtown Los Angeles when a man shot at him with a pistol. Graham has preached to more than 215 million people in person and celebrated his 99th birthday on 7 November 2017.

Appendix D

What Not to Discuss

We are warned about grieving the Holy Spirit and the Scriptures inform us not to discuss certain things because its does not make for peace or edify; such as: fables and endless genealogies which cause disputes, profane old wives' tales, gossiping, disputes and arguments over words which produces envy, strife, reviling, evil suspicions, and irreverent, sinful, wicked and godless chatter, see Ephesians 4:29-30, 1 Timothy 1:4, 1 Timothy 4:7, 1 Timothy 5:13, 1 Timothy 6:4 and 1 Timothy 6:20-21. We are not to strive about words to no profit as it benefits no one and brings ruin to those in earshot. We should shun profane and vain babblings which leads to ungodliness; we should not put up with those who do not endure sound doctrine, having itching ears and those who turn aside to fables, see 2 Timothy 2:14, 16 and 2 Timothy 4:3-4. We are also to disregard Jewish fables and avoid foolish disputes and strivings about the law, see Titus 1:14 and Titus 3:9.

There is a big danger of building a lot on a little especially when that little happens to be a preconceived idea. We are told to warn those who cause divisions and offences and reject them after the second warning, and then avoid them, see Romans 16:17 and Titus 3:10. We should pursue things that make for peace and edify (Proverbs 25:11-12 and Romans 14:19). Do not answer a fool according to his folly, less he despise the wisdom of your words, see Isaiah 5:20, Proverbs 23:9 and Proverbs 26:4-5.

Thank you for taking the time to read this book. Please give a shout out on social media (@ or / ByFaithMedia) and write a short review on your favourite review site. Thank you.

Sources and Notes

Preface
1. *When the Spirit Comes With Power* by Dr. John White, Hodder & Stoughton, 1989, page 137.
2. *Grace, Grit & Gumption* by Geraint Fielder, Christian Focus Publications, 2000, page 200.

Chapter One
1. Dr. Martyn Lloyd-Jones speaking on the centenary of the 1859 revival, at Westminster Chapel, London, boxed cassette, tape one.
2. The word 'awakening' first came into the English language in 1736, when Jonathan Edwards' published a letter referring to a 'general awakening' amongst his flock at Northampton, Massachusetts, New England, during 1734-1735, when virtually the whole town was converted. In the context of Edwards' letter, it meant: an awakening of conscience among the people.
3. *Revival For Survival* by Dr. Fred Barlow, Sword of the Lord Publishers, 1973, page 64.
4. *Opened Windows – The Church and Revival* by James A. Stewart, Marshall, Morgan & Scott, 1958, page 19.
5. See *Global Revival – Worldwide Outpourings* by Mathew Backholer, ByFaith Media, 2010, appendix B.
6. *The Fire of God's Presence* by Owen Murphy and John Wesley Adams, Ambassador Press, 2003, page 13.
7. *Opened Windows – The Church and Revival* by James A. Stewart, Marshall, Morgan & Scott, 1958, page 80.
8. Ibid. pages 73 and 75.
9. Ibid. page 73.
10. *The Price Of Revival* by John D. Drysdale, C. Tinling & Co., Ltd, 1946, page 25.
11. *From Death Into Life* by Rev. William Haslam, Jarold & Sons, 1880, 1904, page 174.

Chapter Two
1. The revival at Nineveh is quite unique, in that God did not come to revive His people first (the Israelites), but He came to give life to those who were dead in trespasses and sins, the Assyrians.

Chapter Three
1. The Scripture is in the context of judgment, but before God can heal and bind up, He often has to discipline His children and judgment has begun at the house of the Lord! See 1 Peter 4:17.
2. This Scripture is in the context of the Messiah's reign but can still be prayed for God to come by His Spirit to meet with His people.

Chapter Four
1. *When the Wind Blows, The Kilsyth and Cambuslang Revivals* by Rev. James Robe, Ambassador Productions LTD, 1985, page 189.
2. *Narrative of Remarkable Conversion and Revival Incidents – Great Awakening of 1857-'8* by William C. Conant, Derby & Jackson, 1859, pages 43-44.
3. *The Half Can Never Be Told*, published by the World Wide Revival Prayer Movement, 1927, page 68.
4. *The Shantung Revival* by Mary K. Crawford, The China Baptist Publication Society, 1933, pages 34-35.

5. *Good News in Bad Times* by J. Edwin Orr, Zondervan Publishing House, 1953, page 258.
6. *This Is That*, Out of Africa Publishers, c.1997, pages 64-65.
7. *The History of Revivals of Religion* by William E. Allen (revival series No. 7), Revival Publishing Co., 1951, page 4.
8. *In the Day of Thy Power* by Arthur Wallis, Christian Literature Crusade, 1956, page 15.

Chapter Five
1. *Opened Windows – The Church and Revival* by James A. Stewart, Marshall, Morgan & Scott, 1958, pages 35 and 89.
2. *This Is The Victory 10,000 Miles of Miracle in America* by J. Edwin Orr, Marshall, Morgan & Scott, LTD, (MM&S) 1936, pages 73-74. The student was called 'Tut' from the Evangelical Theological College, Dallas, America.
3. *Opened Windows – The Church and Revival* by James A. Stewart, Marshall, Morgan & Scott, 1958, page 44.
4. *Can God – ? 10,000 Miles of Miracle in Britain* by J. Edwin Orr, Marshall, Morgan & Scott, LTD, 1934, page 121.
5. *This Is The Victory 10,000 Miles of Miracle in America* by J. Edwin Orr, Marshall, Morgan & Scott, LTD, 1936, pages 127-128.
6. *All Your Need 10,000 Miles of Miracle Through Australia and New Zealand* by J. Edwin Orr, MM&S, LTD, c.1936, page 123.
7. *Revival An Enquiry* by Max Warren, SCM Press LTD, 1954, pages 105-106.
8. *Opened Windows – The Church and Revival* by James A. Stewart, Marshall, Morgan & Scott, 1958, page 92.
9. *Meat For Men, Revival Sermons* by Leonard Ravenhill, Bethany House Publishers, 1961, 1989, page 19.
10. *Rend the Heavens!* by Geoffrey R. King, booklet, 1962, page 15.
11. *Great Revivals* by Colin Whittaker, MM&S, 1984, pages 105-106.
12. *Power No. 2 – Heavenly Power in Wales* – paper, edited by Wm. E. Allen, page 2.

Chapter Six
1. *United Evangelical Action* (Oct. 1970) as cited in *Azusa Street & Beyond* edited by Grant McClung, Bridge-Logos, 2006, page 98.
2. *Revival Sermons In Outline* by eminent pastors and evangelists edited by Rev. C. Perren, Fleming H. Revell Company, 1894, pages 18 and 20.
3. *Memoirs of John Smith*, 1822, as cited in *Missionary Joys in Japan* by Paget Wilkes, Morgan & Scott, 1913, page 225.
4. *Thirsting For God* by Eva Stuart Watt, MM&S, 1936, page 152.

Chapter Seven
1. *White Cane Religion And Other Messages From the Brownsville Revival* by Stephen Hill, Revival Press, 1997, page 21.
2. *Can God – ? 10,000 Miles of Miracle in Britain* by J. Edwin Orr, Marshall, Morgan & Scott, LTD, 1934, page 113.
3. *Mighty Moments* by Lionel B. Fletcher, Religious Tract Society, c.1931, pages 15-16.
4. *Road to Revival – The Story of the Ruanda* Mission by A. C. Stanley Smith, Church Missionary Society, 1946, pages 81 & 111.
5. Ibid. pages 104-105.
6. *Sodom had no Bible* by Leonard Ravenhill, Bethany House Publishers, 1971, page 38.

Chapter Ten
1. *Children in Revival – 300 Years of God's Work in Scotland* by Harry Sprange, Christian Focus Publications, 2002, page 256.
2. *China in Revival* by Gustav Carlberg, 1935, chapter five.
3. Dr. Martyn Lloyd-Jones speaking on the centenary of the 1859 revival, tape ten.
4. *The 'Toronto' Blessing* by Dave Roberts, Kingsway Publications, 1994, page 145.
5. Ibid. page 158.
6. See *Clash of Tongues with Glimpses of Revival* by Hugh B. Black, New Dawn Books (NDB), 1988, page 150 and *Revival Personal Encounters* by Hugh Black, NDB, 1993, pages 73-75.
7. *As At The Beginning, The Twentieth Century Pentecostal Revival* by Michael Harper, Hodder and Stoughton, 1965, page 59.
8. *Prove Me Now! 10,000 Miles of Miracle to Moscow* by J. Edwin Orr, Marshall, Morgan & Scott, LTD, 1935, page 31.

Chapter Eleven
1. *China in Revival* by Gustav Carlberg, 1935, chapter five.
2. *The Korean Pentecost & The Sufferings Which Followed* by William Blair & Bruce Hunt, The Banner of Truth Trust, 1977, page 74.

Chapter Twelve
1. *Road to Revival – The Story of the Ruanda* Mission by A. C. Stanley Smith, Church Missionary Society, 1946, page 49.
2. Ibid. page 104.
3. *Hill Ablaze* by Bill Butler, Hodder & Stoughton, 1976, pages 91-92.
4. *From Death Into Life* by Rev. William Haslam, Jarold & Sons, 1880, 1904, page 257.

Chapter Thirteen
1. *One Divine Moment – The Asbury Revival* by Robert E. Coleman, Editor, Fleming H. Revell Company, 1970, page 24.
2. *This Is The Victory 10,000 Miles of Miracle in America* by J. Edwin Orr, Marshall, Morgan & Scott, LTD, 1936, pages 74-75.
3. *Revival Fire – 150 Years of Revivals* by Mathew Backholer, ByFaith Media, 2010, pages 91-92.

Chapter Fourteen
1. The soul and body are interlinked. Humans have five distinct functions, we are: physical beings, thinking beings, longing beings, choosing beings, and feeling beings (physical, rational, personal, volitional and emotional), which can be placed into three categories: the mind, the will and the emotions, which connect to the body, the spirit and the soul. The different capacities are not designed to work isolated from each other but as part of the whole.... The body and mind are so inextricably connected that what affects the mind affects the body and vice versa. Jesus Christ came to heal the whole man, physically, mentally and emotionally, Isaiah 61:1-2 and Luke 4:18-19. *Discipleship For Everyday Living* by Mathew Backholer, ByFaith Media, 2011, chapter 43.
2. Carol and John Arnott from Toronto Airport Christian Fellowship, interviewed on *The 700 Club* by Pat Robertson for the Christian Broadcasting Network (CBN), September 2008.

Chapter Fifteen
1. *Manifestations & Prophetic Symbolism In a Move of the Spirit* by John Arnott, New Wine Ministries, 2008, pages 22, 26 and 28.
2. *Overcome By The Spirit* by Francis McNutt, Eagle, 1990, 1991 Great Britain edition, back cover.

3. *A Century of Mission work in Basutoland 1833-1933* by V. Ellenberger, Morija Sesuto Book Depot, 1938, pages 320-323 & 348.

4. *Missionary Joys in Japan* by Paget Wilkes, Morgan & Scott, 1913, pages 314-315.

Chapter Sixteen

1. Aired on the God Channel on 24 June 2008.

2. John Wesley, an ordained clergyman never wanted to form another denomination. Methodist class meetings were deliberately set at different times to the local Church of England services and its members were expected to attend them both. It was only after his death in 1791 that the Methodist denomination was officially formed. Father Daniel, a converted Copt monk saw revival in Egypt in 1991, when 20,000 Copts in El-Minya, became born again. He encouraged his people not to leave the church of their fathers but to be the light from within it. Father Daniel was excommunicated from the Coptic Church and for a period of time was in hiding. In 2008 he was an AOG pastor in Cairo, Egypt.

3. *Road to Revival – The Story of the Ruanda Mission* by A. C. Stanley Smith, Church Missionary Society, 1946, page 112.

4. *China in Revival* by Gustav Carlsberg, 1936, chapter five.

In 1934, Miss Erva Moody of the American Lutheran Mission, in Tsingtao, China wrote from personal observation in connection with the revival. She mentioned 'among desirable manifestations the following: Ability to lift the voice in public in prayer to Almighty God; eagerness to witness, whereas formerly there was no desire to witness; deeper appreciation of the meaning of stewardship; enthusiasm for reading and studying the Bible. On the other hand there are the undesirable manifestations such as: babbling, which is called "tongues," and believed by some to be an indication of the fullness of the Holy Spirit; Pharisee-ism, a pious attitude eliciting men's praise; cases of people possessed by evil spirits instead of the Holy Spirit; a feeling of superiority over a person who does not see eye-to-eye in the revival movement.' *China in Revival* by Gustav Carlsberg, 1936, chapter four.

Chapter Eighteen

1. See *Revival Fire – 150 Years of Revivals* by Mathew Backholer, 2010, ByFaith Media, pages 49-62.

2. *The 59 Revival* by Ian R. K. Paisley, Ravenhill Free Presbyterian Church, 1958, 1969, page 175.

3. *Road to Revival – The Story of the Ruanda Mission* by A. C. Stanley Smith, Church Missionary Society, 1946, pages 96-97.

4. Ibid. page 104.

Chapter Nineteen

1. *The Personal Life of David Livingstone* by William G. Blaikie, London – John Murray, 1881, page 51.

2. *From Death Into Life* by Rev. William Haslam, Jarold & Sons, 1880, 1904, pages 81-83.

3. Ibid. pages 67-69.

4. *Billy Bray* by F. W. Bourne, Bible Christian Book-Room, 1877, 1898, pages 32-34 and 36-38.

5. *Billy Bray in his own words* by Chris Wright, Highland Books, 2004, page 90.

6. Ibid. pages 134-135.

Chapter Twenty

1. *As At The Beginning, The Twentieth Century Pentecostal Revival* by Michael Harper, Hodder and Stoughton, 1965, pages 114 and 117.

2. *Religious Affection* by Jonathan Edwards, edited by Dr. James M. Houston, 1984, 1996, page 40.

3. *The Prophetical Ministry* or (*The Voice Gifts*) *in the Church*, 1931, pages 98-99, as cited in *The Welsh Revival of 1904* by Eifion Evans, Evangelical Press of Wales, 1969, 1987, pages 193-194.
4. See *Overcome By The Spirit* by Francis McNutt (1991).
5. *The 59 Revival* by Ian R. K. Paisley, Ravenhill Free Presbyterian Church, 1958, 1969, page 174.
6. *Charisma Reports The Brownsville Revival* by Marcia Ford, Creation House, 1997, pages 124-125.
7. *Pandita Ramabai, A Great Life In Indian Lessons* by Helen S. Dyer, Pickering & Inglis, c.1922, page 102.
8. *Revival An Enquiry* by Max Warren, SCM Press LTD, 1954, page 65.
9. *Revival, Not An Option* – Dr. M. Brown, 1997, teaching tape.
10. *Revival in our Time*, Edited by Fredrik A. Tatford, The Paternoster Press, 1947, page 60.
11. *Road to Revival* – *The Story of the Ruanda Mission* by A. C. Stanley Smith, Church Missionary Society, 1946, page 82.
12. *Pandita Ramabai, A Great Life In Indian Lessons* by Helen S. Dyer, Pickering & Inglis, c.1922, pages 102-103.
13. *Where Lions Feed* by John Kilpatrick, teaching tape, c.1997.
14. The heart is deceitful above all things and desperately wicked (Jeremiah 17:9) and we should be aware of setting up idols in our hearts (Ezekiel 14:1-6). God can also be crushed and grieved by our adulterous heart (Ezekiel 6:9). Those with an evil heart of unbelief will depart from God (Hebrews 3:12) and people do commit sin believing that God cannot see (Ezekiel 8:7-12). We should be aware of having a blasé attitude towards the Word of the Lord, idols and sin (Jeremiah 44:15-17) as it is possible to draw near to God with our lips, yet our heart can be far from Him (Psalm 81:15 and Isaiah 29:13) and God knows the secrets of the heart (Psalm 44:21). We are told to give God our hearts (Proverbs 23:6) because he who trusts in his own heart is a fool (Proverbs 28:26a).
15. Do not fret against God; let Him have His way in your life.

Chapter Twenty-One
1. *The Evangelical Revival in The Eighteenth Century* by J. H. Overton, London, Green, and CO., 1891, page 69.
2. *Times of Refreshing* by D. L Thomson, 1877, page 52 on CD ROM.
3. *The Advance Guard of Missions* by Clifford G. Howell, Pacific Press Publishing Assn., 1912, pages 324-344.
4. *The Life of John Wesley* by Telford, The Epworth Press, 1886, 1929, pages 119-120.
5. *The Evangelical Revival In The Eighteenth Century* by J. H. Overton, London, Green, and CO., 1891, page 17.
6. *Wesley His Own Biography, Selections From The Journals*, Charles H. Kelly, 1890, page 111.

Chapter Twenty-Two
1. *Revival Comes to Wales The story of the 1859 Revival in Wales* by Eifion Evans, Evangelical Press of Wales, 1995, pages 101-102.
2. *The Advance Guard of Missions* by Clifford G. Howell, Pacific Press Publishing Assn., 1912, page 336.
3. *Wesley His Own Biography, Selections From The Journals*, Charles H. Kelly, 1890, page 109.

Chapter Twenty-Three
1. *Revival Year Sermons* – *C.H. Spurgeon, Preached in the Surrey Music Hall 1859,* The Banner of Truth Trust, 1959, pages 73-74.

2. *Revival's Golden Key – Unlocking the Door to Revival* by Ray Comfort, Bridge-Logos Publishers, 2002, page 71.
3. *If Ye Abide 10,000 Miles of Miracle In South Africa* by J. Edwin Orr, Marshall, Morgan & Scott, LTD, 1936, page 104.
4. *Revival's Golden Key – Unlocking the Door to Revival* by Ray Comfort, Bridge-Logos Publishers, 2002, page 73, from (*Finding the Reality of* God by Paris Reidhead, Reidhead Publications).
5. *Spirit of Revival* by I. R. Govan, The Faith Mission, 1938, 1978, page 89.
6. *If Ye Abide 10,000 Miles of Miracle In South Africa* by J. Edwin Orr, Marshal Morgan & Scott, LTD, 1936, page 61.
7. *When the Wind Blows, The Kilsyth and Cambuslang Revivals factually recorded by Rev. James Robe*, Ambassador Productions LTD, 1985, page 140.
8. *Revival Sermons – William C. Burns*, edited by M. F. Barbour, The Banner of Truth, (1869), 1980, pages 178-180.
9. *The Welsh Revival – Its Origin and Development* by Thomas Phillips, 1860, 1989, 2002, Banner of Truth Trust, page 133.
10. *China in Revival* by Gustav Carlberg, chapter five.
11. *The Second Coming of the Church* by George Barna, Word Publishing, 1998, page 121.

Chapter Twenty-Four
1. *White Cane Religion And Other Messages From the Brownsville Revival* by Stephen Hill, Revival Press, 1997, pages 27-30.
2. *The Master and the Multitude* – the magazine of The Open-Air Mission October-December 2007, page 3.
3. *The Revival We Need* by Oswald J. Smith, Marshal Morgan & Scott, 1940, page 83.
4. *White Cane Religion And Other Messages From the Brownsville Revival* by Stephen Hill, Revival Press, 1997, pages 31-35.
5. *The Lewis Awakening 1949-1953* by Duncan Campbell, The Faith Mission, 1954, page 31.
6. *God's Answers, Revival Sermons* by Duncan Campbell, The Faith Mission, 1960, page 24.
7. *Good News in Bad Times* by J. Edwin Orr, Zondervan Publishing House, 1953, page 232.
8. *Opened Windows – The Church and Revival* by James A. Stewart, Marshall, Morgan & Scott, 1958, page 88.
9. *The Revival We Need* by Oswald J. Smith, Marshal Morgan & Scott, 1940, pages 45-48.
10. Ibid. page 47.
11. *The Scarlet Sin And Other Revival Sermons* by John R. Rice, Sword Of The Lord Publishers, 1946, pages 248-249.
12. *China in Revival* by Gustav Carlberg, 1935, chapter three.

Chapter Twenty-Five
1. *The Price Of Revival* by John D. Drysdale, C. Tinling & Co., Ltd, 1946, page 42.
2. *God's Answers, Revival Sermons* by Duncan Campbell, The Faith Mission, 1960, pages 34-36.
3. *Revival Fires and Awakenings* by Mathew Backholer, ByFaith Media, 2009, pages 224-226.
4. *Always Abounding, An Intimate Sketch of Oswald J. Smith of Toronto by* J. Edwin Orr, Marshall, Morgan & Scott, 1948, page 98.
5. *Revival Sermons – William C. Burns*, edited by M. F. Barbour, The Banner of Truth, (1869), 1980, pages 155 and 164.

Chapter Twenty-Six
1. *Thomas Birch Freeman, Missionary Pioneer to Ashanti, Dahomey & Egba* by J. Milum, London, 1894, page 148.
2.www.desiringgod.org/ResourceLibrary/sermons/bydate/1990/711_Are_Signs_and _Wonders_for_Today/.
3. *True and False Revival* by Andrew Strom, Revival School, 2008, pages 56 and 59-60.
4. *America Is Too Young To Die, A Call To Revival* by Leonard Ravenhill, Bethany Fellowship, Inc, 1979, page 63.
5. *Revival Year Sermons – C.H. Spurgeon, Preached in the Surrey Music Hall 1859*, The Banner of Truth Trust, 1959, page v.
6. *When the Spirit Comes With Power* by Dr. John White, Hodder & Stoughton, 1989, page 137.

Chapter Twenty-Seven
1. *Great Revivals* by Colin Whittaker, MM&S, 1984, page 92.
2. *Rend the Heavens!* by Geoffrey R. King, booklet, 1962, page 12.
3. *Soul Obsession* - Nicky Cruz, Hodder & Stoughton, 2005, page 126.
4. *Personal Declension and Revival of Religion in the Soul* by Octavius Winslow, Banner of Truth, 1841, 2000, pages 102-103.
5. *Personal Declension and Revival of Religion in the Soul* by Octavius Winslow, Banner of Truth, 1841, 2000, page 10.
6. *The Enduement of Power* by Oswald J. Smith, Marshall, Morgan & Scott LTD, 1933, 1937, page 40.
7. *Prove Me Now! 10,000 Miles of Miracle to Moscow* by J. Edwin Orr, Marshall, Morgan & Scott, LTD, 1935, page 113.
8. *Revival in our Time*, Edited by Fredrik A. Tatford, The Paternoster Press, 1947, pages 62-63.
9. *The Price Of Revival* by John D. Drysdale, C. Tinling & Co., Ltd, 1946, pages 30 and 31.
10. *Spirit of Revival* by I. R. Govan, Faith Mission, 1978, page 181.
11. *Road to Revival – The Story of the Ruanda Mission* by A. C. Stanley Smith, Church Missionary Society, 1946, pages 74-75.
12. *The Lewis Awakening 1949-1953* by Duncan Campbell, The Faith Mission, 1954, page 30.
13. *Prove Me Now! 10,000 Miles of Miracle to Moscow* by J. Edwin Orr, Marshall, Morgan & Scott, LTD, 1935, pages 116-119.
14. *Prove Me Now! 10,000 Miles of Miracle to Moscow* by J. Edwin Orr, Marshall, Morgan & Scott, LTD, 1935, page 36.
15. *All Your Need 10,000 Miles of Miracle Through Australia and New Zealand* by J. Edwin Orr, MM&S LTD, c.1936, pages 123-124.
16. *If Ye Abide 10,000 Miles of Miracle In South Africa* by J. Edwin Orr, Marshall, Morgan & Scott, LTD, 1936, page 113.
17. *Times Of Refreshing 10,000 Miles of Miracle Through Canada* by J. Edwin Orr, Marshall, Morgan & Scott, LTD, 1936, page 92.
18. Book source unknown, though in the public domain.
19. *The Glory of the Impossible* by Albert D. Helser, Evangelical Publishers, 1940, 1953, pages 138-140.
20. *God's Answers, Revival Sermons* by Duncan Campbell, The Faith Mission, 1960, page 39.

Chapter Twenty-Nine
1. *Wesley His Own Biography, Selections From The Journals*, Charles H. Kelly, 1890, page 575.

Chapter Thirty

1. *Another Wave of Revival* by Frank Bartleman, (*Another Wave Rolls In,* 1962), Whitaker House, 1982, pages 11-12 and 20.
2. What a tragedy it would have been, not only for Christians, but for social historians if John Wesley did not write his *Journal!*
3. *When the Wind Blows* by Rev. James Robe, Ambassador Productions LTD, 1985, pages 35-36.
4. *Edwin Orr The Ubiquitous Ulsterman* by Newman Watts, Uplift Books (Croydon) LTD., 1947, pages 57 and 78.

Chapter Thirty-One

1. *Revival in Brownsville* by Steve Rabey, Thomas Nelson Publishers 1998, page 224.
2. *Opened Windows – The Church and Revival* by James A. Stewart, Marshall, Morgan & Scott, 1958, page 175.
3. *True and False Revival* by Andrew Strom – first listed on Amazon.com on 13 May 2008 and the Lakeland Outpouring began on 2 April 2008, thus published within forty-one days.
4. *Revival An Enquiry* by Max Warren, SCM Press LTD, 1954, page 100.

Appendix A

1. *The Evangelical Revival And Christian Reunion* by Archibald W. Harrison, The Epworth Press, 1942, page 89.
2. *Wesley His Own Biography, Selections From The Journals*, Charles H. Kelly, 1890, pages 139 and 157.
3. *The Life of John Wesley* by Telford, TEP, 1929, page 144.
4. *Wesley His Own Biography, Selections From The Journals*, Charles H. Kelly, 1890, page 238.
5. Ibid. page 374. Facts from appendix A (1-5) from *Revival Fires and Awakenings* by M. Backholer, ByFaith Media, 2009, chapter 3.
6. *The Evangelical Revival And Christian Reunion* by Archibald W. Harrison, The Epworth Press, 1942, page 75.
7. Ibid. page 126. Chapters IX and X are very good.

Appendix B

1. *Exploring Evangelism* by Mendel Taylor as cited in *Revival* by Winkie Pratney, Whitaker House, 1983, pages 114-115.
2. *Catch the Fire, the Toronto Blessing* by Guy Chevreau, Marshal Pickering, 1994, pages 214-215.
3. *Autobiography of Peter Cartwright the Backwood Preacher* edited by W. P. Strickland, Granson and Curts, c.1900, page 51.
4. *The Year of Grace, A History of the Ulster Revival* by William Gibson, Ambassador Productions, 1989, page 218.
5. *The Manifesto* Vol XXI, October 1891, pages 217-220.

www.RevivalNow.co.uk

Social Media

Instagram and Twitter: @ByFaithMedia
Facebook, Youtube and Pinterest: /ByFaithMedia

ByFaith Media Books

The following ByFaith Media books are available as paperbacks and eBooks, whilst some are available as hardbacks.

Revivals and Spiritual Awakenings
Revival Fires and Awakenings, Thirty-Six Visitations of the Holy Spirit: A Call to Holiness, Prayer and Intercession for the Nations by Mathew Backholer. With thirty-six fascinating accounts of revivals in nineteen countries from six continents, plus biblical teaching on revival, prayer and intercession.

Global Revival, Worldwide Outpourings, Forty-Three Visitations of the Holy Spirit: The Great Commission by Mathew Backholer. How revivals are birthed and the fascinating links between pioneering missionaries and the revivals that they saw.

Revival Fire, 150 Years of Revivals, Spiritual Awakenings and Moves of the Holy Spirit by Mathew Backholer. This book documents in detail twelve revivals from ten countries on five continents. Be inspired, challenged and encouraged.

Revival Answers, True and False Revivals, Genuine or Counterfeit Do not be Deceived by Mathew Backholer. What is genuine revival and how can we tell the true from the spurious? Drawing from Scripture with examples across Church history, this book will sharpen your senses and take you on a journey of discovery.

Reformation to Revival, 500 Years of God's Glory: Sixty Revivals Awakenings and Heaven-Sent visitations of the Holy Spirit by Mathew Backholer. *Reformation to Revival* traces the Divine thread of God's power from Martin Luther of 1517, through to the Charismatic Movement and into the twenty-first century.

Understanding Revival and Addressing the Issues it Provokes by Mathew Backholer. Everything you need to know about revival and its phenomena, the good, the bad and the unfortunate.

Supernatural and Spiritual
Prophecy Now, Prophetic Words and Divine Revelations for You, the Church and the Nations by Michael Backholer. An enlightening end-time prophetic journal of visions, prophecies and words from the Holy Spirit to God's people, the Church and the nations. Read about the coming revival, plus the emptying of stadiums, which was witnessed during the Coronavirus pandemic of 2020!

Glimpses of Glory, Revelations in the Realms of God Beyond the Veil in the Heavenly Abode: The New Jerusalem and the Eternal Kingdom of God by Paul Backholer. Find a world beyond earth which is real, vivid and eternal. A gripping and enlightening read!

Heaven, Paradise is Real, Hope Beyond Death: An Angelic Pilgrimage to Your Future Home by Paul Backholer. Come on a journey to another world of eternal bliss, joy and light, in this enchanting narrative which pulls you in and shows you Heaven.

Biography and Autobiography
Samuel, Son and Successor of Rees Howells: Director of the Bible College of Wales – A Biography by Richard Maton. The life of Mr Samuel and his ministry at the College and the support he received from numerous staff and students as the history of BCW unfolds. With 113 black and white photos.

Samuel Rees Howells A Life of Intercession: The Legacy of Prayer and Spiritual Warfare of an Intercessor by Richard Maton, Paul Backholer and Mathew Backholer is an in-depth look at the intercessions of Samuel Rees Howells alongside the faith principles that he learnt. With 39 black and white photos.

The Holy Spirit in a Man: Spiritual Warfare, Intercession, Faith, Healings and Miracles by R. B. Watchman. One man's compelling journey of faith and intercession, a remarkable modern day story of miracles and faith to inspire and encourage.

Christian Teaching and Inspirational
Holy Spirit Power: Knowing the Voice, Guidance and Person of the Holy Spirit by Paul Backholer. Power for Christian living; drawing from the powerful influences of many Christian leaders.

Tares and Weeds in Your Church: Trouble & Deception in God's House, the End Time Overcomers by R. B. Watchman. Tares and weeds are counterfeit Christians used to sabotage Kingdom work; learn how to recognise them and neutralise them in the power of the Holy Spirit.

Jesus Today, Daily Devotional: 100 Days with Jesus Christ by Paul Backholer. One hundred days of two minutes of Christian inspiration to draw you closer to God to encourage and inspire.

The Baptism of Fire, Personal Revival, Renewal and the Anointing for Supernatural Living by Paul Backholer. The author unveils the life and ministry of the Holy Spirit, shows how He can transform your life and what supernatural living in Christ means.

Historical
God Challenges the Dictators, Doom of the Nazis Predicted: The Destruction of the Third Reich Foretold by the Director of Swansea Bible College, An Intercessor from Wales by Rees Howells and Mathew Backholer. Available for the first time in 80 years – fully annotated and reformatted with twelve black and white photos.

Rees Howells' God Challenges the Dictators, Doom of Axis Powers Predicted: Victory for Christian England and Release of Europe Through Intercession and Spiritual Warfare, Bible College of Wales by Mathew Backholer. This is the story behind the story of *God Challenges the Dictators,* Rees Howells' only published book, and is centred around World War II (1939-1945). With twenty-four black and white photos.

Rees Howells, Vision Hymns of Spiritual Warfare & Intercessory Declarations: World War II Songs of Victory, Intercession, Praise and Worship, Israel and the Every Creature Commission by Mathew Backholer. *Vision Hymns* gives a rare insight into the prophetic declarations, hymns and choruses used in spiritual warfare by Rees Howells and his team of intercessors at the Bible College of Wales (BCW). Spanning the pivotal years of 1939-1948.

Britain, A Christian Country, A Nation Defined by Christianity and the Bible & the Social Changes that Challenge this Biblical Heritage by Paul Backholer. For over 1,000 years Britain was defined by Christianity, with monarch's dedicating the country to God and national days of prayer. Discover this continuing legacy and the challenges from the 1960s till today.

How Christianity Made the Modern World by Paul Backholer. Christianity is the greatest reforming force that the world has ever known, yet its legacy is seldom comprehended.

Celtic Christianity & the First Christian Kings in Britain: From St. Patrick and St. Columba, to King Ethelbert and King Alfred by Paul Backholer. Discover this striking history and what we can learn from the heroes of Celtic Christianity.

Christian Discipleship
Extreme Faith, On Fire Christianity: Hearing from God and Moving in His Grace, Strength & Power – Living in Victory by M Backholer.

Christianity Rediscovered, in Pursuit of God and the Path to Eternal Life: What you Need to Know to Grow, Living the Christian Life with Jesus Christ, Book 1 by Mathew Backholer.

Discipleship For Everyday Living, Christian Growth: Following Jesus Christ and Making Disciples of All Nations by Mathew Backholer. Engaging biblical teaching to aid believers in their faith.

Short-Term Missions (Christian Travel with a Purpose)
Short-Term Missions, A Christian Guide to STMs: For Leaders, Pastors, Churches, Students, STM Teams and Mission Organizations – Survive and Thrive! by Mathew Backholer. A concise guide to Short-Term Missions (STMs).

How to Plan, Prepare and Successfully Complete Your Short-Term Mission For Churches, Independent STM Teams and Mission Organizations by Mathew Backholer. This book will guide you through all you need to know about STMs and includes more than 140 real-life STM testimonies.

Biblical Adventure and Archaeology
Lost Treasures of the Bible: Exploration and Pictorial Travel Adventure of Biblical Archaeology by Paul Backholer. Unveil ancient mysteries as you discover the evidence for Israel's exodus from Egypt, and travel into lost civilisations in search of the Ark of the Covenant. With more than 160 colour photos and pictures.

The Exodus Evidence In Pictures – The Bible's Exodus: The Hunt for Ancient Israel in Egypt, the Red Sea, the Exodus Route and Mount Sinai by Paul Backholer. With more than 100 full colour photos and graphics!

The Ark of the Covenant – Investigating the Ten Leading Claims by Paul Backholer. Combining an on-site travel journal with 80+ colour photographs through Egypt, Ethiopia and beyond.

Budget Travel – Vacation/Holiday
Budget Travel, a Guide to Travelling on a Shoestring, Explore the World, a Discount Overseas Adventure Trip: Gap Year, Backpacking, Volunteer-Vacation and Overlander by Mathew Backholer.

Travel the World and Explore for Less than $50 a Day, the Essential Guide: Your Budget Backpack Global Adventure, from Two Weeks to a Gap Year, Solo or with Friends by M Backholer.

ByFaith Media DVDs

Revivals and Spiritual Awakenings
Great Christian Revivals on 1 DVD is an inspirational and uplifting account of some of the greatest revivals in Church history. Filmed on location across Britain and drawing upon archive information, the stories of the Welsh Revival (1904-1905), the Hebridean Revival (1949-1952) and the Evangelical Revival (1739-1791) are brought to life in this moving 72-minute documentary. Using computer animation, historic photos and depictions, the events of the past are weaved into the present, to bring these Heaven-sent revivals to life.

Christian Travel (Backpacking Style Short-Term Mission)
ByFaith – World Mission on 1 DVD is a Christian reality TV show that reveals the real experience of a backpacking style short-term mission in Asia, Europe and North Africa. Two brothers, Paul and Mathew Backholer shoot through fourteen nations, in an 85-minute real-life documentary. Filmed over three years, *ByFaith – World Mission* is the very best of ByFaith TV season one.

Historical and Adventure
Israel in Egypt – The Exodus Mystery on 1 DVD. A four year quest searching for Joseph, Moses and the Hebrew slaves in Egypt. Join Paul and Mathew Backholer as they hunt through ancient relics and explore the mystery of the biblical exodus, hunt for the Red Sea and climb Mount Sinai. Discover the first reference to Israel outside of the Bible, uncover depictions of people with multicoloured coats, encounter the Egyptian records of slaves making bricks and find lost cities. 110 minutes. The very best of *ByFaith – In Search of the Exodus.*

ByFaith – Quest for the Ark of the Covenant on 1 DVD. Join two adventurers on their quest for the Ark, beginning at Mount Sinai where it was made, to Pharaoh Tutankhamun's tomb, where Egyptian treasures evoke the majesty of the Ark. The quest proceeds onto the trail of Pharaoh Shishak, who raided Jerusalem. The mission continues up the River Nile to find a lost temple, with clues to a mysterious civilization. Crossing through the Sahara Desert, the investigators enter the underground rock churches of Ethiopia, find a forgotten civilization and examine the enigma of the final resting place of the Ark itself. 100+ minutes.

www.ByFaithDVDs.org

www.ingramcontent.com/pod-product-compliance
Lightning Source LLC
Chambersburg PA
CBHW070824100426
42813CB00003B/475